Language Use and Language Attitudes in Juárez, Mexico

A Reader

By

Margarita Hidalgo

ORCID 0000-0003-0130-5191

Language Use and Language Attitudes in Juárez, Mexico
A Reader

Acknowledgments and memoirs vii
Prologue xiii

Part I Language Use and Language Attitudes in Juárez, Mexico (1983)

Introduction 1
1 .... Historical background: the beginnings 1
1.1 .... Baptismal records 3
1.2 .... Indigenous languages vs. Spanish 4
2 .... The 18th century: recovery period 6
3 .... Independence from Spain 9
4 .... The Mexico-U.S. war 9
5 .... Two sides of the border 11
6 .... After the wars 12
6.1 .... Benito Juárez in Paso del Norte 13
6.2 .... Benito Juárez in Cd. Juárez 14
6.3 .... The end of the 19th century 14
7 .... The Taft-Díaz meeting of 1909 15
8 .... The Mexican Revolution 15
9 .... The battles of Cd. Juárez in literature 16
10 .... The end of Madero's presidency 20
10.1 ..... Legends and folklore 21
10.2 ..... The novel of the Mexican Revolution 24
10.3 ..... Cinematography 25
10.4 ..... Rural Spanish and residual variants 27
10.5 ..... Social class differentiation 30
11 .... El Paso, U.S.A. 30
11.1 ..... Organizing civil government 31
11.2 ..... Economic activities 31
12 .... Identity and language attitudes 33
12.1 ..... Language and ideology on "the other side" 35
12.2 ..... This side of the border 38
13 .... Population growth 39
14 .... Profile of subjects 41
15 .... The growth of Cd. Juárez from the 1960's on 44
16 .... Reports on local identity 48
17 .... The international border 49
18 .... The final balance 50
19 .... Theoretical considerations: from linguistics to sociolinguistics 51
20 .... Language attitudes and sociolinguistics 53
20.1 ..... Sociolinguistics and the social psychology of language 54
21 .... Direct questions in surveys 56
22 .... The original survey 57

22.1 .....Methodology 58
23 ....The original survey form 60

List of Figures, Part I

Figure 1 .. Madero's victory (1911) 17
Figure 2 .. Revolutionary camp outside Cd. Juárez (1911)..17
Figure 3 .. Rebels took Cd. Juárez at the Customs House 18

List of Maps, Part I

Map 1 ....United States-Mexico Boundaries (1853)..11
Map 2 ....The Central District in the 1960's 47
Map 3 ....Partial view of Ciudad Juárez 1965...48
Map 4 ....Córdova de las Américas Bridge 50

List of Tables, Part I

Table 1 .... Population of El Paso Communities (1744) 6
Table 2 .... Population of El Paso Communities (1750) 7
Table 3 .... El Paso Area Population (1760) 7
Table 4 .... El Paso Area Households by Town and Ethnicity 8
Table 5 .... Fray Andrés Varo Census (1749)..8
Table 6 .... Origin of the Juárez Population (1980-1981) 40
Table 6.1 . Female Subjects 41
Table 6.2 . Male Subjects 42
Table 7.1 . Residential Area by Social Class: Lower-lower 44
Table 7.2 . Residential Area by Social Class: Lower-working 44
Table 7.3 . Residential Area by Social Class: Lower-middle 44
Table 7.4 . Residential Area by Social Class: Middle-middle......................................44
Table 7.5 . Residential Area by Social Class: Upper-middle 44
Table 7.6 . Residential Area by Social Class: Upper-upper 44
Table 8 .... Population growth: 1900-2020 51

Part II Language use and language attitudes in Juárez, Mexico (1983)

Chapter 1: Theoretical considerations 71

1.1 .... Attitudes toward a second or foreign language 72
1.1.1.. Gardner's model..73
1.2.... Evaluations of majority languages and language varieties..................................74
1.2.1 . Other values assigned to languages..77
1.3 .... Attitudes toward mother tongue 78
1.4 .... Speech accommodation 79
1.5 .... Attitudes and behavior 80
1.6 .... Bilingualism and diglossia 82
1.7 .... Summary of theoretical considerations 83
Footnotes..84

Chapter 2 The study and its background 85

2.1 ....Historical background 85
2.2 ....Socioeconomic overview 86
2.3 ....The effects of migration 87
2.4 ....Cultural controversy 88
2.5 ....Languages and language varieties 88
2.5.1 ....English and Spanish outside of their own territory 90
2.5.2 ....Spanglish in Juárez 91
2.5.3 ....Spanglish in El Paso 91
2.6 ....Methodology 92
2.6.1 ....Data collection 93
2.7 ....The respondents 94
2.7.1 ....Socioeconomic characteristics 94
2.7.2 ....Education 96
2.7.3 ....Formal exposure to English 97
2.8 ....Summary and implications 98
Footnotes 99

Chapter 3 English in Juárez 101

3.1 ....The Informal Use of English 102
3.2 ....Predictors of English Use 105
3.3 ....Diglossia and bilingualism 106
3.4 ....Attitudes toward English 107
3.4.1 ....Integrative orientation 108
3.4.2 ....Instrumental orientation 110
3.4.3 ....The values of English 110
3.5 ....Beliefs about Anglo-Americans 112
3.6 ....Predictors of attitudes toward English 114
3.6.1 ....Local identity as a predictor of attitudes toward English 114
3.7 ....Attitudes towards English in other settings 116
3.8 ....Attitudes towards education in English 118
3.9 ....Conclusions 119
Footnotes 120

Chapter 4 Spanish in Juárez 123

4.1 .... The Spanish of the northern frontier 123
4.1.1 . Local versus national Spanish 125
4.1.2 . The capital versus the province 127
4.1.3 . The effects of education and social class 128
4.1.4 . The effects of the border 131
4.2 .... Spanish as the national language 132
4.2.1 . Language loyalty in Juárez 134
4.2.2 . The values of Mexican Spanish 135
4.3 .... Language loyalty and national ethnocentrism 136

4.4. Spanish language loyalty policy in Mexico 138
4.4.1. Language policy in Juárez 139
4.4.2. Language disloyalty: a consequence of modernity? 140
4.5. Conclusions 141
Footnotes 143

Chapter 5 The Mexican-American connection 145

5.1. The inherent values of Spanish-English Code-Switching 145
5.1.1. Predictors of the inherent values of Spanish-English Code-switching 147
5.1.2. Language attitudes and the rejection of Spanish-English Code-switching 147
5.1.3. Sex and the rejection of Spanish-English Code-switching 148
5.1.4. The origins of linguistic value judgements 151
5.2. The communicative values of Spanglish 154
5.2.1. English as a barrier to communication 155
5.2.2. Language loyalty: a predictor of communicative values of Spanglish 158
5.3. Beliefs about Mexican-Americans 160
5.4. Conclusions 162

Chapter 6 Conclusions 165

6.1. Assumptions about language use 165
6.2. Assumptions about the relationship between language attitudes and behavior .. 166
6.3. Assumptions about language attitudes 166
6.4. Implications 169
6.5. Suggestions for further research 170

References 173

Appendix I ..... Questionnaire 181
Appendix II .... Correlation matrix 185

List of Maps, Part II

Map 1 .... English-appropriate Locales in Juárez 108

List of Figures, Part II

Figure 1 .. Summary of Relationships between Demographic and Linguistic Dimensions.. 168

List of Tables, Part II

Table 2.1. Attributes of Spanish, English and Spanglish 89
Table 2.2. Percentages of Respondents by Income, Residential Area and Father's Occupation 95
Table 2.3. Distribution of Respondents by Socioeconomic Status 96
Table 2.4. Percentage of Respondents by Education 97

Table 3.1. Response Percentages: The Informal Use of English in Juárez 102
Table 3.2. Multiple Regression Analysis: The Informal Use of English in Juárez 106
Table 3.3. Scattergram of Socioeconomic Status and English Use 107

Table 3.4. Response Percentages: Attitudes toward English in Juárez 109
Table 3.5. Correlation Coefficient Matrix: Eight Items on Attitudes toward English 111
Table 3.6. Response Percentages: Beliefs about Americans 112
Table 3.7. Multiple Regression Analysis: Attitudes toward English in Juárez 114
Table 3.8. Response Percentage: Local Identity 115

Table 4.1. Response Percentage: Local versus National Spanish 126
Table 4.2. Multiple Regression Analysis: Local versus National Spanish 127
Table 4.3. Some English Borrowings Used in Juárez 131
Table 4.4. Response Percentages: Language Loyalty in Juárez 135
Table 4.5. Response Percentages: National Ethnocentrism 137

Table 5.1. Response Percentages: Inherent Values of Spanglish 146
Table 5.2. Multiple Regression Analysis: Inherent Values of Spanglish 147
Table 5.3. Response Percentage by Sex: Inherent Values of Spanish-English Code-switching . 148
Table 5.4. Response Percentages: The Communicative Values of Spanglish 155
Table 5.5. Multiple Regression Analysis: The Communicative Values of Spanglish 155
Table 5.6. Response Percentages: Beliefs about Mexican-Americans 161

Acknowledgments and memoirs

Forty years after my public three-hour dissertation defense at the University of New Mexico, I still receive queries whether the topic of my research is valid or relevant to the knowledge of sociolinguistics in general and the Mexico-U.S. border, in particular. I take advantage of this opportunity to express my gratitude to those who over the decades have been interested in this rare project. I certainly appreciate the encouragement and patience of my family, my friends, former students, co-workers, and the occasional readers who insist on the need to replicate a study of this magnitude. Unfortunately, not all projects are easily replicated in identical manner. One of the frequent questions was, "Why did you include English Use in different domains but ignored Spanish Use in similar contexts"? My reply is plain and simple: as in the rest of Mexico, Spanish is the language used in all private and public domains of interaction, but English is not. Therefore, there was no need to ask when, where and with whom Spanish speakers were speaking Spanish. This is followed by another pressing question, "Why don't all the inhabitants of Cd. Juárez speak English if they are so close to the United States"? The reply is again redundant: most people in the community under study are native Spanish speakers though there may be speakers of indigenous languages who may be monolingual in the indigenous language or bilingual. At the time I conducted the research, Spanish was *de facto* official in Mexico but not *de jure* official.

One question leads to other relevant issues that implicate and jumble social change. Empirical studies provide evidence of trends and patterns of human behavior and may be validated when various researchers approach the same problem. In the case of my dissertation the problem at hand was language use and language attitudes. My *a priori* assumption was that use and attitudes are not always discontinuous; the paradox of attitudes and use preoccupies researchers in contexts where speakers may say that they like or love the language that they do not use, e.g., any of the U.S. immigrant languages that, by the second generation, are going through shift rather than maintenance. On the contrary, in some communities use and attitudes are linked by various indicators. On the Mexican side of the border most people speak Spanish, and some people may speak other languages such as English or an indigenous language. This explains the inclusion of English Use as an important variable.

After such a long time, are there any relevant changes to these patterns? The answer is affirmative since 2003, when the Law on Linguistic Rights of the Indigenous Peoples was enacted. This bill strips off the status of Spanish as *de facto* official. In other words, speakers of Mexican indigenous languages (MIL) have the right to use their language(s) in all private and public domains within the political borders of the Mexican Republic, where the law is fully applicable and effective. The next question raised to me was, "How about the status of English"? In Cd. Juárez, as in the rest of Mexico, English is an additional language of "high prestige" and "medium or low use". This statement leads to the next item on the agenda, that is, that attitudinally and ideologically, English is in great shape but not everyone uses or speaks English fluidly. I make the difference between attitudes and ideology, the former being expressed verbally by common people who identify other groups or individuals, while the ideology encompasses an expansive machinery of societal values endorsed by the powers that be. Attitudes are shaped in the local or regional community and may vary within the members of any speech community.

I see two major problems in any attempt to repeat this study. The first one relates, as I mentioned above, to social change, which is normally expected. In reassessing some of the major questions about English language use, I consulted and received the feedback of San Diego State University students who were thoroughly familiar with my research. They claimed that I could have added other domains of language use such as video games (in the 1980's) and navigation in cyberspace, more recently. Also, studies involving human subjects must be reviewed by institutional boards that may not allow to raise the questions I raised forty years ago. Human rights activists and college boards have drafted a series of procedures that restrict the freedom of speech, and consequently, freedom of research.

The word "prejudice" that appears in the summary of my dissertation (Hidalgo 1986) is a doubled-edge sword that attracts the reader and mortifies the reviewers working on the protection of human subjects. Thus, while I claimed that speakers of Mexican Spanish have prejudices about or "against" bilingual speakers residing in the Unites States, I failed to advance that the same prejudices are observed on the U.S. side of the border. I have been told that two wrongs do not make one "right", and therefore, the issue of reciprocal prejudice should be a moot point. The scenario is nonetheless inviting to reconsider speakers' actions and reactions on both sides of the border, since the various beliefs appeared to be engraved in stone. This issue comes to the surface when reporting the perceptions of Spanish-accented English and the interpretations and consequences of yet another register available in El Paso. Aguilar's study (2018) exemplifies the case of a candidate for a job as a weather broadcaster; she highlights two variants of English pronunciation and assumes that the words *radar* and *wind* would be a real challenge for some Spanish speakers. A job like this would be offered to a candidate who did not have an accent at all. However, in El Paso, as in any other U. S. city, a job as a physician, nurse, laboratory technician or paramedic would be offered to a person qualified to perform the advertised duties—regardless of accent. In weather broadcasts, artificial intelligence could be used and a robot could be programmed to remove the accent from an attractive announcer, particularly if the announcer is female.

Many a time I have replied that we should distinguish between prejudice and discrimination, the former being perhaps innocuous and the latter truly damaging. Prejudice is not subject to fines or punishment while discrimination has consequences in some specific cases (e.g., education, work, public services, etc.). Forty years ago, I did not anticipate cases of discrimination against speakers of Spanish-English code-switching in Mexico because there were no stories of repatriated children or adults from the United States. These days things have changed so drastically that it is possible to locate thousands of English-speaking minors of Mexican heritage who are attending public schools in Mexico, where education is strongly monolingual in Spanish. Thus, these days we should pay attention to violations of human rights and language rights.

Readers have directed me to explore issues related to immigration, female employment, and neocolonialism, among other relevant topics. When they are related to language as a variable, I certainly tackle those. Societal challenges we observe are not tangential, but they do modify human habits, sometimes massively. In the Introduction to this book, I explore the historical background of the old Paso del Norte community from the beginnings in the mid-late 17th century to the end of the 20th century. The final decade and a half of the past century I saw the change, which occurred immediately after I completed and published my research. Changes are sometimes latent and not readily observable but occur over time and often have long-term consequences for individuals and societies. The alterations in the social order may be paradigmatic and may include a set of transformations affecting thousands of people. The transition from a model of behavior to another model may strike too many individuals at the same time until the "transition" becomes the norm, and another model is emulated or rejected—if anomalous. Local changes are not fortuitous insofar as they derive from actions and reactions provoked by human behavior.

The question about neocolonialism seems to refer to the use of English in Juárez, or in Mexico, in general. The subtle propagation of socioeconomic and political activity by former colonial rulers aimed at strengthening capitalism, neoliberal globalization, and submersion of their former colonies. In reference to Latin America, neocolonialism was a merger of economic exploitation by industrialized countries (Britain, France, Germany, and the United States) and inexcusable military intervention and protectionism. Neocolonialism originates in the praxis of colonialism, and in theory it replaces imperialism, which sounds overpowering. The term neocolonialism is loosely used to describe the resulting connection of imperial powers with their former colonies; it imposes a leash that restrains economic activity to a dependency similar to that sustained during the colonial period, while language and cultural products are thrust on colonial subjects who have few other or no choices at all. A broader question must tackle the issue of neocolonialism to identify the Mexican border in particular, or even Mexico as a former colony of an English-speaking power. Did it happen after the Mexico-U.S. war?

Did the portion of the Mexican territory that was split and annexed by the United States turn immediately into an English-speaking colony? The negative reply leads us to rather pay attention to the emergent bilingual milieu that has fostered attitudes that did not exist before the Mexico-U.S. War. This juncture is thus ideal to explore issues related to expressions of nationalism, ethnicity and language. The consequences of Paso del Norte's partition are still being felt in reactions of enhanced metalinguistic awareness that befog other relevant issues in routine speech acts. Is accent important when buying or selling shoes? Is monolingual / bilingual discourse style determining in consultations with the doctor? Are doctors and patients willing to accommodate and converge as interlocutors, or do they engage in divergence when there is no ethnolinguistic empathy?

I reiterate my appreciation for the notes, comments, and criticism that I have received both personally and in writing. This is the major incentive I have to address the issues in this Reader, which is divided in two major parts: the first one presents the historical background, the theoretical considerations and methodological questions since many find it appalling that El Paso (Texas) or El Paso (U.S.A.) has its own deep roots on the "Mexican side of the border". Some of my sharpest SDSU students noticed that the U.S. side of the border retained an inviting name that keeps attracting people from other places to attempt to cross to the United States. I do recommend advanced students to examine the theoretical and methodological issues presented in the first part before they engage in a major research project such as a thesis or dissertation. I also recommend to study the original survey form in Spanish, which I did not disclose in my study. The second part of this Reader is the dissertation of 1983. I certainly welcome more and more insightful reactions.

In the first part of this Reader, I present short stories about local folklore, pop music and even personal anecdotes that the audience may find entertaining. I do love the corrido "La Adelita", both the lyrics and the music in various styles and performances (corrido, mariachi band, philharmonic, etc.). I also like a few of the songs composed by Juan Gabriel, known as the "divo de Juárez", lots of fun for all students of Spanish. Please review my favorites: "Ya lo sé que tú te vas", "Con todo y mi tristeza", "Buenos días señor Sol", and the one we all enjoyed the spring semester for Mother's Day: "Amor eterno". In passing, I do mention the legend about the origin of the burritos, an insipid meal that I do not recommend to anyone wishing to eat a healthy diet.

I introduce old pictures in black and white because they capture memories better than words. My eyes glaze in vivid remembrance when I watch the images of the Customs House of Cd. Juárez because my parents worked there for many decades (www.museo-de-la-revolucion-en-la-frontera-norte). Sometimes they would take me with them after school, and I would entertain myself by pretending to write on the old Remington typewriters. I waited patiently for them while watching the adults—that is, the language use and language attitudes conveyed at every turn. I also loved to listen to the anecdotes of the adults who worked there. From the anecdotes they moved on to the history of the sumptuous 19th century French-style building. I liked to watch the people who came in to do their paperwork and left happy because they had done well. I observed with delight the visitors' clothing, at times different from ours. Some of the people who visited that office dressed differently and spoke languages that I didn't understand, but I didn't hesitate to ask what language it was. Some adults would clear my doubts, and to this day I suppose that most of the time they were right. Was it Dutch, Low German or Danish? When they could not guess in what language a service was requested, the employees called the person or persons who spoke English. This is the same language policy they have in some the U. S. stores when a customer arrives and doesn't speak English; they call the employee who speaks the needed language.

My interest in the MIL also dates back to the years of childhood and adolescence, as I liked to walk around the city with my friends with whom I shared many memorable moments. We easily recognized Tarahumara and Nahuatl, and we knew when some of the other MIL were neither Tarahumara nor Nahuatl. In those years the boys and girls calmly walked down the street. People were strolling the streets because nothing was happening that could worry them. In public, both insiders and outsiders used to speak the language or languages they knew, and if visitors from the United States or Europe would stumble with Spanish, they would ask: Do you kids speak English? Most of the time we said, "Yes, of course". Spanish-English code-switching is heard in the city, and services are rendered to bilingual customers, though employees in the various locales may not convey the feelings of rejection—if at all concerned. The incipient multilingual and liberal environment of the "Mexican side of the border" inspired both my dissertation and other studies in sociolinguistics and the sociology of language.

The different codes heard in this locality about eighty years ago were accepted with ease because speakers of "other" languages were not massively visible; the natives must have thought that speakers would eventually assimilate to the rest of the Spanish-speaking community. First-generation Chinese immigrants must have arrived in Cd. Juárez *ca.* the 1930's, and settled there, raised families, went to school, and made a living running food businesses, where they served the public in both Chinese and Spanish. They did the math in the native language and gave the change in Spanish. In their premises, among themselves, they spoke Chinese. Many years later, when I was a graduate student at Michigan State University, I took a couple of classes with Dr. Ruth Brend. One of those classes had to do with linguistic fieldwork in non-Indo-European languages, which involved direct interaction with native first-generation speakers of Chinese. The goal was to develop detailed descriptions of language data, particularly in morphology.

In the 1950's and very early 1960's, Spanish-speaking gypsies were roaming the city. The gypsies used to come in the summer months and set up tents where they read the palm of the hand, trying to make a buck via their divinatory prowess. In those days they charged about five Mexican pesos, then equivalent to forty cents on the dollar. On the land that Pronaf later occupied, there was an amusement park and fairground with a carousel, wheel of fortune, roller coaster and other amenities for children. Taking advantage of the fact that there was a public eager for entertainment, the gypsies conducted their business on the land that was almost vacant. I think that the jargon or argot derived from contact between Spanish-speaking and speakers of Romani might be related to itinerant gypsies. The gypsies had made a long journey from Spain to Mexico City, and from there they left for the Mexican side of the border, with the intention of crossing into the United States. Information in academic circles about the *caló* of the gypsies has been published in Spain and the United States but rarely in Mexico. The *caló* jargon was not unknown in the decades of the 1940's, 1950's and 1960's. It was spoken in the Cd. Juárez since the early decades of the 20th century, and actively used and enjoyed by some younger males; it was also understood by almost everyone else as a register of vernacular Mexican Spanish.

How about the spread of English on the other side of the border? Many a time I have been questioned about the role of the spoken media in the dissemination of English. I know as much as everyone else, since the first radio (1922) and television (1953) stations that opened in El Paso have been transmitting programs that are heard and seen in Cd. Juárez. The next item on this agenda has to do with "learning" English through television, and if this means of communication "bombard" the border city on a regular basis. I don't think there has been a media blitz that began in the early 1950's. Rather, viewers around the world found a means of entertainment that didn't exist before. I belong to the generation that was receptive to English-speaking television, since programs for children and adults could be seen in the cities near El Paso. All Walt Disney's programs were seen in Juárez after school hours. One or two weeks later the same programs were dubbed into Spanish and broadcast in the local television station. I guess it was a good review. But as children grow older, they want to be exposed to challenges, and the major challenge for me was to watch directly every single episode of "The Twilight Zone", translated into Spanish as "La dimensión desconocida" and rebroadcast in the local station. This was better than any dumb Halloween movie. The author of the series, Rod Serling, was born and raised in upstate New York. It took me a while to understand his inspiration, creativity, and uplifting sensitivity.

How about teens? Like everyone else I thoroughly enjoyed the irresistible television programs featuring Petula Clark, Diana Ross and the Supremes, The Beatles, The Rolling Stones, and some other singers and musicians that appeared on the Ed Sullivan show Sunday afternoon. How about adults? Like today, adults selected convenient programs like the Hollywood films that became famous around the world. Some of my mother's favorites were "The Wizard of Oz", "Gone with the Wind" and "Madame X". For a Spanish speaker it was a great challenge to watch these movies without the Spanish dubbing. In my dissertation I explored English Use as a variant of a "personal domain".

In closing, I should remark that the Mexican side of the border keeps attracting mostly Spanish speakers that maintain the full-fledged vitality of Spanish and the variations unfolding in the local environment. Spanish-speaking immigrants from Mexico's interior contribute to language strengthening and modeling Mexican identity. Their contributions may come from Mexican states that are very far away from the border. Local sources report 60,000 people from Veracruz living in Cd. Juárez in 2021 (cf. Universidad Autónoma de Cd. Juárez). This is one of the reasons why Spanish always prevails in all private and public domains. Many *juarenses* and *neojuarenses* become bilingual, but to date there is not a single record indicating the proportion of Spanish-English bilinguals, or the degree of individual or collective bilingualism. Since the beginning of the 20th century, official census logs gather language data on the MIL, rather than focusing on other-than-Spanish languages used on the Mexican border sites. Informal reports indicate that as I close the edition of this manuscript, there are about 20,000 speakers of the MIL in Cd. Juárez.

Juárez and El Paso interdependence must be traced to the foundation of Paso del Norte in the mid-17th century. Specialized readers and the general audience are invited to dig into the beginnings of Juárez history in order to understand the circumstances in which Paso del Norte was built. Wise and redolent historians mentioned in this Reader have contributed to setting the record straight by distinguishing the places, protagonists, dates, and sometimes the time in which facts occurred. One of the results of the new bilingual and /or multilingual environment is the use of language as an independent variable from sociodemographic indicators. It seems that in both Juárez and El Paso, people feel free (sometimes even obliged) to pass judgements on language use and language attitudes. As I study the newer reports on sociolinguistics, I gather that the general attitudes are leading the communities to draft an ideology that is associated to values that are above and beyond the speech communities. Hopefully my focus on the speech communities will fortify the understanding of an area of the world that will continue to make headlines for decades to come.

Prologue

Writing about new or innovative issues was not an easy task. Exploring issues of language, identity and ethnicity was until recently a discipline based on a phenomenological experience in all its varieties without any reference to objective or observed behavior. Based on perception and self-conscious description, such approach was the basis of very popular essays on Mexican history, thought and culture, i.e., *El laberinto de la soledad* by Octavio Paz (1950) and *El perfil del hombre y la cultura en México* by Samuel Ramos (1951), respectively. They both grabbed the headlines for many decades, since there was an audience eager to know more about the search for patterns of thought in universal forms of human activity, including the myth and folk fantasies. The emerging trend of structuralism in psychology, anthropology and sociology may have been influential in the use of introspection and self-observation (Wundt 1912 and 1928; Lévi-Strauss 1947/1967), though not necessarily generalizable to all human collectivities and social groups.

The advent of linguistics at the beginning of the 20th century coincides with the foundation of psychology as a science and the holistic approach to human development. The trends of structuralism, a school of thought stressing an understanding of human culture and its components in connection with one another and with a whole system known as structure, became popular in all the disciplines including linguistics, which was best represented by Ferdinand de Saussure and his *Cours de linguistique générale* (1915/1945), known in the Spanish version as *Curso de lingüística general* (1945). In his prologue to the Spanish edition, Amado Alonso extolls Saussure's scientific contributions to the new and exciting discipline that systematizes the study of language (1945:30). Saussure was influential on Roman Jakobson and other leading names in the nascent field of linguistics, insofar as the former had developed an approach focused on the way language structure served its basic function, i.e., communication between speakers. Making significant contributions to Indo-European linguistics, Austronesian, and Amerindian language families, Leonard Bloomfield (1933) epitomizes the most comprehensive description of structural linguistics. American structuralism highlighted the language form to be described in terms of a single, objective, observable, and verifiable aspect of language per se.

Bloomfield's influential role in American linguistics began to be questioned by Noam Chomsky. The basic principles of structuralism—which reject the notion that each language is unique—were challenged by Chomsky, who instead proposed that linguistic analysis presupposes that there are substantial similarities. The notion that a sentence in a language has a deep structure and a surface structure, a dual representation common to all languages, is the major contribution of transformational-generative grammar. Transformations involve two types of rules: phrase structure rules and transformational rules (Chomsky 1957, 1965; Lyons 1970). Deep structures appear as derivational trees and may be transformed into predicted surface structures that sound grammatical to the native speakers of the language under study. Though the interpretation of the times makes structuralism appeared as being divorced from transformational linguistics, a principle common to both schools of thought is a structure perceived as being limitless. The repetitive use of the notion of structure by Chomsky and theoretical linguists makes the field representatives appear as being more *structuralist than the initiators of structuralism.*

The foundations of transformational-generative grammar are accompanied by two main notions, *linguistic competence* and *linguistic performance* (Chomsky 1965: chapter 1), which find equivalents in the Saussurean dichotomy: *langue* or the language system with its meanings, and *parole* or the actual utterances of the language system, both concepts now firmly rooted in the field of linguistics. Chomsky proceeded from a fundamental characteristic of human language, i.e., speakers are capable of producing and comprehending an infinite number of sentences while seeking to gain information into deeper organizing principles (30-31). Primary language data consists of a finite amount of information about sentences and still produce newer sentences. Grammatical transformations are structure-dependent because they manipulate substring in terms of their assignments to categories (57). The theory of language as it is manifested in competence and performance proposes that the former comprises all levels of skills in phonology, morphology, syntax and semantics, and the ability to recognize ambiguous sentences via intuitions of native speakers, or sentences that were never heard before. Performance represents the outcome of competence, may be limited in the number of utterances, and may even be accompanied by errors.

How did we make it from linguistics to sociolinguistics and the sociology of language (SOL)? Was linguistic theory incomprehensible or incomplete? Was it severed from social reality? My aim is to guide the readers through the different topics that I discussed in my dissertation, for they may appear discontinuous to those who are unfamiliar with the development of border studies, its history, and the not-so-new fields of sociolinguistics and the SOL, disciplines that approach language attitudes and language use. I begin with the historical background and consult those works that were unavailable at the time I concluded my research. Over the years students and colleagues have asked me about different aspects of my dissertation and the subsequent articles published in various outlets. The questions raised have been dealing with content, methodology, the instrument used to collect data, and the general assumptions that guided my work.

Part I introduces a guide of 23 concise items that are paragraphed and sub-paragraphed for the audience's convenience. It includes the original survey form in Spanish as it was presented to the subjects. For the convenience of interested students, this section approaches the methodological issues related to the creation of items and the codification of variables. I also discuss how I arrived at identifying six groups of subjects differentiated by social class, a major component of observable reality that is some societies may be a sensitive issue. The belief that quantification is merely descriptive and has no consequences in interpreting social science is open to further study. The advance in technology is moving us closer to undertake empirical studies of smaller or major proportions.

Part II presents the results of my project as submitted to the faculty of the University of New Mexico in 1983. Chapter 1 approaches the theoretical considerations that, far from being outdated, are still insightful to scholars who need to review the foundations of sociolinguistics and the SOL. Chapter 2 affords a view of the speech community and the linguistic codes accessible to speakers of both sides of the border. The historical background of the area is substantially extended in Part I with the carefully select information that, for the most part, was unavailable in 1980-1981. The core chapters 3, 4 and 5 summarize in tables and graphs the results of the survey. Each table represents a language variable or social indicator and presents the replies of the subjects in raw numbers or percentages. Tables and graphs can be replicated in further studies, and the items can be presented in either Spanish or English. The original items in Spanish are organized by variables in paragraph 22 of Part I. Occasional readers and former students have requested clarifications with respect to my conclusions in Chapter 6, where I claim that in a multilingual ambience Language *per se* may be an independent variable from strictly sociodemographic indicators such as social class or its equivalent, i.e., socioeconomic status. The research carried out in the past forty years attests to the hyper-invocation of language use and language attitudes, which in the mouths, tongues, and pens of speakers and scholars finds no boundaries to express what they believe—whether the belief or opinion is politically correct or not.

Part I
Language use and language attitudes in Juárez, Mexico

A Reader

Introduction

This reader is divided into two parts. Part I presents the historical background tracing the origins of Cd. Juárez from the mid-17th century. It examines its evolution to the end of the 20th century. The first part examines, too, the severance of Paso del Norte into two communities, one that stands on the Mexican side of the border, and the other one, El Paso (Texas), on the U.S. side, the result of the Mexico-U.S. War in the mid-19th century. It is clear by now that a single—mostly Spanish-speaking community—was divided since then, and that the newer El Paso has evolved as a bilingual locality that progressively became well-differentiated from its twin counterpart. Part I continues to approach both theoretical and methodological considerations. The aim of this section is to readdress the questions that have arisen in four decades since my dissertation became public. Hopefully, this work will bring to the attention of readers the relevance of language attitudes in general, and those that pertain to the Mexico-U.S. border in particular. This discussion tackles the types of items created for the interviews and the statistical analyses used to present the results.

1 Historical background: the beginnings

One of the most intriguing questions about the history of Cd. Juárez (today in the state of Chihuahua) is the date and circumstances of its foundation, which according to historians occurred on December 8, 1659. Interestingly, El Paso (today in the state of Texas) was founded the same day in the same place by active members of the Franciscan order, who had been successful in the process of converting Indians in central Mesoamerica. Since the mid-1650's, what we know today as El Paso was merely the northern sector of Cd. Juárez; people living north and south of the river made up one single community of speakers of indigenous languages and Spanish. The small village was divided about two centuries later as a result of the Mexico-U.S. war (1846-1848). El Paso (Texas) retained the original name, and the southern part of the village—where the mission was first established—was renamed Cd. Juárez to honor Benito Juárez, who had been Mexico's President while in Paso del Norte (1865-1866). Since 1888, the southern part of Paso del Norte is known as Ciudad Juárez.

The mission of Nuestra Señora de Guadalupe del Paso del Norte was founded with the purpose of converting the Manso people, who were hunters and gatherers living near the Río Bravo or Rio Grande. Another group of natives organized by the Franciscans were Pueblos, known as Piros. The Piros were also from north and central New Mexico villages and their mode of sustenance was agriculture. "The different traditional ways of life led by these two native groups had a major effect on the way the two communities adapted to Spanish rule and colonial society within the setting of the Guadalupe Mission. One community, at the beginning strong in numbers, faded and disappeared. The other, at the beginning small in numbers, grew and persisted for over two centuries" (Reynolds 2011:26). The Manso people spoke an Uto-Aztecan language closely related to that of the Jano and Jacome groups living further to the west in southern New Mexico and northern Chihuahua. By the mid-1660's several hundred natives, mostly Manso, were baptized at the Guadalupe Mission and were encouraged to settle at the Mission where they built "a village south of the Rio Grande on high ground above the river's floodplain opposite the river's crossing. In 1662 these homes were beside the adobe church constructed under Franciscans supervision" (Reynolds, 26). The residence for the friars was built adjacent to the other side of the church, where still stands next to the old Cathedral site in the city center. Today the Cathedral occupies the place where the Franciscans residence once stood. To the other side of the Cathedral complex, the Juárez municipal building occupies some of the land upon which Mansos constructed their original homes. The friars attempted to make the Mission self-sustaining and were engaged in the supervision of the fields, vineyards, and orchards within walking distance on the river's fertile floodplain to the northeast of the church (Reynolds, 26).

The story of the colonization of the region begins towards the end of the 16th century when the Spanish government considered the settlement of a province in New Mexico. Despite the obstacles placed in the way by jealous rivals, Juan de Oñate was assigned to explore the unknown lands, and on April 20, 1598, he reached the Rio del Norte; on April 30 he took formal possession of New Mexico, and only a few days later he reached "El Passo del Rio"; this was the "ford that became the gateway into New Mexico". Proceeding northward to the Pueblo region, Oñate subdued the native groups and planted a mission at a settlement in San Juan de los Caballeros, later abandoned by the settlers. Oñate continued his expedition and by 1609 he re-established a colony "at Santa Fé, the first permanent settlement within the limits of New Mexico" (Hughes 1914:289).

Historians confirm the foundation of Paso del Norte in 1659 by García de San Francisco y Zúñiga, who succeeded in gathering rancherías of the local Manso bands at a site near the mouth of the village, where he dedicated the church made of straw and mud to the Virgin of Guadalupe. Three additional missions and a handful of Spanish colonists provided impetus to the original settlement during the next twenty years. At the time the Spanish conquest of New Mexico was so disastrous due to the Pueblo revolt that about two thousand Spanish-speaking New Mexicans swept southward to Paso del Norte and inundated it in the fall of 1680 with the core of a permanent civilian community of Spanish speakers who had stayed away from the various indigenous groups (Halla 1978:15-18). By 1680 a Spanish civil community had been established under the jurisdiction of Nueva Vizcaya, and the Guadalupe Mission was being administered by the custodia of New Mexico. The original church still stands in the historic center of Cd. Juárez. By the time it was completed in 1668, the mission of San Francisco de Sumas and Nuestra Señora de la Soledad at Janos near Casas Grandes had been built. The three missions were the only permanent settlements when the refugees from the Pueblo Revolt in New Mexico arrived in September (Timmons 1990:17-18).

The Indians from the region were restless and dissatisfied under Spanish rule, and consequently organized a widespread revolt plotting to rise and massacre the Spaniards on August 11. When the conspiracy was discovered, they gradually withdrew southward until Governor Otermin and his advisors reached El Paso and made it the base of operations for the reconquest of the revolted province (Hughes 1914:301). "From Taos to Santa Fe and from Isleta to Zuni there were murder, pillage, devastation, and desecration" (Timmons 1990:17). The leaders of Santa Fe and Isleta, Governor Antonio de Otermin and Captain Alonso García, respectively, decided to flee southward to the safety of Paso del Norte. They reached La Salineta, about four leagues north of the Guadalupe Mission where they received provisions gathered by Father Francisco de Ayeta. The total number of soldiers, servants, women, children, and Indians amounted to 1,946; of these, 317 were Indian groups belonging to the Piro pueblos. Since then, Governor Otermin was planning to reconquer New Mexico (Timmons 17-18). Spanish and Indian settlers witnessed the foundation and the subsequent reprisal of the rioters.

1.1 Baptismal records

Baptismal records of the Cleofas Calleros Collection have been available since the mid-1960's. Twenty-eight Spanish-speaking priests serving the region during the revolt in New Mexico helped the refugees in different ways. Some of them escaped with the refugees or retreated from New Mexico to the lower valley. The surnames of the priests seem to be of Castilian or Basque origin: Juan Aluays, Juan Alvares, Antonio Azevedo, Francisco Ayetta, Juan de Bonilla, Diego Chabarria, Nicolas Echeverria, Francisco Gomez de la Cadena, Pedro Gomes, Antonio Guerra, Sebastian Hanarro, Nicolas Hurtado, Nicolas Lopes, Diego Mendoza, Juan Muñoz de Castro, Benito de la Natividad, Domingo Noriega, Joseph Ormarchea, Diego de Parraga, Francisco Salazar, Garcia de San Francisco (founder of the mission), Augustin Santa Maria, Joseph Spinola, Christobal Toblina, Joseph Truxillo, Joseph Valdez, and Francisco Vargas (McLaughlin 1962: Appendix I:1-2).

The information on those who were baptized is varied. The records provide mostly name, origin, approximate age, family membership, whereabouts, and occupation. At the end of the 17th century, almost 450 natives or inhabitants of Paso del Norte had a connection with the Church, normally through baptism. The roster includes prominent citizens such as Francisco Alvares, governor of the pueblo in 1676, Juana Amata, the wife of the governor of the Mansos. Native and nonnatives are distinguished. For instance, in 1681, Thomas Anacostete, Indian, is followed by Joseph de Apodaca, a 28-year-old Spaniard. His wife was Antonia Martin Zerrano and his daughter was named Josepha. All subjects appear in strict alphabetical order. Random examples illustrate the basics gathered by those in charge of the records.

- Juana de Argüello was the wife of Pedro Martin Zerrano de Salazar; she returned with her husband in 1693 to resettle their old home in La Cañada country and lived at least until 1718.
- Antonio de Avalos was born around 1630, was superintendent of Salina Mint mine in 1660; his wife was Juana Ruys de Caceres; his sons were Pedro Antonio, Juan, and Leonardo. He was a captain with Otermin's expedition.
- Fernando Duran de Chaves was a 30-year-old New Mexico native, married, enrolled as a settler in Otermin's expedition.
- Thomas Coyitletla, Indian official until 1680, when he was replaced by Matheo.
- Alonso de Caravasal had an Indian daughter in 1681 by an Indian woman called Ursula. Later wife was Ana Varela.
- Francisco Dominguez, captain born in Mexico City, married to Juana Rueda. He was old and blind when the revolt of 1680 came.
- Mathias Frias, married to Maria de la Encarnacion, was the father of Jeronimo, baptized October 11, 1679.
- Thomas de la Cruz, husband of Maria de Valencia, had a daughter baptized in 1686.
- Juana Garcia de Noriega, wife of Antonio Dominguez de Mendoza; son Antonio was baptized November 21, 1681.

- Sebastian Garcia, married to Maria Quetzitloma, son Andres was baptized December 22, 1662.
- Alonso Garcia, Governor of Socorro, married to Juana Itilgxa, by whom he had a Piro child, baptized on April 7, 1681.
- Anna Maria Garcia was the wife of Severino Rodrigues de Sabelle, father of Manuel Clemente, baptized January 15, 1682.
- Elvira Jemines was married to Juan Trujillo, mother of Cathalina, baptized November 25, 1680. She returned with husband to New Mexico after reconquest.
- Andres Lopes de Gracia was alferez at San Antonio de Isleta 1638; runs wagon trains between Santa Fe and Mexico City; first alcalde Mayor of El Paso; also, Alcalde at Casas Grandes 1680-1681.
- Teresa Gutierres was the wife of Joseph Lopes de Gracia, mother of Maria, baptized October 30, 1679.
- Maria Lopes de Gracia, daughter of Joseph de Padilla. Their two sons, Cayetano and Luis were baptized on October 16, 1679.
- Antonia Martin Zerrano, wife of Joseph de Apodaca. Daughter Josepha was baptized March 27, 1681.
- Antonio de Otermin, the ill-fated governor of New Mexico who struggled so hard and fruitlessly against the revolt of 1680.
- Cayetano Padilla was son of Captain Joseph de Padilla and Maria Lopes, baptized October 16, 1686.
- Apolonia Montano de Sotomayor was daughter of Antonio Montano de Sotomayor and Ysabel Jorge de Vera.
- Matias Naranjo was son of Pascual Naranjo and Maria Romero, listed in the text as mulattoes.
- Nuenebe, Luis, Indian, was baptized in 1663 at the age of 29.
- Juan Seberino Rodrigues de Saballe was born in Sevilla; husband of Anna Maria Garsia, also called Varela. His son Manuel Clemente was baptized on January 15, 1682. Assistant alcalde of Sandia by 1680.
- Cecilia de Vitoria, was the wife of Christobal Baca. Their daughter Maria was baptized on October 8, 1680.
- Francisco Zerberan, leader of a wagon train that came through El Paso in October 1679.

1.2 Indigenous languages vs. Spanish

The Guadalupe Mission and the El Paso region not only had the best land, but the best site to receive the waters of the Rio Grande. That is why most of the fellows who arrived there looked for the lands near the mission. In the middle of the 18th century, the mission of Guadalupe had almost half the population of the region, although one half was no longer indigenous, and by the beginning of the 19th century it concentrated almost 60% of the regional population. With Hispanic settlers and indigenous neophytes to serve, the Mission functioned as a cross between a proper mission and a parish. The mission was the flower of all because of its fruits, orchards, and climate. Half a league to the east, the residents owned vineyards and fruit trees: peach, apple, plum, and pear (González de la Vara 2009:55-56).

For a long time, the missionaries dedicated themselves to retaining control of the missions and their lands, but during the 18th century activity never stopped in the region. Even though the missionaries had lost a good part of the evangelizing initiative, the Christianization work continued because the various indigenous peoples asked to be integrated into the mission. By 1767 the region presented an interesting racial mosaic, but little by little the population classified as Spanish, mestizo or *'gente de razón'*—the one that was not indigenous—was populating the lands, which were distributed according to the interest of the inhabitants and according to the provisions of the Spanish authorities. Since 1681 the bishops of Nueva Vizcaya tried to place a parish priest in Paso del Norte instead of a missionary, given that since then the indigenous population was a minority and was fully Christianized. This substitution process was called secularization, although the Franciscans refused to abandon the missions. An ecclesiastical census of 1744 reports an indigenous population of 60% versus 37% of Spanish descent. Almost four decades later, a similar report indicates that the numbers had been inverted so that in 1782 there are already 70% Spanish and 30% indigenous. The decline of the indigenous population is most likely associated to provisions advanced by the Spanish authorities and the autonomy of the indigenous from New Mexico that stopped paying tribute to the missionaries. The indigenous was singled out as the individual who spoke his native language, preserved his customs, and was loyal to a traditional authority. The various native groups such as *piros, tiguas, mansos, sumas* or *tompiros* were gradually dissolved or mixed with the Spanish-speaking population (González de la Vara, 57-59).

The decline of the indigenous groups was the result of various intervening factors. During 1682 and 1684, the new governor of Gironza Petiz reorganized, together with the religious authorities, the distribution of the settlements, creating the El Paso region. A good part of the colonists expelled from New Mexico settled in the mission of Guadalupe, and the soldiers of the presidio camped right there. Two years earlier, the king had authorized the presence of the soldiers, which resulted in the mission beginning to lose its indigenous character. For this reason, the missions of San Lorenzo, Senecú, Socorro, Santa Gertrudis, and Isleta, respectively, were founded. These names were copied from the New Mexico missions where the *piros, tampiros,* and *tiguas* came from and coincided with the Spanish settlement of El Paso between 1680 and 1681 (González de la Vara, 43).

The mission maintained its presidio and its character as a town that was beginning to develop with good prospects and was consolidated as the center of the new region; between 1680 and 1692 it became the capital of what was left of the province of New Mexico and "began to function with a municipal government for the service of the inhabitants of the town, it had a representative of the governor with the title of lieutenant governor, and during the 18th century was the seat of the Franciscan custody of the El Paso prison and of the Inquisition in the province of New Mexico" (González de la Vara, 43-44). In the land that already seemed stabilized, conspiracies of local indigenous people arose, and the major leaders were mercilessly executed. Not only El Paso but all northern Nueva Vizcaya was threatened by increasing attacks by rebels and so-called barbarian Indians. Since losing El Paso would mean giving up all of New Mexico, the Spanish authorities sent military reinforcements while the missionaries tried to control the situation by offering to help the Indians return to the missions. In 1686, the revolt was contained, and the various communities survived in a civil settlement. The recolonization of New Mexico began in 1693 (González de la Vara, 44-45).

2 The 18th century: recovery period

For the El Paso region, the reconquest and resettlement meant a loss of population. Around 1693, the region was inhabited by just over a thousand people spread out in five communities that formed a chain of towns on the south bank of the Rio Grande. Between the churches and houses that marked the center of each town, stretched a long chain of ranches located on the banks of the river. This dispersion allowed that throughout the 18th century, Indians and Hispanic settlers of different ethnic groups and classes lived closely together and that the latter settled in the indigenous missions until they became the majority of the inhabitants. During the first years of the 18th century, the situation normalized, and peace attracted new settlers to the northwest of Nueva Vizcaya, thus Janos and Casas Grandes were repopulated. In 1706 the town of Albuquerque was founded, and a nucleus of agricultural development was formed in its surroundings. The El Paso region was not as isolated as it had been before, as the El Pasoans took advantage of the proximity of the river to build irrigation ditches, even though floods occasionally wreaked havoc on agriculture, but the constant efforts to tame the rugged landscape were worth it as they were able to cultivate fruit trees, vineyards, cornfields, and wheat fields. For travelers who arrived in El Paso after long journeys through the desert, that town seemed like a true oasis (González de la Vara, 47-48).

The breakdown of ethnic groups is glaring in the next century. Paso del Norte and San Lorenzo were mostly Spanish speaking, whereas Senecú and Isleta were largely Indian. Table 1 lists the settlements, the Spanish families, and the Indian families by mission. Table 2 presents the population of El Paso communities by ethnicity. The language groups are identified by mission: El Paso proper had speakers of Tigua-Piro; in San Lorenzo there were Sumas, whereas Piro and Tigua were spoken in Isleta and Socorro, respectively (Timmons, 35). The 1760 Bishop's census divided the inhabitants between *'gente de razón'* and Indians. The former label is the colonial hyper-distinction of Spanish speakers and Indians, who were descending in the quantitative and qualitative status of the new northern frontier (Table 3).

Table 1 Population of El Paso Communities (1744)

Settlements	Spanish families	Indian families	Total families
Mission of Nuestra Señora de Guadalupe del Paso	180 (plus 40 presidial soldiers)	40	220
San Lorenzo	12	50 (Sumas)	62
San Antonio Senecú	5	70	75
Nuestra Señora del Socorro	6	60	66
Nuestra Señora de las Caldas and Hacienda El Capitán	n/a	60	n/a
Ranches of Ojo Caliente and El Carrizal	20 (mixed with Indians)	n/a	20
Hacienda de la Ranchería	20	"some"	20
Totals	243	370	613

Source: Timmons (1990:35)

Table 2 Population of El Paso Communutues (1750)

Mission	Whites	Indians
El Paso	1,090	200
San Lorenzo	130	150
Senecú	102	384
Isleta	54	500
Socorro	250	250
Totals	1,646	1,484

Source: Timmons (1990:35)

Table 3 El Paso Area Population (1760)

Bishop's census	*Gente de Razón*		*Indians*	
Mission and language group	Families	Persons	Families	Persons
El Paso del Norte	353	2,479	72	249
San Lorenzo del Real and Senecú	32	192	21	58
Piros	-	-	111	425
Sumas	-	-	18	52
Sumas infieles	-	-	-	28
Socorro (incl. gente de razón at Hacienda de Tiburcio)	82	424	46	182
Isleta	18	131	80	429
Totals	515	3,367	348	1,423

Source: Timmons (1990:40)

The grand total for 1760 reached 4,790 people or about 30% of the indigenous population *vis-à-vis* a solid 70% of the Spanish speaking already established in the very small towns or villages of the El Paso region. Only two decades later, El Paso settlements suffered a decline of the greatest smallpox epidemic in the history of the Southwest, which is registered in the Juárez archives of 1784, "one of the most comprehensive yet to come to light. A total of 4,091 for the five settlements, or about a thousand less than the figure of the 1760s" (Timmons, 55). Table 4 shows the heads of households in the same census log listed by ethnicity. Before New Spain's independence from Spain, the grand total reached 1,006 heads of household of which one half or 51.3% made up a solid Spanish-speaking majority.

Table 4 El Paso Area Households by Town and Ethnicity (1784)

Town	Españoles	Mestizos	Indios (G)*	Mulattoes	Coyotes	Negros	Indios
El Paso	395	46	23	68	20	2	51
S. Lorenzo	41	6	-	-	3	-	22
Senecú	8	17	5	1	2	-	70
Isleta	24	3	7	-	-	-	64
Socorro	48	45	7	-	9	1	18
Totals	516	117	42	69	34	3	225

Source: Timmons (1990:55) *Indios genízaros*

For several years (1784-1788) the population of El Paso area remained slightly more than the 4,100 level and continued to outnumber all the settlements combined. Spanish speakers continued to equal the number of ethnic groups combined. In 1788 the population increased again to 4,782, then to 5,314 in 1789, and again to 5,471 in 1795. The mestizo population increased, too, while the indigenous continue declining. By 1800, immediately before Independence the El Paso settlements reached 6,000 people. During the first decade of the 19th century there was a significant increase from 6,190 in 1804 to 6,845 in 1806. In addition, a public school system was established in Chihuahua with 13 schools in El Paso area; nine of those were in Paso del Norte and one each in San Lorenzo, Senecú, Ysleta, and Socorro with a total enrollment of 856 children (Timmons, 56, 58). The mid-18th century census of Friar Andrés Varo corroborates the proportion of indigenous groups by language. In combination they represent the number of individuals who lived in each pueblo with the Tiguas at the top (Table 5). The language is specified by group and contrasts with the category "Spaniards" who belong to only one group of Spanish speakers (Comar 2015:113).

Table 5 Fray Andrés Varo Census (1749)

1749	Indians	Spaniards	Language group
El Paso	200	1,090	Tewa (Tegua) Piro
San Lorenzo	150	150	Suma
Senecú	384	102	Piro
Ysleta	500	54	Tewa (Tegua)
Socorro	250	250	Not listed
Total	1,484	1,646	

Comar (2015:113)

The colonial census of 1793 reports that all the indigenous groups speak Castilian better than their own language. "Los del Paso que se componen de varias naciones no tienen más idiomas que el castellano y lo mismo sucede a los de Socorro; los del real son Sumas pero muy pocos, y aunque entienden su idioma hablan mejor el Castellano; los a Senecú son Piros, los de Ysleta, Tiguas, unos y otros hablar también su idioma como el castellano" (Comar, 93).

3 Independence from Spain

At the beginning of Mexican independence, the population of El Paso (excluding San Elizario) was about 7,000 and by 1815 had almost reached 8,000. By then, El Paso had been divided into eight districts with a population of 5,854 people of whom 4,839 were Spanish speaking (i.e., criollos and mestizos and 1,015 Indians). In the smallest districts (except in Senecú), Spanish speakers also reached one half of the majority (Timmons, 67).

The struggle for Independence from Spain was not as dramatic as in central Mexico, where the hyper-differentiation between Spanish speakers and criollos was leading to multiple contradictions and rivalries. The only Spaniards known in El Paso region was a priest or a local authority. The conditions of socioeconomic injustice were not exacerbated, and consequently, in this region, the anti-Spanish sentiment was not too strong. El Paso and other northern regions played the role of witnesses rather than protagonists of the independence movement. On September 8, 1821, El Paso celebrated Mexican independence and the municipality proclaimed its support to the Plan de Iguala. Three years later El Paso was situated in the *Estado Interno del Norte* that brought together the old provinces of Nueva Vizcaya and Nuevo Mexico with its capital in Chihuahua; the state of Chihuahua gave a warm welcome to Paso del Norte and ascended it to the category of villa with 8,934 inhabitants (González de la Vara, 66-68).

4 The Mexico-U.S. War

El Paso belonged to the new Mexican Republic for less than three decades; during that time, it had its own municipal council largely dominated by the local aristocracy while the traditional economic activities such as agriculture, stock raising, and commerce continued to flourish and provided a large degree of self-sufficiency though occasionally the various missions were overflowed by the river. The Lower Valley of El Paso made up of Ysleta, Socorro, and San Elizario had a population of 2,850 with the majority of heads of household working on the farms. Each settlement had a silversmith, several carpenters, foremen, a hat maker, and mule drivers. The local council landed grants to Juan María Ponce de León and 29 other citizens. Ponce de León's grant was located just across in what is today the downtown business district of El Paso (Texas), where he built an adobe house. Ponce's second grant (1830) was more successful than the first, and in time he developed it into a thriving agriculture and ranching enterprise (Timmons, 74-75).

Indeed, the *Ayuntamiento* regularly parceled out to suitable petitioners grants of uncultivated municipal land on the north bank of the Rio Grande immediately opposite El Paso, in the valley above El Paso, or on the mesa. Since 1827 Juan Ponce had been in possession of two *caballerías* (about 220 acres) across the river, part of which his *peones* cultivated and part of which was pasture. Luis Cuarón and Rafael Ruelas received substantial grants—the first of a square league (4430 acres) plus a *caballería* and the second of one *caballería*—in the same vicinity in 1847 and 1848. In the early 1850s Guadalupe Miranda, Rómulo Barela, and a Juan José Sánchez, influential *paseños* all, acquired tracts of at least one square league each in the rough marsh and sandhill area of the upper valley, though unfortunately, the real barrier to use the ground beyond the immediate confines of the valley was the constant threat of Apache attacks. Thus, to the ecological factors that influenced the configuration of settlement at Paso del Norte must be added the Apache, for it is misleading to imply that the land surrounding the valley lay unclaimed and unused (Halla, 43-45).

Before the severance of Paso del Norte in two communities, historians highlight the Apache raids as a vexing problem for Mexican officials as they had been for the Spanish, and the reaction of those in charge of the territory. In 1839 Chihuahua's governor formed the *Sociedad de Guerra contra los Bárbaros* to curtail the destruction of the regional resources. Another interesting event is the development of the Chihuahua trade along the Camino Real, a natural extension of the Santa Fe trade. Since then, El Paso became a commercial center of such importance that the Mexican government authorized an annual trade fair in 1842 lasting for eight days. Moreover, since 1835, the Mexican government had established a customhouse in Paso del Norte for the inspection of cargoes, seizure of contraband goods, and enforcement of all customs duties (Timmons, 80-81).

The Mexican era ended with the Mexico-U.S. War (1846-48), and Paso del Norte was split in two villas although they continued to be known as El Paso, but one was in Chihuahua and the other one in Texas. *Paseños* were found on both sides of the "new border", which was not clearly demarcated yet. Both Mexican El Paso in the state of Chihuahua and U.S. El Paso in the state of Texas became isolated from their new respective nations, the uncertainty of the boundaries, and the turmoil of civil wars in both the United States and Mexico. At this juncture socioethnic groups were not differentiated, since differentiation does not occur overnight. *Paseños* were mostly Spanish speakers (and writers) who had maintained family and business networks within the region. There were survivors of the attacks of the indigenous groups. In the mid-19th century, there is no record yet of English use. Terms such as Mexican-Americans, U.S. Mexicans or *fronterizos* were unknown. The group known today as Chicano emerged in the 1960's as a result of the modern civil rights movement.

While the Treaty of Guadalupe Hidalgo formally ended the Mexican-U.S. War in February 1848, disputes between the Mexico and the United States continued to simmer over the next few years. The point of contention was the Mesilla Valley as part of their own territory. The Mexican Government demanded monetary compensation for the violence in the region caused by the U.S. indigenous groups that the United States had agreed to prevent. In 1853 Mexicans evicted U. S. citizens from their property and the Governor of New Mexico claimed the Mesilla Valley a part of the U.S. territory. Finally, U.S. President Franklin Pierce commissioned James Gadsen to renegotiate an open border route for transportation.

> The Treaty of Guadalupe-Hidalgo (1848) pushed Texas beyond the Nueces River, its natural boundary. The Rio Grande became the new international frontier, from the Gulf of Mexico to a point eight miles north of El Paso. From El Paso, a line following the boundary between New Mexico and Chihuahua was to run the headwaters of the Gila then down the Gila to the Colorado River (…). The new boundary, however, did not meet demands in the United States for a level, all-weather route to the Pacific, where the discovery of gold in 1848 had attracted Easterners by the thousands. In 1853 the United States minister to Mexico, James Gadsen, a railroad executive from South Carolina, negotiated the purchase of lands south of the Gila to the present United States-Mexican border (Weber 1982:274).

In the historical juncture preceding the Mexico-U.S. War, El Paso was the safeguard of the frontier settlements of Nueva Vizcaya. Though the relevance of El Paso has been underestimated, "the true beginnings of what is Texas now are to be found in the settlements grouped along the Río del Norte in the El Paso district" (Hughes, 392). After the indigenous languages spoken in both New Mexico and Chihuahua, Spanish was the language spoken and written by the early Spanish colonists who arrived in El Paso from Mexico and New Mexico.

Map 1 shows the new political boundary that began in El Paso and ended on the extreme of the Gulf of Mexico. The current states of Arizona and New Mexico adjacent to independent Texas appear as a territory north of the Gila River, while the current states of Nevada and Utah were the Territory of Utah incorporated to the United States since 1850. Texas was annexed to the United States in 1845 and was admitted to the Union as the 28th state. The argument commonly advanced to justify or explain the early annexation of Texas was that the southern states wanted Texas because it would be inclined to support slavery and the slave trade under the Missouri Compromise. Northerners were against the annexation of Texas because they were not supporting slavery.

Map 1 United States-Mexico Boundaries (1853)

5 Two sides of the border

By the mid-19th century and having converted a good number of local indigenous, Spanish speakers were mostly adhered to Catholicism (see Baptismal records). On the new Mexican side of the border, Catholic priests were determined to maintain the Church's autonomy. Some of the leaders such as Ramon Ortiz struggled throughout his long life of service to maintain the Church's purity of tradition in the face of strenuous challenges from his own government and from an influx of Protestantism, as after 1848, Americans settled across the river from El Paso del Norte (Halla, 95).

Immediately after the Mexico-U.S. War it was difficult to delineate with any precision the boundaries either of the Villa de Paso del Norte itself or of any individual district. Size of landholdings and population density in the districts of Mejia and Juárez in 1880 have been retrieved by Halla (1978). In spite of adversity, the *paseños* remaining on the Mexican side of the border retained some of their properties, to wit: Miguel Aguirre, Dionicio Apodaca, Manuela Ascárate de Jáquez, the Barela family, Emiliano Barrio, the Bernal family, Francisco Carbajal, Manuel Córdova, the Cuarón family, the Delfín family, Pedro Espinosa, the Gallegos family, Teodora Jiménez, the Lucero family, the Madrid family, Francisco Salcedo, José María Sierra, Josefa Velarde de Herrera and 28 other *paseños* who gave the value of their land in pesos rather than listing the dimensions of individual plots. The four largest landholders listed are Epitacio Corral, Inocente Ochoa, Juan N. Ruiz, and Mariano Samaniego, none of whom gave the dimensions of their holdings. It should be remembered that this partial accounting of landholders has no direct correlation with the actual wealth of the individuals listed, or even to the total amount of land owned, since dimension plots were omitted. Many of the plots not fully described were gardens adjacent to homes (327-329).

6 After the wars

In the last decades of the 19th century, the attacks of the Apaches in the territory of Chihuahua, Texas and New Mexico decreased until they disappeared. The cessation of this threat finally opened many lands to cattle ranching and speculation. Agriculture resumed its growth due to the recovery of the markets that had been unstable. By 1878, the production of grains and the wine industry were making juicy profits. Over time, an agricultural and commercial elite emerged in the vicinity of the Guadalupe mission. Simultaneously, the best houses were built, and a class of artisans arose that was connected to both the El Paso (Texas) and the Chihuahua markets. On the other hand, Spanish-speaking merchants from New Mexico passed through Paso del Norte (Chihuahua) to market their products. Some merchants remained active until the railroad arrived. The new merchant class was largely descended from the old class of farmers who survived the vicissitudes of previous centuries. The transactions were carried out in pesos or in the Mexican ounce of gold that had a value of 16 dollars. Spanish was the language of commerce, and since El Paso (Texas) had no banks, banknotes were only seen at Fort Bliss. By 1875 the binational mercantile elite could rival the U.S. counterpart in resources. For the first time, Paso del Norte (Chihuahua) had an embryonic aristocracy that displaced the old patricians who combined political power with prestige. The mercantile leaders consolidated the peace from 1884, when the U.S companies began to build the railroad thus contributing to the social change on both sides of the border (González de la Vara, 108-113).

6.1 Benito Juárez in Paso del Norte

Maximilian of Austria (1832-1867) was a young naval officer and an ally of the French emperor. After the defeat of May 5, 1862, Napoleon III persuaded him to rule Mexico with the support of the Roman Catholic clergy, thousands of French troops, and a group of ultra-conservatives who were hostile to the liberal administration of President Juárez. By 1864, Maximilian crowned himself as Emperor of Mexico, and though the Empire was acknowledged by European powers, the United States recognized Juárez as president. During his reign he managed to form an alternate government. Benito Juárez, the main protagonist of the events and Minister of Justice since October 1855, became the leader of the liberal reforms against the Catholic Church. The Constitutional Reform of 1857 succeeded in separating state from church for the first time, the scission that had provoked a three-year Civil War (1857-1860).

Maximilian and his young wife Charlotte of Belgium had no hopes of ever inheriting a kingdom of their own, since Napoleon III normally prevailed in European politics. Then Maximilian demanded not only financial and military support from France but also the results of a plebiscite showing the Mexican voters' preferences for a monarchy. By April 1864, with the support of his wife, he signed a pact in which he gave up to all his rights as the Prince of Austria. The couple left for Rome to receive the blessings of Pope Pius IX, and shortly after, they embarked themselves to Veracruz on the Austrian war ship *La Novara*. Amid deafening applause, they entered in Mexico City on June 12, 1864. From the beginning, the young emperor tried to earn the goodwill of the liberals and gained their support. Unable or unwilling to annul or modify the Reform Laws, he provoked the wrath of the conservatives. As though there were no political turmoil, the capital of the country turned into the scenario of lavish social functions in the imperial residence of Chapultepec. The squandering of resources reduced the revenue of the new Court and for this reason it was necessary to borrow money from London and Paris (Blasio 1905:187).

In contrast to the opulent life in the capital city, the incessant guerrilla warfare in the interior rural districts caused large losses to Mexican troops. In October 1865, Maximilian ordered that the rebels and any other armed group against Europe be sentenced to death, offered amnesty to those willing to lay down their arms before November 15, and even gave an extension to December 1. The emperor assumed that with this decree, the civil war would end and attract leaders to the liberal cause, but to his dismay he only alienated the party members (Quitarte 1970:27). The Mexican adventure was so costly that at that point Napoleon only wanted to withdraw his troops from Mexico. Empress Charlotte took the initiative to go to Paris and demanded Napoleon to deliver his promises; she also went to Rome to request the influential intervention of the Pope to rescue the imperial cause.

When Charlotte departed from Veracruz on July 10, 1866, she did not suspect that she would not see her husband anymore. She arrived in Paris a month later and went directly to Saint-Cloud. There she met Napoleon with whom she exchanged recriminatory remarks about the political and military fiasco in Mexico. The French Intervention had been an attempt to test the Monroe doctrine, and Napoleon had indeed taken advantage of the fact that the United States was going through the civil war. At the time, the U.S. Secretary of State William Seward was giving him an ultimatum to end the occupation of the Mexican territory. To maintain his dignitary presence and appease the French people who were upset over the cost of the expedition to Mexico, Napoleon decided to withdraw the support he had given to Maximilian (Hamann 1983/1994:21, 171). Aggravated by the many tensions, Charlotte proceeded to Rome and requested the Pope's assistance, but since the Reform Laws had incited hostility amongst the Catholic powers in Europe, he only wanted to return to the Mexican Church the property confiscated by the liberals.

6.2 Benito Juárez in Cd. Juárez

Between August 14 and November 20, 1865, and again between December 18, 1865 and June 10, 1866, President Benito Juárez established his national government in the El Paso region while constantly fleeing from the French invaders. Not only daily life and the region were altered by this event, but its strategic importance became evident due to the need to extend the Mexican population south of what was properly Paso del Norte, so that its resources could be exploited. Thus, he made concessions for ranchers and landowners located about 40 km away south of the village. His performance as president was not exempt from disputes in the administration of different issues ranging from the use of water to the administration of justice. The following years he had to confront another powerful enemy, the dictator Porfirio Díaz (González de la Vara, 106-107).

6.3 The end of the 19th century

After the arrival of the railroad in 1880, both the new city of El Paso and Paso del Norte were well connected with the U.S. northwestern states (Arizona and California) and with the interior of Mexico. On the U.S. side of the border, banks, newspapers (in English), transportation services, public schools, and churches were established. By 1890 it already had 8,000 souls, and by 1920 the population multiplied exponentially so that it reached 80,000. Trade with Mexico increased from more than one million pesos in 1885 to almost 9 million pesos in 1887, and 11 million 400 thousand dollars during 1910. Along with trade and associated services, mining boomed, and thanks to its development, El Paso began to have institutions of higher education. From 1890 it became a strategic point for those who went to Chihuahua or for tourists who wanted to know Mexico. El Paso attracted thousands of Mexicans who worked in the nascent U.S. industry. Other groups of Chinese, Austrian, German-Jewish, and Syrian origin have left their mark on the region (González de la Vara, 105).

With its ups and downs Paso del Norte grew more modestly. On March 23, 1884, the first train from Mexico City arrived at the Chihuahuan border. The *Ferrocarril Central Mexicano* united the region with the center and north of Mexico creating a wide geographical corridor that joined Aguascalientes, Zacatecas, Cd. Lerdo, Torreón and Chihuahua with Paso del Norte. Before the end of the 19th century, the region had strengthened its communication network that extended throughout the state of Chihuahua. Very soon, the duty-free zone contributed to economic growth and was consolidated as the main Mexican population center with a checkpoint for the entry and distribution of foreign merchandise and as an export checkpoint. Commercial activity encouraged the urbanization process around the new Customs House built in 1887 in the most flamboyant French style (Gonzalez de la Vara, 115 and ff). The building was inaugurated with great pomp on September 10, 1889, and is currently the City History Museum. A year earlier it had changed its name to Ciudad Juárez, and by the beginning of the 20th century, it began to enjoy public services such as electricity, drinking water, telephone lines, trams, schools, markets, etc.

Having established Paso del Norte as the provisional capital of the country (1865-1866), regional leaders were motivated to change the name from Paso del Norte to Ciudad Juárez. Chihuahua Governor Carrillo not only proposed the change but elevated its status from villa to ciudad to honor the memory of President Juárez. The change was effective in 1888, and since then the El Pasoans (in English) retained the original demonym in Spanish and are distinguished as paseños from El Paso (Texas). The neologism juarenses, derived from Ciudad Juárez, was probably coined and spread in the course of the 20th century, while the term neojuarense ('established newcomers') emerged at the end of the past century.

Since 1880, the newspapers El Progresista and El Centinela circulated intermittently. Years later, publications such as El Clarín, edited by the businessman from Juárez, Espiridión Provencio, came to light. This magazine was joined in 1896 by El Agricultor Mexicano and El Hogar, both founded by the Escobar brothers. In 1903 the construction of the Juárez Theater began. The development of the end of the century contributed to the consolidation of a mature Mexican mercantile elite that allied itself with U.S. merchants such as the Oppenheimers, Webers, and other entrepreneurs. Despite the increasing scarcity of water, some horticultural crops, fruit trees, corn and wheat continued to be cultivated while the free zone made commercial agriculture competitive. In 1906, the Hermanos Escobar School of Agriculture was founded, from which well-qualified agronomists graduated (González de la Vara, 136).

7 The Taft-Díaz Meeting in 1909

The great event of the beginning of the century was the encounter celebrated between the presidents of the United States and Mexico, the first one between two heads of state of the respective countries. On October 15, 1909, Porfirio Díaz arrived in Juárez. The next day, at 11 a.m. Don Porfirio crossed the border to meet William Taft at the Chamber of Commerce, where they spoke privately. In the late afternoon of October 16, Taft was received by Don Porfirio at the Border Customs building where a sumptuous French-style dinner was served (González de la Vara, 135). The details of the interviews are described by Timmons (198-202). The interpreter at both meetings was Enrique Creel, interim governor of Chihuahua. According to Terrazas, the then governor took the content of the interview or interviews to his grave (2005:130).

8 The Mexican Revolution

The Mexican Revolution is the sequel to the lengthy Porfirian era and the defining stage of a good part of the 20th century, which contributed to the destruction of the oligarchic and neocolonial state of the late 19th century. The Porfirian regime provoked a crisis in the sociopolitical, economic, diplomatic, and cultural sectors that generated oppositional movements between various social classes and political actors. The censorship came from the Catholic Church, which showed its discontent with the excessive concentration of agrarian property in the hands of a few families. Other sectors questioned foreign investment, especially from the United States. Among his opponents was Francisco I. Madero, a businessman and rancher from Coahuila, who organized anti-reelection clubs. The campaign against Díaz's re-election helped Madero ran as a candidate for the presidency, but was arrested and confined to prison in San Luis Potosí. Madero fled from prison and took refuge in San Antonio (Texas), and from there he drafted the Plan of San Luis. Coming from the urban middle class, it was inconceivable that he would incite the armed struggle. Despite the opposition, the idea was welcomed in the northern states: Chihuahua, Sonora, Durango, and Coahuila, where the rebels were few and poorly armed. In February 1911 Madero returned to Mexico to assume leadership of the struggle, since the Díaz government was weak and poorly organized. Ciudad Juárez was the first town to succumb to the forces of Madero and his allies (Garciadiego 2004 /2016:225-228).

The defeat of the *federales* (troops commanded by the military in power) in Ciudad Juárez accelerated the talks between the government and the insurgents and paralyzed the federal government. The unexpected events led to the Treaties of Ciudad Juárez in which it was agreed to replace the three-decade dictator Díaz with his Secretary of Foreign Affairs Francisco León de la Barra. At the end of 1911, Madero's victories in the north helped him gain the presidency of the Republic, and immediately confronted the armed rebellion of Emiliano Zapata in Morelos (Garciadiego, 229-232). Madero's triumph was enlightened by the participation of Pascual Orozco and Francisco Villa, the northern leaders who took control of Ciudad Juárez and besieged the city in what is known as the first decisive battle. The success of Madero and his allies was accelerated by the ready access to weapons coming from the United States, an appalling event that presumably intimidated Porfirio Díaz (Portilla 1997).

9 The battles of Cd. Juárez in literature

The beginnings of the Mexican Revolution (1910-1921) have been reported in countless sources. Writings on the armed movement illustrate not only the heroes and their battles but also the sociopolitical consequences caused by such a long war. The narrative of this period includes a wide range of genres like pamphlets, short stories, biographies, and documented testimonials of witnesses who were present at the battlefield at different times. According to critics the creative writers born under the Porfiriato belong to the first generation of narrators of the Revolution. Mariano Azuela (1873-1952), José Vasconcelos (1881-1959), Martín Luis Guzmán (1887-1976), and José Rubén Romero (1890-1952) contributed to the history of literature creating a nationalist trend that has had a permanent effect in popular and classic culture. Luis Leal (1964) gathered the works of representative authors and excerpts that narrate the battles of Ciudad Juárez: *La revolución y Francisco I. Madero* by Roque Estrada (1912, Guadalajara); *Memorias de Pancho Villa* by Martín Luis Guzmán (1938-1940); *Pancho Villa* by Teodoro Torres (1929, San Antonio, Texas); *Ulises criollo* by Vasconcelos (1935-1936); *Los de abajo* by Mariano Azuela (1915); *Villa en pie* by Ramón Puente (1937), and *Fuego en el Norte* by Rafael F. Muñoz (1960). These works were brought together at the First Cultural Festival in Cd. Juárez on August 22, 1963.

Figure 1 Madero's victory (April 7-May 10, 1911)
Source: Library of Congress (Grantham Bain Collection)

Figure 2 Revolutionary camp outside Cd. Juárez (1911)
Source: Wikipedia

Figure 3 Rebels took Ciudad Juárez in front of the Building of the Customs House
Source: Museo de la Revolución de la Frontera (Cd. Juárez)

As Madero had stipulated in his Plan of San Luis, the armed revolution arose on November 20, 1910. Roque Estrada asserts that the rural class of Chihuahua was the only serious focus of insurrection in the first two months, and it is perhaps to its citizens in arms to whom the Republic owes a work of enormous collective necessity. Madero was, at that time, in the United States, where he remained until February 1911. After finishing his commission in Coahuila, Captain Aguilar said, "I left San Antonio for El Paso, with the purpose of indicating to Mr. Abraham González to arrange the entry of Mr. Madero into national territory as soon as possible". Meanwhile, Pascual Orozco had made a brilliant march on Ciudad Juárez, the vicinity of which he arrived on January 2, 1911. Orozco's remarkable march fell short of expectations. On February 5, Colonel Antonio Ribago arrived with his forces, while Orozco, seeing the impossibility of taking the city, had to withdraw (Leal 1964:231).

In El Paso, President Madero formed a Strategic Council made up of José Garibaldi, Raúl Madero, and Roque González Garza. Accompanied by said Council, Madero passed into Mexican territory, in a place very close to Ciudad Juárez, on the night of February 13 and 14, 1911. The first battle in which Madero participated was that of Casas Grandes, on March 6 of the same year. Having been defeated and Madero wounded in the arm, the insurgent column withdrew to the Hacienda de Bustillos. There they were joined by Francisco Villa and shortly after remaining in Bustillos, the revolutionary column set out, presenting itself in front of Ciudad Juárez in the first days of the second half of April (Leal, 231).

A famous author who followed Francisco Villa to his camp in Ciudad Juárez was Martín Luis Guzmán. In the first part of his *Memoirs of Pancho Villa*, Guzmán tells how Pascual Orozco and Francisco Villa formulated a plan in April 1911, to take Ciudad Juárez. Once they obtained Madero's consent, Orozco and Villa put their plan of attack into execution. Guzmán narrates the event in the words of Villa, whose version tells that

Orozco would enter the river with five hundred men until he took the Customs House and advanced with two hundred more men where the *federales* and "our men" were already seized. At that point Villa would attack from the southern part, where the Central Railroad station is located. That day, May 8, 1911, should not be forgotten among revolutionary men, because Orozco and Villa were the direct commanders of the troops of the Revolution and had managed to fix the facts in a proper way for their action. In the following chapter Villa continues recounting that:

> For the attack on Ciudad Juárez, I made my course along the hill that leads to the pantheon. I spent the whole night near said pantheon, stuck with my forces in one of the streams that flow there. In that place I began to meditate on how I would do the most convenient thing to fight the enemy well at four in the morning. At four in the morning of May 9, 1911, I managed to get with my people as far as the Kételsen winery, and there I broke the fire. Since they knew we were in that spot, from the school that is in front of the warehouses, they yelled at us 'who is in there'. There was a machine gun that caused some casualties and disrupted my ranks a bit. I then tried to continue. But as soon as I saw that I was outflanked in that corralled yard, I decided without further ado to retreat to the Central Railroad station (Leal, 232).

Villa continues saying that he was strong behind that shelter and was able to calmly develop his attack against the school and other fortifications. The *federales* proceeded to withdraw in the direction of their headquarters. Advancing through the interior of the houses, they served as a parapet and shelter, and we were drilling through wall to wall to pass from one house to another. That was a very long and very hard night fight; they did not sleep much and continued in the light of dawn. It was already the next day, May 10, 1911, very close to ten o'clock, when the *federales*, already in frank retreat towards their headquarters, left me with all the wounded and prisoners that they had taken on the early morning of the 9th in my advance towards the cellars. Villa continued advancing until he managed to trap the enemies in the headquarters. General Juan N. Navarro, head of the federal forces, decided to surrender along with his staff of 400 soldiers, handing over the intact weapons and an enormous number of cartridges to the enemy. The surrender of Cd. Juárez took place at three in the afternoon on May 10, 1911. The Battle of Juárez was the most intense of the Maderista plan (Leal, 234).

The other well-known writer who was politically interested in the development of Madero's actions and reactions in Cd. Juárez was José Vasconcelos, the author of *Ulises criollo* and ambassador of Mexico in Washington. His viewpoint is summarized by Leal (1964:235).

> The moral effect of the siege of Juárez was great; it was necessary to take advantage of the precarious situation that the movement demanded. As soon as Customs fell into the hands of the rebels, the diplomacy of Porfirio Díaz managed to close the border. Our mission in Washington was to obtain recognition of belligerence with the resumption of international traffic. If the Porfirian Embassy triumphed, the Maderistas who had just conquered Ciudad Juárez would not be able to stock up on war munitions or food. The interests of American border trade were in our favor. The two days it took for a favorable statement to come out of the State Department were the most intense of my stay in Washington. The reopening of the international bridge on the American side implied the recognition of our party. After the triumph, a conflict arose between Madero and his bosses. These leaders, but especially Orozco for personal reasons, asked for the head of General Navarro, who was in a critical situation. It was believed that he would almost certainly be executed by the rioters. Though

personally in risk, Madero resolved to save the General's life, took him out of his lodgings on the night of May 11 or 12, and hauled him to the bank of the Bravo, where the President and General said goodbye. The latter then passed the river by swimming in the direction of U.S. territory. Before Madero released Navarro, a drama worthy of appearing in the annals of universal history had occurred.

Leal (1964) ends his article with an inspiring story about Dr. Mariano Azuela, who arrived in Cd. Juárez in October 1915 with his first notes for what was to be his great novel, *Los de abajo*. Azuela reports his residence in Juárez twice and his having breakfast at *Delmónico*, a popular restaurant in El Paso. The last occasion he was there, famine was already raging in all the places occupied by the armed forces. General Villa paid for food in gold to his top bosses in said restaurant, and naturally, absolute preference was given to the military. Azuela adds that there he met a deeply unpleasant waiter: short, round-faced, chubby-cheeked, and fiery, his eyes injected with blood. He was extremely active, presumed to be on first-name terms with the most famous leaders, and treated us civilians with disdain and even insolence. From that hateful guy the character known as el güero Margarito was born in Azuela's fiction (240-241).

Azuela read the first part of the novel to his friend Enrique Luna Román, a lawyer, who moved to El Paso a few days later. He had already finished the second part, when he wrote to him and assured him that he had a publisher for his book. As his resources were running out, he left Juárez for El Paso with ten dollars in his bag. Azuela claimed they visited various publishing house agents, and they asked him to send the original version. But since he had immediate urgency for money, he had to accept the offer from *El Paso del Norte*: one thousand overprint copies and three dollars a week on account while printing was made. Within a month of distributing the printed manuscript to book and magazine stands, five copies had been sold. Meanwhile, without fighting, the Carrancistas took Ciudad Juárez. Azuela thus took advantage of the confusion of the first few hours to go to Mexican territory. He bought a railway pass from a soldier and with José Montes de Oca, he returned to Guadalajara. He never knew the end of the one thousand copies of his novel that Mr. Gamiochipi—owner of *El Paso del Norte*—published, but he did know that he owed him twelve dollars.

Azuela concludes that "El Paso lingers in my memory as a foodie paradise. I laugh at those who tell of their great sufferings as exiles with many hundreds and even thousands of dollars, which I never even dared to dream of. With ten dollars I got to El Paso and with fifty cents I did my daily expenses" (Obras III, 1083-1091). In the famous novel, Azuela satirizes exiles: Luis Cervantes takes refuge in El Paso and from there he writes his famous and burlesque letter, dated May 16, 1915, to his dear friend Venancio. The heroic period of the Mexican Revolution is the one that goes from 1910 to 1915. During those years, no city in the Republic played such an important role in the development of its history as Cd. Juárez (Leal, 241).

10 The end of Madero's presidency

Madero's allies suspected from the beginning that because he was president and was able to abuse his power, he had let General Navarro—who had killed many of the revolutionaries—escape or had hidden in his house. In the short time that Madero was in Juárez, both his allies, that is, Pascual Orozco and Francisco Villa and his enemies appeared in the premises, and among them a young supporter of Porfirio Díaz, known as Victoriano Huerta. The unexpected incident involving the release of General Navarro shook Madero's victories and led him to dig his own grave. The many conflicts between pioneering leaders put Madero at risk, and when he returned to Mexico City, his presidency was abruptly interrupted by a coup fabricated by Victoriano Huerta, one of the allies of Porfirio Díaz. Huerta remained in power and was seemingly loyal to Madero, who entrusted him to defend Mexico City from the fighting survivors of the Díaz regime. Having control of the armed forces, Huerta took advantage of this opportunity to assassinate Madero and his vice-president José María Pino Suárez in 1913. Consequently, Huerta was appointed President for a short period of time until he himself was overthrown. It is assumed that other leaders such as Venustiano Carranza participated in the plot to eliminate Madero. The struggles of the Mexican Revolution continued in the south until the end of the Movement in 1921.

10.1 Legends and folklore

From the heroic deeds of the Mexican Revolution, the legend of "la Adelita" and the famous corrido composed in her honor by Colonel Antonio Gil del Río have survived. The image of the brave woman who participated in bloody battles has been used as the symbol of national identity throughout the 20th century and has not disappeared in the 21st century. Gutiérrez (2019) gathered relevant information on "the real Adelita".

Adela Velarde Pérez was born on September 8, 1900, in Ciudad Juárez, Chihuahua, where she studied basic education and later dedicated herself to nursing. From this moment until she triumphed as a heroine of the Mexican Revolution, it is known that she was a rebellious woman, one of those who carry courage in her blood. Not all the information is confirmed by historians since they were seasoned with some of the "romanticism" of her character. Adela was the daughter of a wealthy merchant from Juárez, who disobeyed her father to join the Mexican Association of the Red Cross to be a nurse; she was known for her efficiency and skill in caring for the wounded and that was what made her become the darling of the troops. From her appearance it is known that she was a very beautiful woman, who stood out for the generosity with which she acted, always restless, happy, and curious. She was motivated to join the group of nurses that Leonor Villegas de Manón had founded, to support the armies that were fighting in the revolutionary joust.

Since she was 14 years old, Adela Velarde had been a militant supporting wounded soldiers in the Northern Division under the command of General Carlos Martínez, as well as in the Northeastern Army in the Chihuahua regions, in Zacatecas, Aguascalientes, Morelos and Mexico City. In February 1913, Adelita appeared at a hospital in her hometown, and said that she wanted to work in the ranks of the revolutionary army. She soon adapted to the obligations in her work, and as a noble and determined young woman she captivated the fighters; there she met the love of her life, a man named Antonio Gil del Río Armenta, a sergeant in Francisco Villa's forces, who is supposed to have been the composer of the piece we know today as "La Adelita". Antonio accompanied Adelita during Villa's triumphs in 1913 and 1914 until, in Gómez Palacio, the man was wounded and died in the arms of his lover.

He highlighted Adela's participation against the usurper Victoriano Huerta, who desired to become president of the country; for all these reasons she was officially considered a veteran of the Revolution on February 22, 1941, and a member of the Mexican Legion of Honor in 1962. Thanks to her, female soldaderas are known as "Adelitas" for their role as caretakers, but also as war fighters. After the death of her love, Adelita continued in the Mexican Revolution until it ended. She then moved to Mexico City where she worked as a typist at the Post Office. In December 1961, the Congress of the Union granted her a life pension as a veteran of the Revolution. In 1965, Adela would have married Colonel Alfredo Villegas, with whom she met again after her years in the Army. Villegas was the boss of the late Antonio. Adelita lived in her first marriage until she passed away on September 4, 1971, in Texas.

Corrido "La Adelita"

In the style of the Spanish romance, the *corrido* narrates the epic of the men who fought in the rebel camps and highlights the participation of Adela Velarde and the illusions she awakened in the enamored sergeant, who dreamed of taking her to dance in the barracks, as was customary. The grim fate of the men involved in the hard fighting anticipates the end of the soldier who will die on the battlefield. The improvised composer expresses his justified jealousy thinking that Adelita "is going to flee with another guy", but that if this happened, he would follow her by land and by sea. The first two stanzas of four twelve-syllable verses with alternating rhyme and nine-to-ten syllable choruses have a recurring pattern of metrical length with the long refrain: "people knew that the sergeant was moaning in aching love".

En lo alto de la abrupta serranía,
Acampado se encontraba un regimiento
Y una moza que, valiente, los seguía
Locamente enamorada del sargento

Popular entre la tropa, era Adelita
La mujer que el sargento idolatraba
Porque a más de ser valiente, era bonita
Y hasta el mismo coronel la respetaba

Pues sabía que decía
Aquel que tanto la quería

Adelita se llama la joven,
A quien yo quiero y no puedo olvidar
En el mundo yo tengo una rosa
Que con el tiempo la voy a cortar

Si Adelita quisiera ser mi novia
Y si Adelita fuera mi mujer
Le compraría un vestido de seda
Para llevarla a bailar al cuartel

Una noche en que la escolta regresaba
Conduciendo entre sus filas al sargento
En la voz de una mujer que sollozaba
La plegaria se escuchó en el campamento

Al oírla, el sargento temeroso
De perder para siempre a su adorada
Ocultando su emoción bajo el embozo
A su amada le cantó de esta manera

Y se oía que decía
Aquel que tanto la quería

Si Adelita se fuera con otro
Le seguiría la huella sin cesar
Si por mar, en un buque de guerra
Si por tierra, en un tren militar

Soy soldado y la patria me llama
A los campos que vaya a pelear
Adelita, Adelita de mi alma
No me vayas, por Dios, a olvidar

Y después que terminó una cruel batalla
Y la tropa abandonó su campamento
Por las bajas que causara la metralla
Muy diezmado, regresaba el regimiento

El sargento recordando los quereres
Los soldados que volvían de la guerra
Requiriéndoles su amor a otras mujeres
Entonaban este himno de la guerra

Y se oía que decía
Aquel que tanto la quería

Y si acaso yo muero en campaña
Y mi cadáver, en el campo, va a quedar
Adelita, por Dios, te lo ruego
Que, con tus ojos, me vayas a llorar

Toca el clarín de campaña a la guerra
Salga el valiente guerrero a pelear
Correrán los arroyos de sangre
Que gobierne un tirano jamás

Que si Adelita quisiera ser mi novia
Y si Adelita fuera mi mujer
Le compraría un vestido de seda
Para llevarla a bailar al cuartel.

Los burritos

Another note on folklore refers to popular gastronomy. The versions about the origin of the burrito are varied, but what they all have in common is that it is served rolled in a flour tortilla, not corn. Because wheat is the main ingredient, it is believed that it is a northern dish and originally from Ciudad Juárez, precisely marketed during the years of the Revolution. The men who sold meals in the camps loaded their bundles of food onto small donkeys and came to distribute them to the combatants. The troops waited for the vendors and passed the news from mouth to mouth: "Ahí vienen los burritos" ('Here come the burritos'). The notice referred to pack animals. It is possible that more rolled flour tortillas were consumed in the camps or in the city because the cooks could put more food on them, and the food was kept hot.

10.2 The Novel of the Mexican Revolution

The novel of the Mexican Revolution became an innovative genre. Its precursor was Heriberto Frías, in the beginning a soldier fighting with the troops of Porfirio Díaz. Heriberto Frías inaugurated the revolutionary epic with the celebrated and iconic story on the rebellion taking place in Tomóchic in 1892, the town in the western Sierra of Chihuahua. The author found inspiration for *Tomóchic* (1896) in the reaction of the villagers who expressed their opposition to the oppressive regime still led by the dictator. The *tomochitecos* resisted allegiance to the government and vowed to obey a teenage folk saint, Teresa Urrea, known as the Saint of Cabora, who had been preaching social reform in the neighboring state of Sonora. About half of the 300 villagers did not concur with this millenarian vision and abandoned the town, but those who remained began to develop their own utopian dream. In September 1892, after failed efforts to negotiate a peaceful resolution to their intransigence, government troops sought to crush the movement but were defeated by the devout townspeople. In retaliation, intimidating army units besieged Tomóchic, and for about a week the protesters resisted heroically though they lost the battle due to the unequal distribution of resources. In the end, the *tomochitecos* released their women and children to federal custody, then fought fearlessly to the last man. On the eve of the Mexican Revolution, the events spread rapidly throughout the country, and Tomóchic turned into a legend of courageous Mexicans combating against the dictatorship of Porfirio Díaz.

Three major works belonging to this genre appeared before 1950. Mariano Azuela was the pioneer with his short novel *Los de abajo* (1915-1916), unfortunately translated as "The Underdogs" and adapted to the big screen in 1939. *La sombra del caudillo* ("The Shadow of the Strongman") by Martín Luis Guzmán (1929) deals with the power struggle amongst the triumphant military leaders who wanted to attract the masses to specific presidential candidates. Almost two decades later *Al filo del agua* ("On the Edge of the Storm") by Agustín Yáñez (1947) narrates the life stories of men and women who are disoriented and queasy about their own strange beliefs in religion vs. fanatism. The nebulous events take place in a village of Jalisco, where the protagonists linger over the events of their lives immediately before the outbreak of the Revolution.

A participant in the Mexican Revolution and following President Madero, the author of *Los de abajo* served as a field doctor. At the time the armies led by Francisco Villa, Venustiano Carranza, Álvaro Obregón, and by peasants under Emiliano Zapata, joined forces against General Victoriano Huerta, who eventually resigned as president and fled to Spain. Provoked by *federales* who were hunting rebels, Demetrio Macías, a peaceful farmer, gathered a band of discontent men and turned into the antagonist who fled to the mountains to support the rebels. Demetrio joined Villa, the northern leader whose troops were gaining ground in Chihuahua and Cd. Juárez; after only a few victories he was awarded the rank of colonel and was promoted to general.

Demetrio worked closely with the outlaws who had little or no military training and helped them to drive off twice numerous *federales*. In one of the initial battles two of his men were killed, and Demetrio was shot in the leg. For two weeks, the outlaws remained hidden in an isolated village populated by Indians, where Venancio, a barber-surgeon, attempted to treat Demetrio's wound, while Camila, an attractive young woman, was playing as his personal nurse. One day, Luis Cervantes, a medical student and follower of the outlaws' cause, appeared at the camp saying that he had deserted the *federales* because he was assigned to menial duties. Distrusting Cervantes' explanations, the rebels attempted to condemn him to death, but he was eventually accepted as a trustworthy comrade. Cervantes flattered Demetrio with grandiose expectations while Camila fell in love with Cervantes though he did not bother to lead her on. At the same time Demetrio fell in love with Camila but she did not encourage his romantic advances. In the end, the love triangle sparked the final tragedy.

Cervantes resorted to astute verbal strategies to persuade Demetrio and his men to prepare themselves for more attacks by the *federales*, and following his advice, Demetrio planned a surprise assault on one of the towns along their march. At this point, Demetrio's drags failed to take Zacatecas and were forced to retreat, throwing away their booty along the road. Celebrating a major victory, Demetrio met *el güero* Margarito and a woman known as *la Pintada* in a tavern. The audacious *Pintada* played a persuasive role in Demetrio's actions and talked him into occupying a house belonging to landowners. During the ransacking of Don Mónico's ranch, Cervantes collected jewelry and some money that wanted to hide from Demetrio's followers, but the leader reiterated he was not interested in material possessions, he was just dreaming of Camila. Cervantes then promised to bring Camila for Demetrio and returned to the village to pick her up. Camila mistakenly believed that Cervantes was in love with her. The next morning *la Pintada* discovered that Camila was close to Demetrio and wanted her to leave; at this point Camila refused to quit because she liked Demetrio and decided to stay with him and the rebel army.

A sensitive young woman who is appalled by the ruthlessness and cruelty of Demetrio's allies, Camila advances remarks about their despicable actions. In consultation with Cervantes and others, Demetrio decides to fire *la Pintada* from the camp, and reacting angrily she stabs Camila in the back. Demoralized and fatigued, Demetrio's fellowmen hear that Villa and Carranza, once allies, were fighting one another and that the *federales* had defeated Villa. After Villa's defeat, Demetrio is discouraged and decides to return home; on his way home, he attempts to crush again the *federales* who are strategically positioned into the uplands and shoot fast and precisely at the outlaw band (*los de abajo*), who are marching along the lowlands. Outnumbered, the drags perish on the spot where they had won their first victory. At the end of the battle, the soldiers find Demetrio's body with his dead eyes fixed on his gun. Knowing at this time that their enemies would be merciless with Demetrio's allies, Cervantes escapes safely across the border. From El Paso, he writes to Venancio telling him that *el güero* has shot himself. Cervantes then invites the barber-surgeon to join him in Texas where they can have their own business.

10.3 Cinematography

Three films produced during the golden age of Mexican cinema illustrate some of the social conflicts that ensued during and after the Revolution. First, *Los de abajo* (1939) is one of the best films representing the genre of the Mexican Revolution. The novel drafted hurriedly by Azuela was adapted to cinematography, and the film is loyal to the literary work; the combination of magic images and rural space is more seducing than the representations in writing. The successive scenes and agile dialogues captured both the nuances of rural speech and the drama that unfolded during the upheaval. The variants used by the protagonists are authentic ways of speaking of peasants living and working throughout the country, including the northern region.

María Candelaria (1943) was the first Mexican film to be screened at the Cannes International Festival, where it was awarded the first Latin American Grand Prix. The golden age of Mexican cinema (1935-1962) was both influential in Mexico and around the world. The director Emilio Fernández shows the indigenous characters embodied by María Candelaria and Lorenzo Rafael, two pristine souls facing their community's prejudice. María Candelaria, a flower seller working around the floating gardens of Xochimilco, is in love with a peasant, Lorenzo Rafael. In prerevolutionary Mexico, María Candelaria was ostracized by the local community because her mother had been a prostitute (killed in the past by said community to absolve the town of shame). She finds herself in trouble when a debt is called in, and events triggered by the locals conspire against her possible happiness. María Candelaria's only true ally is her sweetheart, Lorenzo Rafael, and the couples' pet piglet. They are honest and hardworking but are bullied by those around them. The story begins when local cacique Don Damián refuses to accept produce as payment in kind, instead demanding either money or the newborn pig. His authority is undermined when he refers to Lorenzo Rafael as a "damned Indian" and refuses to give him the quinine he is supposed distribute to the locals to protect them against an outbreak of malaria—setting into motion the events that will be the couple's undoing. Don Damián, the antagonist, is a jealous mestizo and storeowner who wants María for himself and is determined to sabotage her loving relationship. For this reason, Don Damián kills María and Lorenzo's piglet, their source of sustenance. When María falls ill with malaria, Don Damián refuses to give them the medicine they need to fight the disease. In desperation, Lorenzo Rafael steals the medicine and ends up in prison.

The depiction of the dogmatic villagers is undisguised, although the negotiations with the priest show a more flexible view between delusion and Christian compassion. Village women, perpetually giving the evil eye contrast with the 'innocent' beauty of María Candelaria according to a visiting painter, who plays a significant role in the unfolding tragedy. María Candelaria's fellow peasants make life miserable for her because they mistakenly believe she is a wicked woman—like mother like daughter. This suspicion became alarming when word gets around that María was the model for a famous nude painting, though actually she only posed for the head. All the tensions unleash the full hatred of the peasants. From this point on, María Candelaria is under pressure to pose nude for a painter who is eager to show the portrait of a naked woman that he is keeping in his study. The artist begins the painting, but when he asks her to pose nude, she becomes terrified. Finally, when the people from Xochimilco see the complete picture, they assume that it is María Candelaria, who is stoned to death. In the end, Lorenzo Rafael escapes from prison and carries María's lifeless body through the Xochimilco canal. The speech of the major protagonists, María Candelaria and Lorenzo Rafael represents the rural variety of the speech community, where other characters such as the journalist, the judge, the doctor, and the court secretary speak the variety of Spanish that was used amongst the schooled people living in the small village. Diglossia is observed due to the glaring compartmentalization of societal roles, occupational activities, and the restricted space in which the speakers live and interact.

Also directed by Emilio Fernandez, *Maclovia* (1948) exploits a similar topic. In the middle of the Pátzcuaro Lake lies the Janitzio Island, populated by a group of Indians who are disdainful of outsiders. Maclovia, the beautiful daughter of a Purhepecha community leader loves José María López, a poor young Indian, rejected by Maclovia's father, who prohibits communication between them, due to José María's lack of means. José María strives for a better life and wants to earn some money to buy his own fishing boat. At the time, a brutal Sergeant de la Garza is the head of the federal troops stationed in the island, and Maclovia's physical assets catch his eye. Determined to follow his lower instincts, he imprisons José María, thus facilitating the request of Maclovia's favors. All the existing tensions unfold on the Night of the Dead. *Maclovia's* main protagonists are José María, who struggles for the well-being of his fellowmen; Maclovia, the obedient daughter who has no options; Genovevo, the insolent trooper that contributes to tragedy; Father Jerónimo, the marginal but persevering priest, and the schoolteacher who is supportive of José María. The scenario is staged in 1914.

The film unfolds in slow motion and captures the exotic landscapes of the island which are connected to the protagonists' emotions. In a difficult situation, Maclovia finally makes up her mind and determines that she may accept the Sergeant's indecent proposals to free José María, though she admits that José María will not accept such resolution. The townspeople are aware that José María and Maclovia are breaking all the rules, arm themselves with countless flaming torches, and chase the couple around the lake. This film highlights the difficult relationships that existed between the Mexican federal government and the indigenous peoples of Michoacán. Class separation and the conflicts inherited from colonial times were still disturbing the peace of many small towns, even after one hundred years of independence. The discourse of identity and the strife that convoluted post-revolutionary Mexico were more patent in the rural areas than in the cities. Fusing the images and the words, the film shows the values and contradictions of a speech community divided by abusive leaders who disdain the indigenous.

10.4 Rural Spanish and residual variants

The subsample of speech traits listed below represents the variety spoken by peasants and farmers living mostly in rural areas throughout Mexico and other Spanish-speaking countries. The Spanish spoken in El Paso / Cd. Juárez at the beginning of the 20th century was akin to the rural variety of other Mexican regions. Immigrants from Mexico's interior moved north when the railroads were efficiently working for transportation and communication. The origins and evolution of most popular variants have been traced to Hispanic and Romance trends and have maintained continuity through the present day. Some of the recurrent dialect variants have been registered in the Area of Nahuatl Iinfluence and Nahuatl-Spanish contact (e.g., residual variants such as *vide, vido, trujo, mesmo, ansí, ansina, muncho, besita, priesa*); aspiration of initial F, as in *jumo* (< Latin *fumus*), *juimos* (< *fuimos*); palatalization, as in *praitico ~ practico, destruición ~ destrucción*, accent shift as in *lléguemos, sáquemos, téngamos, sépamos*, and the reverential use of *vuestras personas* and *vuestras personitas de ustedes* (see Hidalgo forthcoming). Variants may be classified in two groups that differentiate the vocalic and the consonant contrasts between the dialects and the normative form.

Vowels. Open vowels in modern Spanish are realized as closed vowels derived from late medieval Spanish as in: *consiguí ~ conseguí; insiñó ~ enseñó; dicirte ~ decirte*. Similarly, closed vowels alternate with open vowels as in *escrebir ~ escribir* and *mesmos ~ mismos* in **Los de abajo**, and *siñor ~ señor; medecina ~ medicina; creminales ~ criminales; mesma ~ misma* in **María Candelaria**.

In *Maclovia*, the protagonist's father firmly but diplomatically states that he does not want to see her daughter talking to her suitor. The verb QUERER is frequently highlighted in various passages:
>—No *quero* [quiero] volver a verlos juntos.
>—No quero [quiero] que vuelvas a hablarle.

In *Los de abajo*, dissolved diphthongs are used by the characters who are close to the leader Demetrio Macías; in this case Camila raised the same question to Demetrio when he was ill:
>—¿No *quere* [quiere] más?
>—¿No *quere* [quiere] leche?
>—Está regüena [muy buena] la leche. *Prébela* [pruébela].

The verb *querer* ('to want' or 'to love') is not diphthongized but appears with the stem vowel:
>—A ti es al que *quero* [quiero].
>—Demetrio me *quere* [quiere].

Except for Luis Cervantes, the medical student living and trekking with Demetrio Macías, all the protagonists use one or several of the variants that distinguish rural Spanish.
>—*Anque* [aunque] a mí me parece.
>—Tengo *esperencia* [experiencia].
>—Por eso no *peliamos* [peleamos].
>—[Luis Cervantes] *cai* [cae] con los polvos del amor.

In *Maria Candelaria*, hiatus may be dissolved, as in "*limosniarme*" [limosneame], *pasiar* [pasear] and *pior* [peor]. Also, the following fragments of dialogues show the coalescence of two strong vowels into diphthongs.
>—¿Qué gente *trai* [trae] usted?
>—Lorenzo *Rafáil* [Rafael], *traite* [tráete] agua pa' [para] los indios.
>—Que *sian* [sean] tres *riales* [reales].
>—No *m'iba* [me iba] a dejar que me *ninguniara* [ningunerara].
>—Como si me hubieran *apaliado* [apaleado].
>—*Crio* [creo] *que's* [que es] mejor.

The merging of two syllables into one—known as *sinalefa*—is accurately emulated by the protagonists of *Maria Candelaria*, who pronounce two words in one, making vowels coalesce in one single utterance:
>—Está *retiamolao* el *probe* [El pobre está muy mortificado].
>—*Ojalá 'i* [ojalá y] me hubieras hecho caso.
>—Mayormente *qui 'asido* [que ha sido] tan bueno
>—¿Por qué no *mi 'ogo* [me ahogo]?
>—Es *l 'único* [el único] que tengo.
>—Que *mi 'oiga* [me oiga] Dios nuestro señor.
>—¿Qué *hac iusté* [hace usted] aquí en la iglesia?

Consonants. Velarization of the sequence /bwe/ derives from Mexican Colonial Spanish (MCS) and persists to this day. The protagonists of *Los de abajo*, of rural extraction and culture, clearly reproduce the velarized form.

—Sabe lo que es *güeno* [bueno].
—Tan *güenos* [buenos] zapatos que *m 'iba* [me iba] yo a avanzar.

In *Los de abajo* the initial or medial sequence /fwe/ may be realized as an aspiration [h] or as a velar [x] in:

—Me agarra la mano *juerte juerte* [fuerte fuerte].
—Ya le *jueron* [fueron] a *dicir* [decir] a mi mamá que mañana salen.

A voiceless aspiration may be strongly or weakly velarized in *María Candelaria*, as in *fuereños* [xuereños], or may start with a velar and end with an aspiration

—Pa' [para] que *te ' che* [te eche] *xhuera* [fuera] la enfermedá [enfermedad].
—¡Voy a *esperar* aquí *xhuera*! [fuera].
—No *xhue* [fue] posible.

Verb forms. In *María Candelaria*, the actors and actresses successfully imitated the features of the social dialect in question. Two types of verb forms are used in speech communities with a high index of rurality. The first one appears in preterit indicative of the second person singular informal *tú* in which <s> is deleted before <t> and is added at the end of the word, as in *vites, tuvistes*, etc.

—¿Por qué me *dejates* [dejaste]?
—¿A dónde *juites* [fuiste]?
—¿Por qué *salites* [saliste]?
—¿De modo que *juites* [fuiste] tú?

The second verb form is found in the first-person plural of the present subjunctive *nosotros*, as in *tengamos ~ téngamos*, where there is a stress shift.

—Lo mejor es que nos *váyamos* [vayamos] donde *puédamos* [podamos] vivir en paz.
—No *quere* [quiere] que *váyamos* [vayamos] a dar la vuelta como todas las lunas llenas.
—A ver si *quere* [quiere] que le *páguemos* [paguemos] con las verduras.
—¿Cómo *queres* [quieres] que nos *váyamos* [vayamos]?

Other verb forms are used in nonstandardized varieties, as in the following sentences retrieved from *Los de abajo*:

—Lo que *haiga* [haya] con él, hay conmigo.
—Los poquitos que *semos* [somos].
—Esta currita que *usté* [usted] *trujo* [trajo] es igualita a *usté* [usted].

Reduction of *para* to *pa*. In *María Candelaria*, the frequent reduction of *para* to *pa* in combination with *naide, hartos, medecina*, and conjugated verbs (e.g., *puédamos*) portray features of the social dialect used in rural communities, where there can be bilingual speakers of Spanish and indigenous languages, and / or monolingual Spanish speakers:

—*Pa'* que *naiden* [para que nadie] se fije en mí y *puédamos* [podamos] vender flores.
—*Pa'* que [para que] crezcas pronto y nos des *hartos* [muchos] cochinitos.

—Voy a otro lado *pa' vender* [para vender] las verduras.
—Sólo tenemos flores y verduras *pa' pagarle* [para pagarle].
—No *trai* [trae] *pa' pagar* [para pagar] la *medecina* [medicina].
—*Pa' qué* [para que] hacernos guajes

Popular residual variants. In ***Maclovia***, the young fisherman wants to learn to read and write and asks permission to attend classes with children. The teacher welcomes José María and praises his desire to become a literate person. José María addresses the teacher with the honorific *su merced*, a residual variant derived from MCS; he also uses *merced* with the ancestral meaning of "favor".

—Quería hablar con su buena *mercé* [su merced]
—Perdóneme su buena *mercé* [su merced].
—Que *mi aga* [me haga] la *mercé* [merced] de *escrebirme* [escribirme] una carta.

10.5 Social class differentiation

Social class in films and literature is informed by personality types belonging to the in-group or the out-group. The individuals who were not allied with the revolutionaries were known as *catrines*, *curros*, *copetones*, *pelones* or *cuicos* (schooled middle-class types) like Luis Cervantes, *el curro sacamuelas* "the so-called doctor" in ***Los de abajo***. The standpoints of the privileged class are infused with knowledge acquired in a distinct environment, and therefore, do not fit in with the causes of the outlaws. The lexicon of the outlaws may refer to people and experiences that convey solidarity amongst those identified as the fighting in-group, who use various verbs for the action of killing: "te manda *quebrar*", "lo *trueno*", "se los *echó*". The frequency of the verb *querer* with the stem vowel in the present tense (*quero*, *quere*, *queren*) in combination with all the other residual variants (e.g., intrusive -N as in *nadien*, *ansina*, *muncha*) still distinguishes rural from nonrural Spanish.

11 El Paso, U. S. A.

A few decades after the Mexico-U.S. War (1846-48), El Paso witnessed serious tensions between Anglo-Americans and Mexican-Americans. By the 1880's, the city had experienced the first noticeable population explosion; while most of the newcomers were Anglo-Americans, a wave of immigration from Mexico in the 1890's gave the Mexican-Americans much of the city's population. In the late 19th century, El Paso became a significant railroad, smelting, ranching and commercial center, as well as the main arrival terminal for Mexican immigrants, who contributed to the economic boom of the city with their muscle. The meager population of El Paso grew from 736 people in 1880 to 10,338 in 1890 and to 15,906 in 1900 (García 1975:58, 61). Between 1910 and 1921, El Paso served as a refuge for those displaced from Mexico's interior by the turmoil created by the Mexican Revolution (1910-1921). Although the refugees fleeing to El Paso "represented all economic levels and the city profited especially from the presence of the affluent, most of the newcomers were poor..." (Luckingham 1980:49), and happened to settle in the oldest part of the city—or literally the wrong side of the tracks. As a result, the population of El Paso increased to 39,000-45,000 in 1910 and continued growing to 78,000-89,000 in 1920 (Luckingham 1980:49, 52; García 1975:58). By 1930, Mexicans had made up 66.9% of the total population (68,476) of the city, but in 1940 their number dropped to 55,000 or 56.8% (Luckingham 1980:63).

The most interesting question at this point is whether El Paso's swift Americanization contributed to the conflict observed by historians. Martínez (1980), García (1981) and Timmons (1990) advanced various explanatory models regarding sociocultural transformations that separated the communities that once happened to be one single Spanish-speaking villa or ciudad. According to Timmons (1990), less than two weeks before the signing of the Treaty of Guadalupe-Hidalgo, gold was discovered in California. "Within a short time, this brought into El Paso hordes of adventurers, opportunists, characters larger than life, discharged soldiers, outlaws, wife deserters, debtors, and the first Anglo female resident" (Timmons, 103). Paso del Norte seemed like a true oasis with its cottonwood trees, gardens, vineyards, town plaza, and some other commodities (104). Then by mid-1849 four thousand emigrants remained in the area, and by late 1849 five settlements were founded by Anglo-Americans, roughly a mile or two apart, along the left bank of the Rio Grande. The Old Mexican sites of Ysleta, Socorro and San Elizario were declared to be within the U.S. jurisdiction (105).

Very soon the new authorities removed local Mexican officials and warned Mexicans south of the river not to trespass U.S. territory. A permanent military post was installed during the years of transition, and once the international border was established, consulates and customhouses along with a small crew of new bureaucrats were opened to serve the demands of the inhabitants. The transitional period was not favorable to commercial activities due to new regulations and tariffs (Timmons, 117). "At the same time El Paso County was organized with the appointment of Magistrates and Judges. With the organization of El Paso County in March 1850, the civil jurisdiction of Texas was extended into the area north of the Rio Grande" (Timmons, 120).

11.1 Organizing civil government

Before the end of the 19th century, El Paso Mayor Joseph Magoffin and his council had made substantial progress in law enforcement, public health, transportation, flood control, drainage and utilities. There was also a streetcar connecting El Paso (Texas) with its twin cities across the river. His administration was so modern and efficient that telephone, gas, and electricity were introduced in the early 1880's. In 1881 a church was still missing, and Catholic parishioners would cross the river to worship in Paso del Norte (Chihuahua). By 1882 Methodists, Episcopalians, Presbyterians and Baptists had organized their congregations until they were able to complete their church building. By 1882 El Paso had a street railway, two banks, three newspapers, four churches, an established city council, and the largest hotel in the state (Timmons, 172-173).

11.2 Economic activities

Between 1880 and 1920, the years of its greatest economic growth, this border site supplied jobs for large numbers of Mexican workers as it surged as an "instant city". As El Paso and the Southwest contributed to the new industrial state, Mexican immigrants augmented its multiracial working class. El Paso became not only the main arrival terminal for Mexican immigrants but an occupational center linked to both the United States and Mexico. The connections and proximity to Mexico and southwestern mines made it a perfect site to receive ores from surrounding fields, and by 1910, El Paso's trade became the focal point for increased international commerce. The various economic sectors stimulated enterprises such as wholesale and retail trade, manufacturing, tourism and construction. The western boom would not have been possible without the Mexican labor. As the shortsighted Porfirian regime benefited national and foreign investors in agriculture, thousands of Mexicans migrated to Chihuahua, Sonora and Coahuila, where they found work in railroads, mines, and ranches. Before the Great Depression about one million Mexicans entered the United States first arriving in El Paso. The economy of the city was dependent on the Mexican labor force engaged in transportation, smelting, manufacturing, retail, construction, and a variety of activities. Others found work in the garment industry or as clerks in both U.S. and Mexican-owned stores (García 1981:3-4).

From the start, El Paso public school system followed a policy of segregation. "School administrators argued that until Mexicans learned an adequate amount to English, they would have to remain in their own schools, which provided classes solely through the early grades. However, most who did learn English failed to enter integrated classes after the sixth grade because they had to seek work by then to augment the family income" (García 1981:5). Consequently, school officials directed their attention to manual and domestic education. Americanization was promoted to make citizens more patriotic and able for future work while English was one of the foundations fostering socialization. For those years Mexicans lived apart from Americans. Over time and subsequent generations, Mexican Americans became Americanized via the process of socialization and by sharing many of the values common to a middle-class Anglo-Saxon family (202).

Since the early years of the 20th century, a portion of the destitute Mexican population remained concentrated in South El Paso, a blighted slum, an area inhabited by the lumpen proletariat, a neighborhood without comparison under U.S. standards. A separate world, a condensation of all the racial, economic, and political problems facing El Paso and the Southwest, South El Paso was the glaring example of poverty, an area shunned by all groups and a source of tension that has erupted into violence at different times (Márquez 1985). Moreover, the history of the city implies that El Paso was born and evolved with a strong anti-Mexican/anti-Spanish sentiment, due not only to the presence of South El Paso, but to the incessant migration of Mexican descent that 'took over' the city since the early 1900's.

In contrast, as in other borders, in the Old El Paso area, the attempts to take control of the land brought the two groups into conflict and sharp divisions among the townspeople along ethnic lines were not avoided. While it is admitted that racial animosity exists across the Southwest between Mexican-Americans and Anglo-Americans, the form in which intergroup relations have manifested themselves from city to city depends upon each area's development (Márquez 1985:54). The residential patterns of the Mexican population changed dramatically in the four decades before the end of the 20th century, and those who became upwardly mobile generally left South El Paso. In 1960 Mexicans accounted for 45.4% of the total population of El Paso, only to become the majority with 57.5% in 1970, 62.4% in 1980, and two full thirds (67%) in 1990. At the end of the century, the total population reached 679,222 of whom 78% were "Latino". It thus seems that the population of Spanish-speaking origin recovered the density it had in the 1930's.

As a result of the population growth and other socioeconomic changes experienced in El Paso before the early 1900's, native Mexican-Americans became "subjects of a new country, and soon the Anglo minority that moved in relegated them to a position of relative powerlessness" (Martínez 1980:7). To make matters worse, the newcomers ignored local rules and traditions in their drive to acquire property; the losses were reflected in farm land, timber, and salt (Martínez, 7). Martínez focusses on the people from El Paso, whose "low-cost labor has been a strong factor in luring employers to the region", where cattle, copper, cotton, and climate provided an early and continuing impetus for growth since the beginning of the 20th century (8).

Martínez (1980) summarizes the employment structure of the Chicano and Anglo communities of El Paso between 1910 and 1970, one decade before I started my project on language attitudes. The data examined shows "a protracted concentration of Chicano workers in low skill (and low paying) jobs throughout the period, while the opposite is true for the non-Spanish surnamed labor force" (9). Socioeconomic mobility among Chicanos was "limited and slow, with most gains coming after 1940, principally at the low white-collar, semi-skilled, and service levels" (10). Only a minuscule proportion of Spanish surnamed individuals entered into high white-collar positions: 3.4% in the late 1960's, improving slightly to 6.3% by 1970. "The recent modest increase of Spanish surnames in high white-collar jobs indicates that there are more Chicano bureaucrats, managers, businessmen, and professionals in the 1970s". Nevertheless, "proportionally these individuals still lag far behind their Anglo counterparts, and Chicanos are largely absent from influential and policy-making positions in El Paso" (10-11). The disadvantages reported by scholars are observed, too, by common people and by Mexicans who reside "on the Mexican side", which may be "safer" to express opinion about the U.S. economic and political system and to speak Spanish in all the public domains.

12 Identity and language attitudes

Data provided by researchers appear to indicate that between the Great Depression and World War II, Juárez and its twin city became well-differentiated. Cd. Juárez was solidly entrenched in the Mexican institutional system, where Spanish was the predominant language in all private and public domains. By contrast, El Paso began to develop bilingual modes of interaction, where English did not prevail but turned into a powerful ideological tool that was gaining space or spaces in various domains. While English has not been the only language spoken or written in El Paso, its international prestige after War World II has made it persuasive. These phenomena have motivated innumerable studies on language use and language attitudes in many world contexts.

Language use and language attitudes are called out in studies of education, sociolinguistics, the social psychology of language, and the sociology of language. In all cases, the issues at hand are both the shaping of identity and the focus on self-definition via the interaction with the group or groups of the speech community and "other" communities with which speakers may be in direct or regular contact. The specific case of the Mexican borders that are demarcated as of the mid-19th century is challenging and provocative, for it is certain that border sites are not like all the other sites that are missing an international border. An international border was erected in a limited physical space that divided a group into at least two groups, namely Mexicans to the south ('this side of the border') and Mexicans to the north ('the other side of the border'). The arrival of a third group aggregated a variable of new forms of interaction in a newer space "across the border". The border to the north became bilingual and bicultural in a matter of decades and fostered the shaping of alternate identities erected in opposition to one another. Mexicans to the north ended in a social and economic disadvantage and were submerged in a construct of ethnic-social identity that did not unfold on the Mexican side of the border. In juxtaposition with the northern side of the border, inhabitants "to the southern side of the border" sculpted their own national and local identity.

The first Mexican writer to indulge in calm introspection and gain knowledge about the "international border" is José Vasconcelos, author of *Ulises criollo* (1935). The author defines *criollismo* as the Hispanic-type culture involved in an unequal fight against falsified indigenist and Anglo-Saxonist postures that are disguised with the rouge of the most deficient civilization known to history. The author's soul wages his ideological combat, which is the same that in each of his compatriots (Prologue). His lengthy autobiographical novel invokes new realities that did not exist before the Mexico-U.S. War. Vasconcelos was from Oaxaca and moved to Piedras Negras (Coahuila) when he was a toddler. His presence in Piedras Negras and Eagle Pass (Texas) gives him the opportunity to describe and narrate his feelings about the new environment, where people have to cross the bridge ('el puente'), a thing that is not part of his imagination but a real wood structure built over a body of water, an obstacle that separates two people. The bridge is permanently there to either reduce the gap or to get rid of it when it is unlikely that the two sides will bridge their differences. Vasconcelos narrates the adventure of a young guy who identifies himself with the emerging class of criollos (Mexicans differentiated from indigenous people), who speak Spanish in post-revolutionary Mexico.

The author of Ulises criollo hyper-distinguishes the perceived human types that he meets in his journeys: Indians, mestizos, criollos, Mexicans, and gringos. His hero was Francisco I. Madero, a leader who had contributed to frame the national identity. "Social unrest had finally taken hold in the conscience of a Mexican who had courageously examined the past and the immediate present" (Vasconcelos 1935:362). Vasconcelos admires Madero's in the difficult task of becoming President. The candidate's name and circumstances appear more than 200 times. The expected battlefield was the border ('la frontera'), the desired space where the idea, the action-and-reaction of being Mexican is concocted in the 20th century. In Piedras Negras, the author mentions in passing the native but tasteless dish of flour tortillas, a lousy diet that contrasted with the exquisite and sophisticated Oaxacan cuisine.

But to compensate for the simplicity of Piedras Negras, the locals knew they had some options if they crossed to the "other side" (20). Piedras Negras is compared with Eagle Pass, where "progress" was moving fast. The author was partially educated in Eagle Pass crossing the river in rafts. At the time he lived in Piedras Negras he noticed that people from both sides of the border respected one another's space and circumstance. The 'other side' was distinguished from 'this side'. On the other side there were different things, forms of entertainment not known on this side, different food, tasty fruit (41-42). The other side is not a construct or the product of his imagination but a different place that is contrasted in tacit opposition to this side, where *fronterizos* (border people) reside. Border people are judged acrimoniously in Mexico's interior primarily because they live in the middle of the desert and lack 'high culture' (118). When Vasconcelos was the First Minister of Public Education, he introduced the literature of the classical antiquity in both Mexico and Latin America. The other border known to Ulises, the self-proclaimed criollo, is Ciudad Juárez, where the old Franciscan mission stood. The chapter about Ciudad Juárez occasionally mentions the weather, the streets, or the people. When his father was transferred as a customs agent from the neighboring state of Sonora, the criollo Ulises was still thinking of Paso del Norte, though he feels that the place is ancient. El Paso (Texas), tangible on the other side, was an impressive place, which was called the metropolis of the desert. The streets and buildings were "modern" for the time, the commerce was vibrant, and in general, the landscape and some commodities were very attractive without being fascinating (180). The protagonist Ulises noticed enthusiastically the availability of luxury items and a large selection of garments for all tastes and budgets, the same impression that people have had over decades.

His memoirs about Ciudad Juárez are conflated with the image of Madero and the treaties of Ciudad Juárez, though he is not fond of Benito Juárez, who opened the path for the incursion of various religious denominations (e.g., Protestantism). The treaties of Ciudad Juárez were not respected, and egregious Madero was assassinated by unscrupulous enemies that were only thinking of themselves. Adventurous Ulises does not resolve his conflicts and paradoxes. He rejects both Mexican *indigenismo* and the U.S. progress; according to Ulises, the latter is admirable but has a hollow spirit or no spiritual hallo. Strained by his own limitations, he feels empathy and sympathy for those who are similar. Vasconcelos reinforces the primordial concept of being Mexican and celebrates the glorious adventures of the Mexican people ('el pueblo'). Everything was better in Mexico—or at times, even much better on the "Mexican side" of the border.

The remembrance of the events of the Mexican Revolution with a tinge of self-celebration exacerbated the feeling of nationalism that prevailed for decades. In real life Vasconcelos became bilingual in Eagle Pass but he claimed to be loyal to Spanish and to Hispanicized Nahuatl names. The child attending a school with both Mexicans and Americans expresses his frustrations as he attempted to learn the English language, which interfered with his learning of Spanish (87, 182). The criollo Ulises was bullied at school and got involved in scuffles with English-speaking teens for whom the Mexico-U.S. War was still an issue of contention (36). Putting his frustrations at school aside, the author reiterates his love of languages and his admiration for multilingual people (375, 470). Vasconcelos is the pioneer of introspection and phenomenology on the Mexico-U.S. border. Introspection is the process by which he forms beliefs about his own mental state, a conscious experience based on judgement and observations that trigger thoughts, feelings, or perceptions. Though the literature of the Mexican Revolution and the autobiographies of the times did not turn into 'best sellers', they were influential in casting opinions that were spread to many people via different outlets.

12.1 Language and ideology on "the other side"

The Anglo-American power that prevailed in El Paso since the 1880's was not challenged until the 1960's, when militant movements proliferated among young people from the *barrios*, who had lost enthusiasm for acculturation and English monolingualism; they moved Spanish from the despised lower-class language to the "in" language. Spanish became prestigious in Mexican-American circles and social, religious, and political organizations. In addition, the emerging of a Mexican-American middle class was not as concerned about Anglo-American acceptance as before (Knowlton 1982:221, 223). At the turn of the century, El Paso seemed to be a city that was tailor-made to serve the Mexican population of its twin city, Juárez. And although Spanish is still somewhat 'marked' in the city, no 'pure' neighborhoods nor exclusive-English areas are encountered in this border (Teschner 1995). In El Paso, Spanish is no longer the focal point for intense *overt* conflict, although ambivalent attitudes towards Mexican normative values and identification orientation remain a source of *covert* conflict. According to the reports of the 1990's (Bills et al. 1995; Teschner 1995), El Paso is a city of high and intense language maintenance and vitality, because (a) residents of Mexican origin have outnumbered Anglo-Americans, and (b) almost all types of services and forms of interaction may be conducted in Spanish.

The estimated number of Mexicans commuting to El Paso to work only was 50,454 in 1980 (Herzog 1990:7), accounting for almost one-third of all border crossings in the nine most populated municipalities. According to Martinez's (1990) typology, the commuter worker is a kind of transnational *fronterizo*, who varies according to their sources of socialization, lifestyle, culture formation, and sustenance: (1) the settler migrant is partially acculturated to U.S. life, but her/his lifestyle/culture are basically shaped in Mexico; (2) the worker commuter lives a predominantly Mexican lifestyle with family and social networks and support systems mostly located on the Mexican side; (3) the binational consumer is thoroughly embedded in Mexican society with consumerism being its stronger tie in the U.S.; (4) the bi-culturalist is also entirely embedded in Mexican lifestyle and society but maintains very strong and substantive links and exposure to U.S. culture through the domains of education, social interaction, employment, consumerism, core culture and popular culture; (5) the bi-nationalist is equally shaped by both cultures and functions well in all the former domains in both societies.

Before 1848, Paso del Norte was entirely monolingual in Spanish and Mexican monoethnic. The arrival of Anglo-Americans changed the profile of the border communities giving rise to Spanish-English contact for the first generations of Anglos and Mexicans. Historians (Sonnischen 1968; Hamilton 1976) indicate that the second generation of Anglo-Americans was bilingual. The beginning of Mexican-Anglo contacts in most southwestern communities is distinguished by elite intermarriages (Gonzales 1989), thus making us assume that not only in El Paso but throughout the Southwest at least some of the pioneers of both groups were bilingual. As Anglo-American groups increased in number of individuals and the control of the community was almost exclusively in the hands of speakers of English, English became the general language of communication throughout the 20th century; so strong was the influence of English and the wave of Anglicization that Mexican-Americans became well differentiated from Mexicans on "this side of the border". This is the noticeable trend in the pre- and post-World War II decades.

Nonetheless, the 1960's and 1970's made English retreat as the most preferred language of communication in the community. In the last decades of the 20th century, El Paso was defined as a border of stable bilingualism, given the geographically contiguous co-existence of native speakers of Spanish and native speakers of English. El Paso was so intensely bilingual that the universal sociolinguistic occurrence of bilingualism with diglossia may be indeed contradicted, at least in some areas of the city. In El Paso, as well as in other 'twin border cities' (e. g, San Ysidro, Calexico, Yuma, Eagle Pass, Nogales,

Laredo, and Brownsville) researchers observe a rare case of shared domain (Sánchez 1983:44). Following Sánchez (1983) "there are domains where both languages may be used. For example, in the commercial area, both English and Spanish may function without altering the stability of the two language communities" (49).

The shared domain is more noticeable around South El Paso, discussed above. Physically intermediate between Juárez and El Paso, the neighborhood is isolated from other sections of the city and from Anglo-American culture. Almost the only Anglo-Americans seen in South El Paso are service personnel. Very few young people in South El Paso have any permanent contact with Anglo-Americans except through television and the schoolroom (Knowlton 1982:228-229). According to some observers, Spanish is the language of South El Paso and very little English is ever spoken. An inability or unwillingness to speak Spanish would be taken as 'cultural treason' (Knowlton, 229). In the experience of other researchers, in South El Paso, Spanish and English are indistinctively used for the same purposes and by the same people, depending on the personal preferences of the speakers (Valdés 1990:56). This communicative strategy, which was not as usual before the 1960's and 1970's, may extend to other areas of El Paso (Teschner 1995), which were, at the time, as heavily populated by Mexican-Americans as South El Paso. The shared domain occurrence is one of the many strategies of divergence that are in operation in this community. It may be only a transitional experience towards a more categorical shift in the direction of the ancestral mother tongue, albeit other variables such as socioeconomic status might indicate the overall preference for English in various domains. The conditions normally identified for language maintenance in El Paso are present, to wit: continued in-migration from Mexico that replenishes previous generations of anglicized Mexican-Americans, isolation from the American mainstream, ready access to the country of origin, and availability of services in Spanish, though English may overpower various domains of interaction. In turn, all these conditions have a strong impact on the intergenerational transmission of the mother tongue, the *sine qua non* condition of reversing language shift (Fishman 1991:8).

The severance of Paso del Norte after the Mexico-U.S. War transformed the region, which became an international border giving rise to two speech communities that were progressively differentiated not only by the political infrastructure but by religious, discourse, and ideological values that commonly—when it was convenient—overemphasized the importance of language (Spanish vs. English). The newspaper where Azuela published *Los de abajo* circulated weekly in Spanish between 1904 and 1918, a few years before the end of the Revolution. People of Mexican descent were exposed to the English language most likely in informal domains until public education programs admitted Spanish speakers in integrated classrooms.

By the 1940's and 1950's, the waves of Anglicization of El Paso caused the equally emphatic reaction of its twin city. The Juárez residents' boundaries turned out to be hyper-nationalists and ultra-(language) loyalists (Bustamante 1983 and 1985; Hidalgo 1983 and 1986). My publications of the 1980's gathered the replies of adults who were born and raised between the early 1920's and the early 1960's. The dissertation documents the opinions of a group of locals who voluntarily participated in the survey, which is based on the findings of previous studies that used direct items presented on the Likert scale to prompt the reaction or reply that was later quantified using simple analysis of frequencies and other methodologies. The advantage of presenting direct questions is that they can be quantified and interpreted with more precision than open-ended questions and narratives. The description of the local activities and economy is presented in chapter 2 "The study and its background".

12.2 This side of the border

If some of the oldest subjects I interviewed in 1980-81 were alive today, they would be about a century old; those who were middle age are in their seventies or pushing eighties, and the youngest are in their late fifties. My sample therefore captured traditional beliefs reflected in a new nationalism that rejected some of the values of the neighbors, and who felt stress-free to express their thoughts and opinions about language. A frequent question that has been raised to me is, why was language so important? I have replied that it may be an independent variable because most residents "on this side of the border" have at least heard of the position of the Spanish language *vis-à-vis* the English language "on the other side of the border". The "other side of the border" may offer different commodities for unlimited consumption, entertainment, and even free access to some public services (e.g., libraries), but when it comes to U.S. public education, residents from the "Mexican side" may have to give up a precious commodity, language-and-identity.

My language attitudes survey coincided with the steady development of the maquiladora industry in Ciudad Juárez and the general perception that the economy was going through a healthy period of growth. Local dailies routinely advertised various positions for bilingual personnel. Public safety was not a major concern, and rarely did my subjects express a feeling of distrust or discomfort. In those few cases, I did not proceed to administer my survey or simply omitted the survey in the quantification of the results. The major difference between today and forty years ago resides in the strength of the social networks that were sharing common values and expectations. Acting like a *fronterizo* was a positive trait, though most *fronterizos* were confronting ambivalent reactions from fellows in Mexico's interior. Foreign automobiles locally registered and licensed to freely circulate within the city boundaries were *fronterizados*, that is, they had their own local identity, just like people. The year that I starting collecting data, two songs by local singer and composer, Juan Gabriel, joyfully described the border: "El Noa Noa" (a late mixed twist-and-rock) and "En la Frontera", a ballad that describes border people as sincere, positive, trouble-free and living a happier life with higher (material) standards. People were also discreet, respectful, and solidary. Because Juan Gabriel was originally from Michoacán, he and his family experienced the uprooting from their native land and went through a lengthy process of adaptation to a place that the singer later considered his own and represented as his own.

"En la Frontera"

A mí me gusta más estar en la frontera
Porque la gente es más sencilla y más sincera
Me gusta cómo se divierte y cómo lleva
La vida alegre, positiva y sin problemas
Aquí es todo diferente, todo todo es diferente
En la frontera, en la frontera, en la frontera.

A mí me gusta más estar en la frontera
Porque la gente es más feliz y siempre espera
Vivir mejor estar mejor y se superan
Y todo logran porque aquí la gente es buena
Aquí es todo diferente, todo todo es diferente

En la frontera, en la frontera, en la frontera
La gente no se mete en lo que no le importa
Todo respetan cada quien vive su vida
Lo más hermoso de la gente en la frontera
Es que es mi gente y cada vez es más unida
Aquí es todo diferente todo, todo es diferente

Porque la gente es más feliz y siempre espera
Vivir mejor estar mejor y se superan
Y todo logran porque aquí la gente es buena

A mí me gusta más estar en la frontera
Porque la gente es más sencilla y más sincera
Me gusta cómo se divierten, cómo llevan
La vida alegre, positiva y sin problemas

13 Population growth

When I collected my data in 1980-1981, the number of families totaled 113,338 with an average of 5.52 people per family. The labor force amounted to 432,408 workers over 12 years of age, while the economically active population reached 171,581 people or 39.7% of the labor force. The underemployed and unemployed represented smaller figures. Most of the economically active population worked in Juárez (88.2%) compared to 11.2% of those who earned a living in El Paso. The socioeconomic study of the Municipality of Cd. Juárez shows the number of 606,426 inhabitants in 1980 and 628,500 in 1981. The place of origin of the inhabitants is divided into three large groups: those who were natives of the city outnumbered nonnatives as shown in Table 6. At the beginning of the 1980's, the local and regional population had reached an overwhelming majority of 77.4%, represented by those who reported Cd. Juárez as their place of origin—and some others who were El Paso-born— but were raised and educated in this locality or elsewhere in Mexico. The age of the gainfully employed population ranged from 18 to 60 years of age, whereas the distribution by sex was 96,429 (52.2%) males and 75,152 (43.8%) females. Inhabitants from Chihuahua's interior were well represented with a 16.5%. The rest of the locals were originally from the state of Durango (an important province of Nueva Vizcaya) in the 18th century. Zacatecas represents the boundary from central and northern Mexico, while Coahuila is adjacent to Chihuahua. A small proportion of the *juarenses* at the time were immigrants from Mexico City, some other places in Mexico, and foreigners, all together representing ten percent of the entire official estimate. In sum, locals outnumbered nonlocals, female and male workers—at least in appearance—had reached a healthy balance, and because unemployment rates were low, crime did not flash in neon lights.

Table 6 Origin of the population:1980-1981

Origin	Amount	%
Cd. Juárez	382,757	60.9
Another place in Chihuahua	103,702	16.5
Durango	42,110	6.7
Zacatecas	20,112	3.2
Coahuila	17,598	2.8
Mexico, D. F.	10,056	1.6
Other places in the country	33,929	5.4
Foreigners	18,226	2.9
Total	628,500	100.0

Source: Desarrollo Socioeconómico (1980-1981)
Municipio de Cd. Juárez

The active economic sectors were agriculture, livestock and fruit growing (3.85%); the extractive, transformation, export maquila, construction, and electrical and oil energy industries together reached a little more than one third (37.06%). The assembly plants employed 43,776 workers. Trade was both wholesale and retail (16.5%), transportation occupied 4.05%, while banking and financial, educational (private), professional, private health, tourism, and some other services accounted for 26.25%. Finally, government services were positioned at 7.63% and other unspecified sectors at 4.40%. The abovementioned data appear to indicate that the city was growing and that the family structure was still solid. One decade later, in 1990, the number of assembly plant workers increased to 130,000-140,000, presumably with a large proportion of young females working for low wages (Desarrollo Socioeconómico, Municipio de Ciudad Juárez, 1980-1981).

    The promotion of industrial and cultural development in Cd. Juárez was derived from initiatives advanced by both the federal government and local entrepreneurs. Between 1970 and 1990, seven municipalities that are adjacent to U.S. cities registered an annual population growth above the national average. In 1980 the national growth rate was 2.9% and decreased to 2.1% in 1990, whereas the nine most important cities of the northern frontier reported an increase to 2.6% and 3.2%, respectively. The largest increase was observed in Tijuana (5%), Nogales (4.7%), Ensenada (4.2%), Juárez (3.7%). Piedras Negras, Matamoros, Reynosa, Mexicali, and Nuevo Laredo grew more slowly than all of the above. Between 1980 and 1985, the industrial plants increased in Tijuana from 123 to 192; in Cd. Juárez, from 121 to 168; and in Nogales, from 49 to 59. By contrast, in Matamoros and Nuevo Laredo this type of activity decreased. In the next quinquennium the assembly industry continued growing, and in some cities, it was doubled. This is the case of Tijuana,

Mexicali, Ciudad Juárez, Nogales, and Matamoros. Between 1980 and 1990, employment increased in Ciudad Juárez from 39,402 to 122,231 and in Tijuana from 12,342 to 59,870. As of the 1990's the industrial sector integrated sophisticated organizational systems of very high and competitive technology (Santiago Quijada 2013:164-165).

14 Profile of subjects

For decades I have saved the additional information I gathered from my subjects. Tables 1 and 2 itemize the data related to variables such as age, years of formal education, and residential area. The notes on residence are useful to reconstruct the stratificational patterns of the 1980's, when the "colonias" were different from the modern "fraccionamientos". The former were older and more traditional than the newer eastern communities that were enjoying services such as telephone landlines, easy access to a large variety of restaurants, stores, clinics, pharmacies, hospitals, schools, and the international bridge "Puente Córdova de las Américas" that was opened in the 1960's. The Universidad Autónoma de Cd. Juárez and the local museums were also established in this part of town; the older "colonias" and the historic Customs House remain to the west of the railroads in the central district and closer to the Santa Fe bridge that connects the city to the historic center in El Paso and its traditional landscape.

Table 6.1 Female subjects

F Ss	Age	F. Ed.	Residence	Code
1	16	9.0	Colonia Hidalgo	3
2	16	9.0	Colonia Hidalgo	3
3	19	12.0	Las Rosas / Fracc. Colegio	5
4	19	15.0	Colonia Hidalgo	3
5	20	15.0	Fracc. Margaritas	4
6	20	15.0	Primera Burócrata	4
7	18	12.0	Colonia Hidalgo	3
8	20	10.0	Infonavit Casas Grandes	3
9	20	13.0	Los Nogales	6
10	20	15.0	Fracc. Emiliano Zapata	4
11	21	14.0	Melchor Ocampo	3
12	21	14.0	El Campestre Juárez	6
13	22	14.5	Fracc. Arecas	3
14	22	11.0	Fracc. Jardines San José	3
15	23	14.0	Unidad Benito Juárez	3
16	23	14.0	Fracc. Olimpia	4
17	24	15.0	Segunda Burócrata	4
18	24	9.0	Colonia San Antonio	2
19	24	9.0	Leyes de Reforma	2

20	24	15.0	Colonia Sta. Rosa	2
21	21	9.0	Fracc. Tecnológico	3
22	25	8.0	Colonia López Mateos	1
23	26	12.0	Colonia del Carmen	2
24	26	8.0	Colonia 16 de Septiembre	1
25	26	10.0	V. Guerrero y Argentina	3
26	26	10.0	Segunda Burócrata	4
27	27	6.0	Paso del Norte	1
28	30	17.5	Córdova-Américas	5
29	31	10.0	Bella Vista	3
30	32	13.0	Campestre Juárez	6
31	32	8.0	Ex Hipódromo	4
32	33	15.0	Colegio Teresiano	5
33	35	12.0	n. a.	0
34	37	17.5	Infonavit	3
35	37	6.0	Colonia Hidalgo	3
36	48	9.5	Tercera Burócrata	4
37	50	10.0	Los Nogales	6
38	54	11.0	Fracc. Villa del Norte	5
39	60	6.0	Colonia Margaritas	4
40	68	10.0	Colonia Centro	3

Table 6.2 Male subjects

M Ss	Age	F. Ed.	Residence	Code
41	16	10.0	Colonia Cuauhtémoc	4
42	16	2.0	Chaveña / Concho	3
43	17	7.0	Ex – Hipódromo	4
44	17	6.0	Colonia Altavista	1
45	18	11.0	Zona Centro Camionera	4
46	18	12.0	Ex – Hipódromo	4
47	19	13.0	Colonia Hidalgo	3
48	19	15.0	Colonia Margaritas	4
49	19	11.0	División del Norte	1
50	19	11.0	Cuauhtémoc	4
51	19	11.0	Independencia	1
52	19	11.0	Melchor Ocampo	3
53	21	11.0	La Cuesta	2

54	21	14.0	Melchor Ocampo	3
55	22	15.0	Los Nogales	6
56	22	11.0	Francisco I. Madero	1
57	22	10.0	Anexas	1
58	23	16.0	Colonia Centro	3
59	24	6.0	Colonia Hidalgo	3
60	24	16.0	Colonia Los Lagos	4
61	24	14.0	Barrio Cuauhtémoc	4
62	24	12.0	Satélite	2
63	24	16.0	Calzada del Parque / Hidalgo	3
64	25	14.0	Infonavit	3
65	26	17.0	Los Nogales	6
66	26	6.0	Fracc. Granjero	2
67	26	12.0	Fracc. Pradera Dorada	5
68	27	6.0	Colonia Hidalgo	3
69	27	16.0	Melchor Ocampo	3
70	27	16.0	Colonia Hidalgo	3
71	27	6.5	Colonia Obrera c. Chaveña	2
72	28	15.0	Unidad Benito Juárez	3
73	28	9.0	Colonia Hidalgo	3
74	28	9.0	San Antonio	2
75	30	15.0	Primera Burócrata	4
76	31	18.0	Bellavista	3
77	31	16.0	El Roble	4
78	31	17.0	Unidad Emiliano Zapata	4
79	33	7.0	Colonia Santa Rosa	2
80	33	16.5	El Campestre Juárez	6
81	34	13.0	Sector Centro	3
82	34	3.0	Colonia Obrera	2
83	37	15.5	Colonia Galeana	1
84	48	6.0	Los Lagos	4
85	61	11.5	Niños Héroes / Insurgentes	2

The subjects who responded to the survey reported the residential area in which they lived. A total of 43 neighborhoods classified in six groups were recorded. They are presented in Tables 7A through F and codified from 1 to 6. The six groups listed separately attest to the diversity of social strata and the various commodities they had access to in the early 1980's. The neighborhoods can be divided in two major ascending groups: Groups 1, 2 and 3 total

26 neighborhoods along the lowest ranks, while the second group (4, 5 and 6) comprises only 17. The two highest clusters in the ranking 5 and 6 amount to seven neighborhoods located to the southeastern section, where the city has grown consistently since the 1960's. The community may be divided into two major sectors demarcated by the old railroad construction and the historic center where the Franciscan Cathedral, the plaza, the park (Monumento a Juárez), and the Customs House were initially located. The landmarks to the west still have easy access to El Paso, where the oldest international bridge was built in 1882. The Puente Santa Fe has been refurbished a few times since then.

Table 7.1 Group 1 Lower-lower
1. Colonia Galeana
2. Altavista
3. División del Norte
4. Independencia
5. Francisco I. Madero
6. Anexas
7. López Mateos
8. 16 de septiembre
9. Paso del Norte

Table 7.2 Group 2 Lower-working
1. La Cuesta
2. Del Carmen
3. Satélite
4. Granjero
5. Colonia Obrera
6. San Antonio
7. Santa Rosa
8. Leyes de Reforma
9. Niños Héroes

Table 7.3 Group 3 Lower-middle
1. Chaveña
2. Colonia Hidalgo
3. Colonia Melchor Ocampo
4. Colonia Centro
5. Infonavit
6. Unidad Benito Juárez
7. Colonia Bella Vista
8. Arecas
9. Jardines de San José
10. Tercera Burócrata

Table 7.4 Group 4 Middle-middle
1. Cuauhtémoc
2. Colonia Ex-Hipódromo
3. Central Camionera
4. Colonia Margaritas
5. Los Lagos
6. Primera Burócrata
7. El Roble
8. Unidad Emiliano Zapata
9. Segunda Burócrata

Table 7.5 Group 5 Upper-middle
1. El Colegio Teresiano
2. Fracc. Villa del Norte
3. Pradera Dorada
4. Olimpia
5. Córdova-Américas

Table 7.6 Group 6 Upper-upper
1. Los Nogales
2. El Campestre

15 The growth of Cd. Juárez from the 1960's on

The territorial dispute over 600 acres on the border between the two cities is known as "El Chamizal", an issue that entangled the relations between the United States and Mexico for almost a century, though not a major conflict, it "was a constant emotional irritant which has plagued both nations and had frequent reverberations throughout Latin America" (Jessup 1973:423). In 1867 Mexico began to question the legality of El Chamizal's belonging to the United States. The Rio Grande changes its course frequently "as floods come and go, tearing land from one bank and depositing it on the other side as it winds around its bends and corners" (Jessup, 423). Several conventions followed for about one hundred years, including the presidencies of Porfirio Díaz and William Taft. The conflict was finally resolved in 1963 when the U.S. Congress introduced the American-Mexican Convention Act of 1964, and the settlement was formally proclaimed (Hill 1965). A park and museum were built for public recreation and just recovering a piece of land that had belonged to "the other side" made some people feel appease on the "Mexican side". The local space was expanded to the northeastern sector when the dispute was resolved.

Gutiérrez Casas (2009) explains the transition of the 1960's and the extension of the city to the southeastern section. From a place with a central district as the major nucleus of the community, both the occupational activities and the residential area were expanded to the southeast, where other nuclei were built. In the 1960's the central district did not house the majority of the large industrial enterprises within its polygon, but was the supply center due to the location of the international bridges and the route of the railway tracks. In this small center, merchandise imports and exports were commonly taken place. Between 1961 and 1965, new neighborhoods were built where the middle and upper classes settled their properties. Urbanization continued in the same section where other dense colonias were growing. The road infrastructure was utilized to access another zone with new constructions, beautifying landscape, and strategic public installations. The Border Industrialization Program (BIP) was the engine behind the change. Between 1966 and 1970, the assembly plants settled towards the southeast, where more than 20 factories were concentrated, primarily electronics, fertilizers, packing, and wood. Some of them remained in an intermediate position between the central district and the newer industrial park (132-138).

Part of the land that belonged to the BIP served as the equipment to which the investment was destined. A museum, a performance hall, a hotel and the very new self-service stores were the first tourist and commercial works. The need to attract family-oriented tourism required a more agile connection between the Córdova Island and the new commercial area. In this way, the Lincoln Avenue circuit and the López Mateos Avenue were built, which would reach the new international crossing. The delivery of the El Chamizal land allowed the creation of a true open space for the city. The newer territory was accompanied with investments in the Córdova bridge and urban beautification works in the surrounding area. The innovative intraurban nucleus was conveniently connected to the main street, 16 de Septiembre, and adjacent streets. The new infrastructure replaced the monocentric layout of the border city (Gutierrez Casas 2009:143-145).

By the 1980's, there were already several urban nuclei with efficient roads for communication and transportation. The growth had stimulated the older speech community that was sharing common attitudes and values with newcomers. My informants are distributed along the two main nuclei of the old central district and the innovative extension to the southeast. Map 2 shows the layout of the city from west to east during the transitional period. The "mancha urbana" is known as the dispersion of a city and its boroughs to rural zones that are reaching the western periphery of the urban center. The landmarks are located to the east of the "mancha urbana", where the railroad yards still stand. Next, Map 3 shows the central district, mostly dominated by commercial activities and services of all kinds. In the central district there were also residential sectors, hospitals, pharmacies, parks, monuments, movie theatres, bookstores, television stations, public and private schools, and some other constructions. The central district ends where the industrial zone begins (see Map 2).

The transformation of the city was consolidated in the 1990's. The urban structure was modified from monocentric to dual-centric as of the 1970's, and at the end of the 1980's there was a second central district located in the Programa Nacional Fronterizo zone to the southeast, very close to the international Córdova bridge that connects roads and traffic to El Paso. The investment in infrastructure, both large and cost-effective, stimulated tourist-related activities and assembly plants growth. The resulting consequences are observed in varied occupational and economic activities, stable employment, and concomitantly, the attraction of more people motivated to immigrate and work in the city.

These factors are closely related to the incessant population growth. Fuentes Flores (2001) describes in detail the changes experienced between the 1960's and the end of the 1990's with the location of the industrial parks as of the late 1960's and on. The newer central district catered to diverse services such as department stores, malls, finances, real estate, medical and dental plans, radio, cinematography, theatre and television. At the end of the 1980's the two subcenters were well-connected with a large area representing about ten percent of the urban zone (107-108).

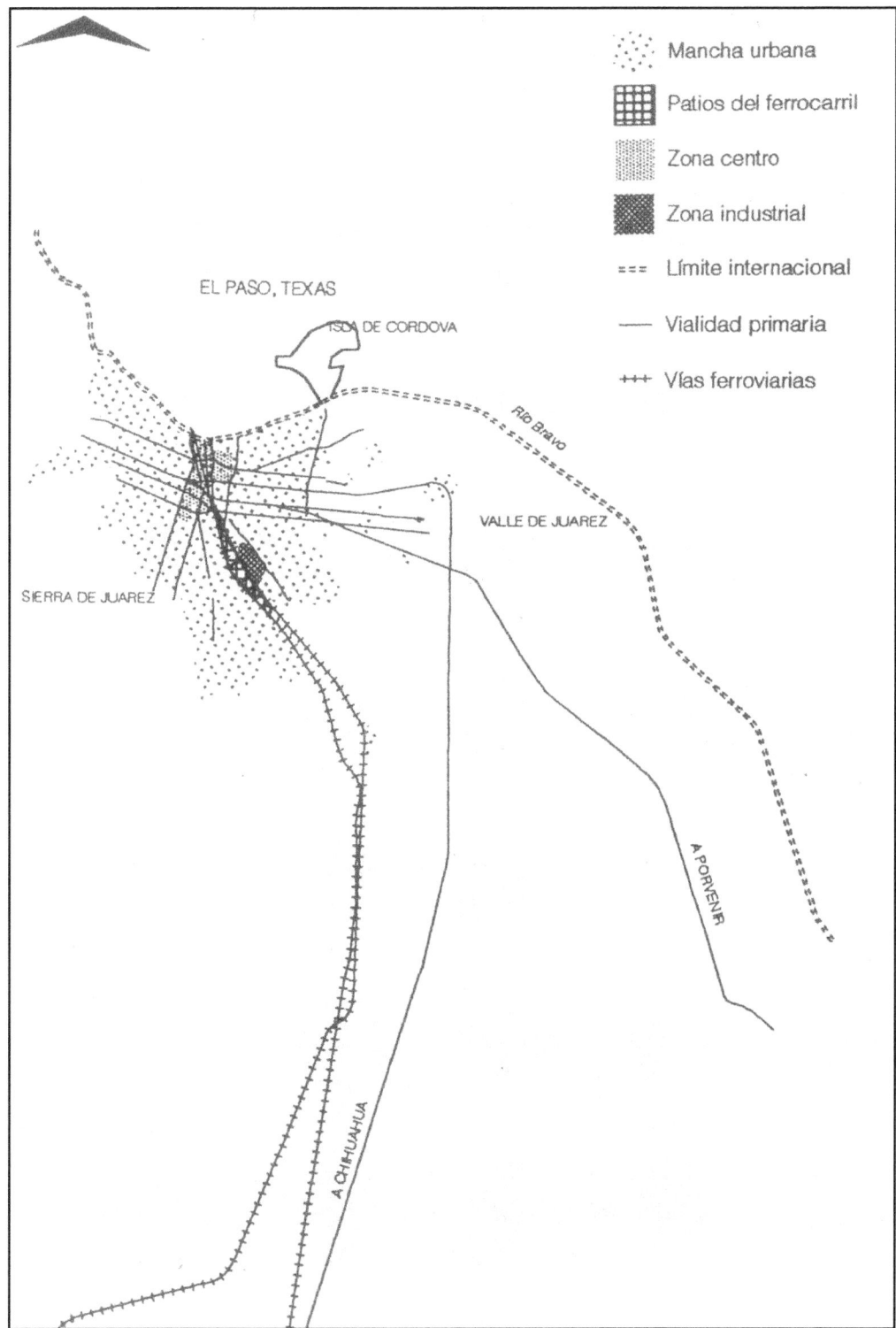

Map 2 The central district in the 1960's
Fuente: Gutiérrez Casas (2009:136)

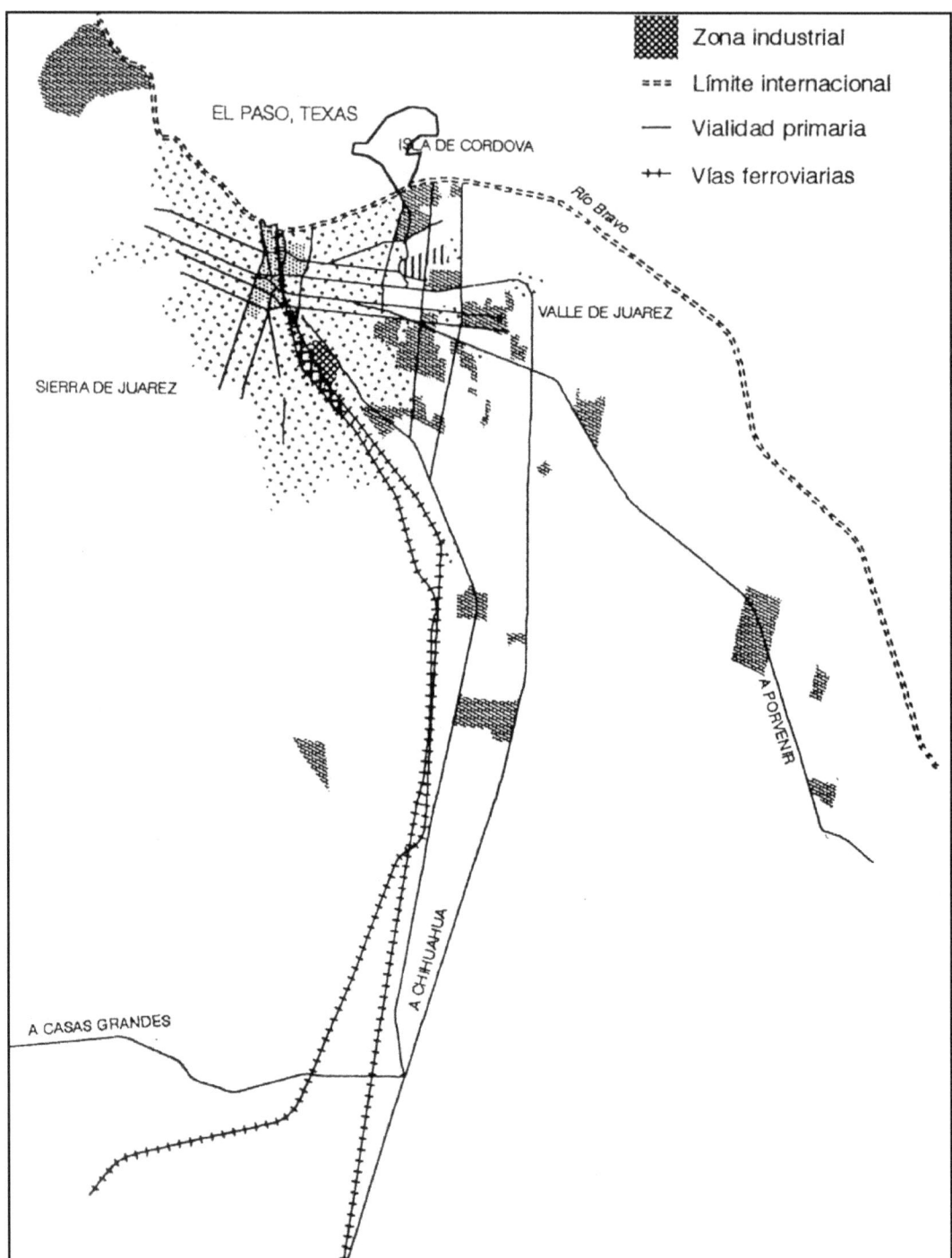

Map 3: Partial view of Ciudad Juárez 1965
Fuente: Gutiérrez Casas (2009:144)

16 Reports on local identity

My reports on local identity are not exclusively based on phenomenology but on empiricism, a methodology that may be rejected by those who question the accuracy of survey results, for it has been observed that subjects may change their replies with no warning. Empirical studies, nonetheless, have become a major source of information on public health, national, state and local elections, buyers' preferences, and consumer habits. It is thus difficult to reject *a priori* the design and results of small and large surveys. Identity has been defined as a subjective notion that leads to understanding the position of the self *vis-à-vis* the position of the concerned other(s), primarily in the context that surrounds the individual. Identity may or may not change across the history of a speech community or the individual's lifespan. This notion may or may not be corroborated by empirical means. The early 1980's research items directly requested a reply on the 5-point scale on local identity, that is, the subjects' feeling who were living at the time in the border ambience. In all cases, they replied positively to being proud of their position, corroborating that the border was the best place to be or to belong to, and to perceiving advantages just for living there. The larger and more encompassing identity is associated to their insertion in a nation-state that still keeps an institutional leash on life, education, and all matters of routine. I have been asked, what is then so different? The major difference is glaring. Some border inhabitants have maintained their bonds across the border, "the other side" that now belongs to the United States, where another system of values prevails.

Almost a decade after I collected data on this issue and a few years before the neozapatista uprising in Chiapas (1994), a representative of the Instituto Nacional Indigenista conducted a survey at the Universidad Autónoma de Cd. Juárez. A sample of 341 very sharp students replied to questions calling for attitudes on the contributions of immigrants, in general, and indigenous, in particular, to the city (Pérez Ruiz 1991). Two thirds of the enrollees in the public university were born in Juárez and / or Chihuahua, and about two thirds were male. The opinions read as follows: more than one-third replied that immigrants do not contribute to anything positive, and less than one-third considered that immigrants do contribute to labor, industry and trade. Almost one-half of the respondents considered that the itinerant indigenous are extremely vulnerable due to lack of opportunities and cultural differences, a perspective that is presumably promoted by the local media, whereas the proximity to the United States is partly a factor in the attraction of immigrants. Though some of the respondents' parents were immigrants, those immersed in local routines viewed themselves as common *juarenses* who must assert their identity in a positive manner.

The neozapatista uprising coincided with the enactment of the North American Free Trade Agreement (NAFTA, 1994). It is thus possible that after three decades, there will be more residents who understand, read and speak English for personal reasons, for education, work and businesses. This implies that more bilingual individuals and more bilingual types may be found in younger generations.

17 The international border

The international border is not part of the imagination of fronterizos, and language is an issue overtly verbalized but not abundantly tackled in scholarly journals and books. Many years before starting my survey, I identified three linguistic codes: Spanish, English, and Spanish-English code-switching, which was common to my ears and eyes since the time I have a memory, that is, the mid- and late 1950's. On the other side of the border (El Paso, Texas), Mexican-Americans used intrasentential code-switching in both private and public domains. The "third code" is intelligible to bilinguals, but those who are monolingual cannot easily imitate native "code-switchers". It is a spontaneous speech style of those who are raised in the bilingual ambience of the U.S. southwestern cities and towns. The physical distance between El Paso and Juárez is insignificant. People just have to cross the bridge to the other side and find different domains of interaction between people who speak different codes. Map 4 shows the eastern section of the two cities connected by the international bridge known as Córdova de las Américas, which was free of charge. For this reason, it was also known as "el puente libre".

Map 4 Córdova Bridge
Source: Google Instituto Nacional de Estadística, Geografía e Informática (INEGI)

18 The final balance

The population growth of Cd. Juárez since 1900 has exceeded half a million inhabitants in 1980. The 1940 decade shows less than 50,000 people that were multiplied to more than 500,000 in 1980. Since then, it has been rising to reach a million and a half people at the end of the 20th century (see Table 8). Following World War II, the city shaped their community values that were strengthened by their common origin. High employment rate, better wages, recreation, and the U. S. proximity turned Cd. Juárez into a magnet where both locals and immigrants perceived opportunities inaccessible in other parts of the country. This explains the disproportionate unabated growth that continues today. Between 1950 and 1970, it doubled as a result of the industrial and services drive. At the end of the 20th century, a community of well-adjusted newcomers, identified themselves as *neojuarenses*, have picked up the main values of the older community of *juarenses*. Internal migration has contributed to the vitality of Spanish with thousands of full-fledged native mostly monolingual speakers, who also bring miscellaneous cultural innovations from Mexico's interior.

Table 8 Population growth

1900	8,218
1910	10,621
1920	19,457
1930	39,669
1940	48,881
1950	122,566
1960	262,119
1970	407,370
1980	544,496
1990	789,522
2000	1,187,275
2010	1,321,004
2020	1,501,551

Source: INEGI (2020)

19 Theoretical considerations: from linguistics to sociolinguistics

How did we make the transition from linguistics to sociolinguistics? It seems that it was in the 1960's that the crossover occurred simultaneously with the growth of theoretical linguistics. The Chomkyan revolution was making strong inroads in those schools that were building programs in linguistics, and it became a topic of conversation amongst those who were not in the field. Those of us who were working on phrase structure trees in transformational grammar were persuaded one way or the other to direct our attention to the nascent field of sociolinguistics, which in the beginning was overlapping with the sociology of language. The works of Joshua Fishman (see references in Part II), William Labov (see references in Part II), John Gumperz (1971), and some pioneering protagonists (see Bratt Paulston and Tucker 1997) were assigned or referred to in the innovative courses of sociolinguistics. When I was in graduate school in the 1970's, two books were popular in the courses of sociolinguistics: one of them was Joshua Fishman's *The Sociology of Language* (1972) and the other one was William Labov's *Sociolinguistic Patterns* (1972).

In the "Addendum for nonlinguists", Fishman (1972:201) discusses the underlying tenets of structural linguistics (equivalent to descriptive linguistics). He pays particular attention to Chomskyan principles, equivalent to an adequate theory of the human ability to acquire and use language, a principle that in turn yields a theory of what language itself is. A major statement puts in bold relief the goal of sociolinguistics, which may "ultimately serve similarly basic purposes in the on-going quest of the social sciences to understand communicative competence as a fundamental aspect of the social nature of man" (208). He adds that "many sociologists and social psychologists now realize (...) that the norms that apply to and may be thought of as generating human verbal interaction pertain not only to the communicative content and context of that interaction, but to its linguistic form as well" (209). Finally, Fishman makes the difference between generative-transformational linguistics (GTL) and the sociology of language (SOL), the former focusing upon the similarities between the deep structures of all human languages and upon the underlying linguistic competence of human speakers. By contrast, the SOL is concerned with the differences between surface characteristics of varieties in the repertoires of speech networks or speech communities. Whereas GTL has focused upon syntactic structure devoid of communicational intent, the SOL is concerned with communicative appropriateness relative to diversified social functions. GTL has stressed innate communalities while the SOL has stressed socialized differences (211). In the debate between theoretical linguistics and sociolinguistics, one major difference emerged: the analysis based on intuition, mainly on the intuition of the researcher, and the analysis based on data collected in speech communities, where the researchers have an opportunity to observe the diversity of attitudes and behavior. The insertion of the social sciences in linguistics has overrun structural linguistics.

Hymes (1973 and 1974) focused on the difference *between* and *within* the speech community, its boundaries and the organization of language as a part of communicative behavior (1973:65). The study that leads to reconsider the basis of linguistics itself and the scientific and social concerns of linguists lead to a reconstruction of linguistics and sociolinguistics as a discipline that accepts the social constitution of its subject matter (1974: vii-viii). The societal life of language and the social meaning assigned to specific variants is highlighted in sociolinguistic studies. Communicative competence is equivalent to sociolinguistic competence, i.e., the ability to participate in the speaker's society not only as a speaker but as a communicating member in a broader sociolinguistic description (75).

Differentiating between the SOL and sociolinguistics has been a valuable goal amongst scholars concerned with this type of research. In the "Introduction" to the *Linguistic Bibliography* (Teschner et al. 1975:ix), the distinction is made between the sociology of language and sociolinguistics; the studies based on the former have focused on determining the domains of usage of Spanish and English and the factors associated with Spanish language loyalty and maintenance, while the correlation of specific linguistic elements with sociological variables (i.e., Labovian socio*linguistics* as opposed to the Fishman variety, language *sociology*) has rarely been explored.

In the 1980's the distinction between the sociology of language and sociolinguistics was still a subject of debate. The themes approached in the *Sociolinguistics of Society* (Fasold 1984) include multilingualism, the miscellaneous positions that language(s) may have along with their uses, attitudes to language, maintenance and shift, and the principles on language planning, especially as they relate to education. The analysis of quantitative language data as well as data derived from census logs and experimental studies are examined. The topics in the *Sociolinguistics of Language* (Fasold 1990) cover the semantic differentials of pronouns of address, the ethnography of communication, discourse analysis, language and sex, pragmatics, pidgins and creoles, and linguistic variation. In their *Memories and Reflections,* Bratt Paulston and Tucker (1997:4) state that sociolinguistics is mainly concerned with an increased and wider description of language, whereas the sociology of language is concerned with explanation and prediction of language phenomena in society at a group level.

An integrated theory and praxis of sociolinguistics and the SOL may be feasible in the future under one umbrella concept, that is, Sociolinguistics. A renewed integrated approach may be possible in the new globalized speech communities, where all sociolinguistic phenomena *per se* can be observed and examined. Globalization has plunged formerly monolingual speech communities into unsuspected forms of language and ethnic contact that are in turn conducive to innovative outcomes such as multiculturalism, multilingualism and differentiation, while emerging populations struggle to understand or at least reflect upon newer forms of co-existence.

20 Language attitudes and sociolinguistics

The field of language attitudes had a good start in the late 1960's (see references in Part II). According to Agheyisi and Fishman (1970), it has grown to encompass the relevance of attitude studies to sociolinguistic topics, as in for instance, "language choice in multilingual societies, differential allocation of codes, dialect differences and mutual intelligibility" (137). The authors proceed to review the various theoretical and methodological definitions: in the first place, the mentalist approach implies that attitudes are not directly observable but have to be inferred from introspection; next, the hypothetical construct is related to the overt behavior or verbal responses to any given set of stimuli. The advantage of this approach lies in the fact that attitude remains as an independent variable. Attitude may be, too, a system of beliefs, which in turn embraces cognitive, affective, and behavioral components, though most researchers gauge only the affective component (137). It is conventional wisdom that attitudes are learned from previous experience that somehow are connected to action and/or behavior, and that are not easily modified. The sociolinguistic studies of the times dealt with three major topics: (1) language-oriented or language-directed topics; (2) community-wide impressions toward particular languages or language varieties; (3) those concerned with the implementation of different types of language attitudes (139).

Language attitude studies in the first category report primarily on evaluations or ratings of language or language varieties as 'rich' or 'poor', 'balanced' or 'reduced', 'pretty' or 'ugly', 'smooth' or 'harsh'. These studies fall into two thematic subdivisions: (a) Classical / Standard/ Official vs. Modern/ Nonstandard/Vernacular varieties, respectively; (b) Creoles, Pidgins, and Trade languages. Reports in the second category are concerned with the social significance of languages or language varieties, attitudes towards speakers of peculiar language varieties; attitudes towards speakers of different languages in multilingual settings, etc. Finally, studies in (c) deal with all kinds of language behavior, or behavior toward language, resulting, at least in part, from specific attitudes or beliefs. Major topics in this category include language choice and usage, language reinforcement and planning, language learning, expressed views about interdialect mutual intelligibility, etc. The highest number of studies relevant to language attitudes fall within the topic areas of the social significance of language varieties, and language choice and usage. Also, studies within these substantive areas have employed almost all the different types of data-gathering techniques (144).

Closed-question items used in these studies contain three main dimensions: the focal object, the dimension of appraisal, and a set of rating terms from which the respondents are required to choose. The rating scale differs in degree of complexity: some items require only a 'yes/no' reply, others a choice on a 5-point (e. g., Likert scale) or 7-point scale. Some models of closed-question items require subjects to rank them according to the representation of their own viewpoint or to complete sentences. Closed-question items must be carefully constructed, usually after special pilot studies using open-question items.

Validation of attitude studies may be particularly problematic because of the very nature of attitudes as properties of the psychological or mental process. Studies using commitment measures commonly tap the action component of attitudes, and thus have been found to be useful predictors of overt behavior; for this reason, studies are easily tested for validity by comparing results with actual behavior in circumstances similar to the research situation. Nonetheless, studies focusing on either the cognitive or affective components of attitudes, or those that define attitude as consisting of only an affective dimension, need as criteria, behavior of a rather subjective nature. In actual research practice, the use of special operational definitions seems to overlook or underrate the problem of validity (150-151).

When applied to data collection the operational definition is the precise statement presented by the researcher to gauge attitudes and behaviors utilizing a rating scale (e.g., Likert scale), which is then defined as a specific score. My methodology in Part II has considered the direct observation of attitudes and behavior of the community under study as well as the ready understanding and spontaneous reaction of the subject to the items presented on a 5-point scale. In American daily life, this practice has been perpetuated in surveys of all sorts (e.g., student evaluations, opinion polls, reviews of medical practitioners, etc.), though the familiar problem of the low degree of consistency between attitude measures and overt behavior remains unresolved.

20.1 Sociolinguistics and the social psychology of language

The need for a diversity of social and cultural perspectives found its expression in the past few decades in a variety of new research developments. The perspective implies that social psychology can and must include in its theoretical and research preoccupations a direct connection with the relationship between the functioning human psychological and the large-scale social processes and events which shape this functioning and are shaped by it. Post-war social psychology was concerned with society at large and has been at the fringes of mainstream development since World War II. Connections can be made between this neglect of a sociopsychological integration and the sociocultural background of most of the post-war social psychology (Tajfel 1981:7). The focus was on the construction of social identity, which should be understood as that part of the individuals' self-concept deriving from direct knowledge of their membership of a social group (or pertaining groups) together with the value of emotional significance attached to that membership (Social Identity Theory [SIT]). This implies that the image or concept that an individual has of himself or herself is more complex, and that the individuals' view of the self in connection with the surrounding world derives from membership in certain social groups or categories, where membership may be more salient, and may vary in salience according to a variety of social situations. Social identity is thus used to describe limited aspects of the concept of the self which are relevant to certain aspects of social behavior. The social psychology of intergroup relations is concerned with intergroup behavior and attitudes; intergroup behavior derives from belonging to a group and interaction with another group (Tajfel 1982:2-3).

To reformulate the significance of language and ethnicity, the SOL and the social psychology of language have been integrated most noticeably in Giles and Johnson (1987). Ethnolinguistic Identity Theory (EIT) draws on the SIT while the former considers sociocultural influences on groups in contact and the indispensable variable, self-perception. The major proposal of the SOL reads that language maintenance is a function of ethnic identification. Language is factored in the equation when a group regards its own as a dimension comparable with the language of the out-groups and when membership in a group becomes a component of social identity, except when select language features are highlighted. Vitality accentuates the salience of group identity and may intensify the inclination to exacerbate the saliency of group speech markers. Ethnic solidarity may be week or moderate and ethnic groups are inclined accordingly (Giles and Johnson 1987:72, 84 and ff).

The need for a diversity of social and cultural perspectives found its expression in the 1960's and 1970's in a variety of new research developments. The perspective implies that social psychology should include in its theoretical and research preoccupations a direct concern with the relationship between human psychology and the large-scale social processes derived by it. This concern with society at large has been at the fringes of mainstream development since World War II (Tajfel 1981:7).

"Social identity should be understood as that *part* of the individual's self-concept which derives from their knowledge of their membership of a social group (or groups) together with the value of emotional significance attached to that membership" (Tajfel 1982:2). It is implied that the image or concept of an individual self-concept is more complex, and that his / her view in connection with the surrounding world stems from membership in certain social groups or categories. In certain social groups membership may be more salient and may vary in salience according to a variety of social situations. Social identity thus describes limited aspects of the concept of the self that are relevant to certain aspects of social behavior. The social psychology of intergroup relations is concerned with intergroup behavior and attitudes generated by belonging to a group and by interaction with another group (2-3).

A major spin-off from SIT has been the "theory of speech accommodation" expounded since the early 1970's (see Part II) and the ethnolinguistic identity theory (EIT). Interpretations on the meaning of language and ethnicity aid in the understanding of perceived ethnic conflict in interpersonal relationships. According to Giles and Johnson (1987), language maintenance is a function of ethnic identification. Under this framework language is highlighted when a group regards its own as a dimension comparable with other out-group's and when membership in a group becomes a component of social identity. An enhanced level of perceived vitality intensifies the salience of group identity and increases their inclination to accentuate group speech markers. The "theory of speech accommodation" is concerned with underlying motivations and consequences arising from linguistic adaptations to communication patterns towards others. This framework has stimulated empirical studies across disciplines and sociocultural situations. In *Contexts of Accommodation*, Giles and Coupland (1991) trace the growth of accommodation theory from its origins as a strictly sociopsychological model of speech-style modifications to its status as an integrated, interdisciplinary statement of relational processes in communicative interactions. Accommodation appears as a complex set of alternatives available to interlocutors in face-to-face communication; it is also utilized to gauge and achieve solidarity with or dissociation from a conversational partner. Such framework is open to micro and macro contextual communicative concerns. As applied sociolinguistics advanced, scholars have found sufficient situations conducive to address pragmatic concerns in medical services, legal discourse, and radio broadcasts. Accommodative processes can facilitate or impede language learner's proficiency in a second language as well as immigrants' acceptance by the host community or communities; accommodative processes influence job satisfaction and productivity, affect reactions to defendants in court and the nature of the judicial outcome, etc. The main concepts and relationships imply that "the accommodation model holds out the possibility of inferring underlying similarities in the relational options and tensions that render them researchable as key dimensions of our social lives" (4).

Ethnolinguistic vitality theory (EVT) emerged as a tool to analyze systematically the relative sociostructural positions of ethnic groups being examined in the growing range of intergroup studies worldwide. Objective assessment of vitality thus serves to compare and contrast the different groups under examination (Harwood 1994:171-172). The theories that followed "speech accommodation" are not suitable to examine the communities that have grown along the Mexican side of the border, where most of the population is monolingual Spanish-speaking and predominantly of Mexican descent. EVT is better applied to the U.S. side of the border in the context of bilingual or multilingual communities where the identified variables stand out in bold relief. As a case in point the study by Jaramillo (1995) offers an invaluable model of the sociolinguistic vitality of Spanish in a U.S. quasi-border community. Studies on language and identity have addressed numerous topics such as the relationship between language use, language choice and identity as a process of defining or acting out conventions of behavior lying at the root of elementary school children feelings of social identity (Heller 1984); they are also related to learning and knowing English as an international language (Norton 1997); the ways in which males and females use language with the intention to mark gender boundaries, for instance, phonological variants, stylistic devices, etc. (Holmes 1997); and, finally in identity in literacy and learning practices in multicultural societies (Bell 1997), to mention a few works.

21 Direct questions in surveys

The most frequently used items in surveys are known as interval scale questions that measure opinions. The space between each option, whether it is a number range, or a feeling range should be equal. This type of scale is used in student evaluation forms that ask about agreement or disagreement. These items are presented to subjects when the researcher wants to gauge the opinion of the respondents. College students have a lot of experience with these surveys and respond with ease. Other subjects may have never seen an opinion survey about language attitudes or any other topic. Taking this issue into consideration, I presented the questionnaire to my subjects and gave them sufficient time to understand both the content of the question and the interval scale. A group of four of five items can be summed and later represent a variable.

Additionally, the ratio scale measures the order of variables and reveals the difference between the items. This is helpful to understand the intervals, values, and the relevance of calculating ratios. This scale is one of the most informative methods of measurement because the items are organized in an ordinal format and later added, subtracted, multiplied, and/or divided. For example, when the researcher asks *How often do you go to the gym?* the respondent has several options that can be quantified and inputted as one single codified variable. Item B is equivalent to 1, item C is equivalent to 2, item D is equivalent to 3, item E is equivalent to 4, and item A is equivalent to zero. It is necessary to have a zero.

A. Never
B. Only one day
C. 2 days a week
D. 3. days a week
E. 5 days a week

22 The original survey

Section I of the original survey in Spanish gathered basic demographic data including regular activities in El Paso. This question is contextually specific to Juárez residents. Section II is also specific to Juárez residents, who may or may not be interested in acquiring or learning English in either Mexico or the United States. Occasionally, they do study this language in a different environment. Section III divides the items on attitudes into several groups, which consistently comprised four questions that are treated as variables. The different grouped items make up a set of codified variables that are used to determine their strength and directionality. Students and colleagues have indicated that my dissertation is about the English language, but it is about the interrelationships between the linguistic codes, Spanish, English, and code-switching that are heard, spoken, written, liked, or disliked in the border region. This question is appended with another question referring to the "difference" between border communities and non-border sites. My reply has been that border communities have more boundaries that non-borders, such as an international border, where other rules and regulations are applied, although there are collectivities who believe that we reside in a world without borders. The extra boundaries add variables that are not examined in non-borders. I have been questioned about the choice of language attitudes (e.g., integrative vs. instrumental). These are the dimensions explored in other contexts and appear in the lengthy bibliography previous to 1982-1983.

The next item on the agenda of readers and critics is Spanish-English code-switching. Since the publication of my dissertation and related papers the research has grown exponentially. I have been asked why code-switching is so swiftly rejected. I have replied that most people dislike mixed languages because they are inversely associated to language loyalty, another variable that has been reported in many parts of the world where language contact is common. Some groups tend to adhere more staunchly than others to the first tongue or mother tongue. In my study this variable is correlated to the values of Spanish-English code-switching but it is immaterial when it comes to evaluate Mexican-Americans. It then seems that subjects separate the linguistic code from the people who speak it. There are thousands of people from Mexico who have relatives and friends in the United States and maintain significant personal bonds. Also, thousands of relatives working in the United States send a good part of their earnings to Mexico, where the remittances are used most of the time for basic commodities. Despite the fact of maintaining close ties, some individuals still reject code-switching.

The question of language loyalty is the most important in this research since subjects assumed both a primordialist and a constructive perspective. Primordialism is justified because after the decline of the local indigenous languages, Spanish was the most common language spoken in Paso del Norte. Reports show that the indigenous who survived under very stressful circumstances in the region went through language shift in about a century (see Table 5). By the end of the 1800's, they were not only outnumbered by Spanish speakers, but Spanish was used in writing since the mid-17th century. The members of the Franciscan order left the evidence in the baptismal records, which are re-microfilmed and archived at the University of Texas at El Paso Library.

Returning to the emergence of bilingualism and the issue of who uses which language and where, I have stated that the partition of Paso del Norte was the trigger that allocated the languages of the new border region. Though the indigenous languages occupied the physical space before any European language, the various indigenous groups were dispersed, and did not have the opportunity to spread or to transliterate the oral code to Romanized writing. This contrast sharply with other Mesoamerican languages, particularly Nahuatl, the lingua franca of the Aztec Empire, used by the Franciscans and other mendicant orders in the process of Christianization. From historical records and interpretations, it seems that Spanish speakers built a small community around the main landmark, that is, the church that later became the cathedral. Spanish speakers had in common the linguistic, cultural, and religious background until the Mexico-U.S. War split the village. The U.S. side of the border developed the orientation that the United States was taking in the mid-19th century. Since at least the late 19th century, English was in a good position to spread into local domains. The resulting consequences have had great worth of significance. Spanish has remained as the common language on the Mexican side of the border, whereas English found a niche or domain on the U.S. side of the border, which was already populated by Spanish speakers, who in turn became bilingual at different junctions. I have been asked why English is not the common language in Ciudad Juárez, "if it is so close". I have replied that languages have their own domains.

Also, through the centuries, the archives of the city council of old Paso del Norte and modern Ciudad Juárez are drafted in the Spanish commonly used in both New Spain and independent Mexico. The Mexico-U.S. War severed the community into two distinct political entities; the net effect of this separation has enhanced the feelings of loyalty on the Mexican side and the emergence of a linguistic code on the American side: code-switching. Language loyalty is processed in the collective mind by both primordialism and constructivism. Having been transplanted to the "newer" border environment, the personification of Vasconcelos, *Ulises criollo* (1935) engages himself in meditation and explores his inner self, since he feels his situation is unique. His language loyalty is the reaction to the perceived change when he goes to Eagle Pass. While he is physically in Piedras Negras, he feels more at ease with himself. The *criollismo* of his main character epitomizes interpretations of "a border-native", a way of being Mexican—if extreme and ethnocentric. As compared to Piedras Negras, the valuable evidence of the Western civilization is the presence and rewarding activities of the Franciscans in Ciudad Juárez, because in this old site, Catholicism and the heritage of the Latin language were rooted and established a tradition that supports the Spanish language and the modern Mexican civilization, according to the author of *Ulises criollo*.

22.1 Methodology

From the beginning I thought that all variables preexamined for my survey were somehow interrelated. Some of the results may be predicted by observation while others by intuition. I could not ignore the three distinct linguistic codes and their association with at least one group of speakers, though not all researchers had identified the groups with piercing clarity. Border Mexicans were lumped together as though there were no cultural or linguistic differences; likewise, border Mexican Spanish was identified as a mixed code, though the mixture is objectively distant from speech communities in the U.S. Southwest. Ciudad Juárez was a speech community connected by only one bridge to El Paso, which was a different speech community. Other bridges were added in the mid-20th century.

The issue of social class is recurring in research related to Latin America. Elsewhere I have briefly discussed the differences between approaches to stratification in North American and Latin American societies. Like most sociologists, I selected groups of subjects based on similar social indicators like formal education, residential area, and father's occupation. I divided all subjects in six functional clusters that are associated with one another in correlations that can be identified objectively. I did not mean to give the impression that there are six distinctive social classes. In order to complete this task, I added the scores obtained in each indicator and later computed the z-scores, which describe the position of a raw score in terms of its distance from the mean, when measured in standard deviation units. The z-score is positive if the value lies above the mean and negative if it lies below the mean. A z-score is simply the raw score minus the population mean, divided by the population standard deviation. This methodology allowed me to identify six groups with mathematical precision. The results show that less than one-quarter of the subjects lies in the upper-upper (12%) and middle-upper classes (12%), though they can be defined as social strata only because a numeric score is available to plot the correlations and multiple regression with the other variables. I have not claimed that Cd. Juárez in particular, or Mexico in general have such high percentage of upper classes (see Chapter 2, Tables 2.2 and 2.3 in Part II).

One frequent question has been how I arrived at the score for social class or socioeconomic status. This is obtained by following the formula, where Z is the standard score, x is the observed value, μ is the mean of the sample, and σ is the standard deviation. Z is the number of standard deviations by which the value of the raw score is above or below the mean value of the three variables (formal education, residential areas, and father's occupation) that are summed. Raw scores above the mean are positive and those below the mean are negative.

$$Z = \frac{x - \mu}{\sigma}$$

The association of all the sociodemographic and language variables was assessed via Pearson Product Moment correlation coefficient obtained for the 85 subjects. When applied to a sample, Pearson's is represented by the letter r and may be referred to as the sample Pearson coefficient. In statistics, the correlation coefficient r measures the strength and direction of a relationship between two or more variables, with a value -1 and 1. The formula is obtained by estimates of the co-variances and variances based on a sample of subjects. Therefore, if there is one dataset {SCS}containing n values, another dataset {Formal Education}, {Use of English} containing n values and the scores of n obtained in the attitudinal variables {AV}, then there is a number of pairs of observations of variance and co-variance ready for the *r* formula, which is represented by the $\sum$ of X and Y. To obtain the correlation coefficient, it is necessary to sum the products of the paired variables $\sum xy$, then sum the X scores and the Y scores ($\sum x$ of the X scores and the Y scores $\sum y$), and finally sum the squared X scores $\sum x^2$ and the Y squared $\sum y^2$ scores. The strength of the correlation appears in the coefficient obtained. A number above .400 with degrees of freedom larger than 0.1 and 00.1 is significant.

Finally, multiple regression is a methodology used when we want to make predictions. According to the *Statistical Package for the Social Sciences* (SPSS) this is an extension of simple linear regression. It is used when we want to predict the value of a variable based on the value of two or more other variables. The variable we want to predict is called the dependent variable (or the outcome, target, or criterion variable). The variables used to predict the value of the dependent variable are called the independent variables (or the predictor, explanatory or regressor variables). The SPSS has grown in sophistication, and these days students can find multiple sources of information and short articles with graphic explanations. Check *Simple Psychology* and the Excel program where data can be inputted directly; then you interpret the results right away. The original survey form was administered in Spanish. It is divided into three major sections: (I) demographic information, (II) English language learning and acquisition, (III) attitudinal variables, and an open-ended question related to education in English. The survey items were inputted into scantron sheets.

23 The original survey form

I. Información demográfica

1. Nombre (opcional)
2. Sexo   F   M
3. Edad
4. Lugar de nacimiento
5. Nacionalidad del padre
6. Nacionalidad de la madre
7. Ocupación del padre
8. Ocupación de la madre
9. Número de años de residencia en Cd. Juárez
10. Otros lugares de residencia
11. Ocupación en Juárez
12. Ocupación en El Paso
13. En total, contando primaria, secundaria, vocacional, preparatoria y universidad, ¿cuántos años ha trabajado en México?
14. En total, contando primaria, secundaria y universidad, ¿cuántos años ha trabajado en EE. UU.?
15. Salario mensual
16. Si no trabaja, ¿cuál es el salario del jefe de familia? Para 1981, espero un aumento del – %.
17. ¿Vive Ud. en casa propia?   Sí   No

18. ¿En cuál colonia está situada su casa?
19. ¿Cuál de las siguientes actividades realiza Ud. en El Paso?
    - **a.** Compras **b.** Diversión **c.** Trabajo
    - **d.** Educación **e.** Negocios **f.** Visitas a familiares y / o amigos
20. ¿Cuál es la frecuencia de sus actividades en El Paso?
    - **a.** Diariamente **b.** 2 ó 3 veces por semana **c.** 2 ó 3 veces por mes
    - **d.** De vez en cuando **e.** Nunca

II. Información sobre la adquisición y aprendizaje del idioma inglés

1. ¿Ha estudiado inglés alguna vez en su vida?   **Sí**   **No**
2. Si su respuesta es negativa, puede decir ¿por qué no?
3. ¿Dónde ha estudiado inglés?
    - **a.** El Paso **b.** Juárez **c.** Otro
4. ¿Qué tipo de cursos ha estudiado y por cuántos meses o años?
    - **a.** Los que se ofrecen en la escuela primaria o secundaria en las escuelas mexicanas
    - **b.** Los que se ofrecen en las academias de El Paso o Juárez
    - **c.** Escuela primaria en El paso
    - **d.** Escuela secundaria y preparatoria en El Paso
    - **e.** Universidad en El paso
    - **f.** Otro (especifique)
5. En total, ¿cuánto tiempo ha estudiado inglés?   **Meses**   **Años**
6. ¿Con qué frecuencia habla inglés con hablantes nativos de inglés?
    - **a.** Diario **b.** 2 ó 3 veces por semana **c.** 2 ó 3 veces al mes
    - **d.** De vez en cuando **e.** Nunca
7. ¿Con qué frecuencia habla inglés con hablantes nativos de español?
    - **a.** Diario **b.** 2 ó 3 veces por semana **c.** 2 ó 3 veces al mes
    - **d.** De vez en cuando **e.** Nunca
8. ¿Con qué frecuencia escucha la radio en inglés?
    - **a.** Diario **b.** 2 ó 3 veces por semana **c.** 2 ó 3 veces al mes
    - **d.** De vez en cuando **e.** Nunca
9. ¿Con qué frecuencia ve la televisión en inglés?
    - **a.** Diario **b.** 2 ó 3 veces por semana **c.** 2 ó 3 veces al mes
    - **d.** De vez en cuando **e.** Nunca
10. ¿Con qué frecuencia ve películas en inglés?
    - **a.** Diario **b.** 2 ó 3 veces por semana **c.** 2 ó 3 veces al mes
    - **d.** De vez en cuando **e.** Nunca
11. ¿Con qué frecuencia lee libros y revistas en inglés?
    - **a.** Diario **b.** 2 ó 3 veces por semana **c.** 2 ó 3 veces al mes
    - **d.** De vez en cuando **e.** Nunca

12. ¿Con qué frecuencia escribe en inglés?
    - **a.** Diario
    - **b.** 2 ó 3 veces por semana
    - **c.** 2 ó 3 veces al mes
    - **d.** De vez en cuando
    - **e.** Nunca

13. En general su conocimiento del inglés es:
    - **a.** Excelente
    - **b.** Bueno
    - **c.** Regular
    - **d.** Malo
    - **e.** Nulo

III. Variables referentes a las actitudes

Se explicó la siguiente clave a los sujetos informantes: **1** significa que Ud. está absolutamente de acuerdo; **2** significa que está más o menos de acuerdo; **3** quiere decir que no está seguro (a) (excepto en la Variable E, español local vs. español nacional donde significa que son lo mismo); **4** significa que más bien me opongo; **5** quiere decir que me opongo totalmente. También se presentó la clave opuesta.

Actitudes hacia el inglés, americanos e identidad local

A. Plano de integración (Intervalo: 5=Absolutamente de acuerdo; 1=Totalmente opuesto)
   1. Estudio inglés o he estudiado el inglés para entender mejor a la gente de los Estados Unidos y su estilo de vida
   2. Con el inglés es más fácil o será más fácil hacer amigos entre los americanos
   3. Sabiendo inglés empezaré a actuar y a pensar como la gente de los Estados Unidos
   4. El inglés me ayuda o me ayudará a conocer y a conversar con gente diferente e interesante

B. Plano de uso práctico (Intervalo: 5=Absolutamente de acuerdo; 1=Totalmente opuesto)
   1. Necesito el inglés en el área de El Paso-Juárez para conseguir un buen trabajo
   2. Necesito el inglés para conservar el trabajo que tengo
   3. Necesito el inglés para relacionarme con la gente en el área de El Paso-Juárez
   4. En esta área ninguna persona es educada a menos que sepa inglés

C. Evaluaciones de los americanos (Intervalo: 1=Absolutamente de acuerdo; 5=Totalmente opuesto)
   1. Los americanos son más sinceros que los mexicanos
   2. Los americanos son más alegres y creativos que los mexicanos
   3. Los mexicanos son más organizados y eficientes que los americanos
   4. La educación americana es superior y más disciplinada que la mexicana

D. Identidad local (Intervalo: 1=Absolutamente de acuerdo; 5=Totalmente opuesto)
   1. Yo encuentro difícil vivir en esta área donde hay dos culturas tan diferentes
   2. Soy juarense y me siento muy orgulloso de ello
   3. A pesar de los problemas de delincuencia y desintegración familiar, la frontera es para mí el mejor sitio de México
   4. La frontera tiene la ventaja de que la gente puede conocer otra cultura

Actitudes hacia el español, etnocentrismo y lealtad lingüística

E. Español local frente a español nacional (Intervalo: 0=No supo; 1=Me opongo totalmente; 3=Son iguales; 5=Absolutamente de acuerdo)
   1. El español que se habla en la Cd. de México es más correcto que el de Juárez
   2. El español que se habla en Juárez es más correcto que el de Chihuahua capital
   3. El español que se habla en ciudades importantes de México es más correcto que el de Juárez, por ejemplo, el de Guadalajara
   4. El español que se habla en Juárez es más correcto que el de la Cd. de México

F. Lealtad Lingüística (Intervalo: 5=Absolutamente de acuerdo; 1=Me opongo totalmente)
   1. Es muy importante que los mexicanos de la frontera mantengan el español como todos los otros mexicanos
   2. Los mexicanos de la frontera pueden hablar español como los demás mexicanos, aunque sepan inglés
   3. En Juárez la gente también habla la mitad en inglés y la mitad en español
   4. Yo a veces hablo mezclando los dos idiomas

G. Etnocentrismo (Intervalo: 5=Absolutamente de acuerdo; 1=Me opongo totalmente)
   1. Creo que lo más importante para México es ser un país independiente de cualquier otro
   2. México no es un país perfecto, pero es el más estable de América Latina
   3. La proximidad de los Estados Unidos ha perjudicado la cultura mexicana
   4. Es cierto que México está muy lejos de Dios y muy cerca de Estados Unidos

Actitudes hacia el cambio de código y hacia mexicano-americanos

H. Valores inherentes (Intervalo: 5=Absolutamente de acuerdo; 1=Me opongo totalmente)
   1. El español que se habla en El Paso es más correcto que el de Juárez
   2. Se oye muy bonito cuando la gente en El Paso habla la mitad en inglés y la mitad en español
   3. Me molesta que los mexicanos de El Paso hablen mitad en español y mitad en inglés
   4. Los mexicanos de El Paso deberían imitar a los mexicanos de Juárez cuando hablan español

I. Valores de comunicación (Intervalo: 5=Absolutamente de acuerdo; 1=Me opongo totalmente)
   1. Los mexicanos que emigran a El Paso nunca se olvidan de su idioma
   2. Los mexicanos de Juárez realmente no necesitan sabe inglés porque se pueden comunicar en español con los mexicanos de El Paso
   3. Es imposible entender lo que dicen los mexicanos de El Paso cuando mezclan los Dos idiomas
   4. Se pueden mezclar los dos idiomas, el inglés y el español como hacen los mexicanos de El Paso y de cualquier forma entender lo que dice la gente

J. Evaluaciones de mexicano-americanos (Intervalo: 5=Absolutamente de acuerdo; 1= Me opongo totalmente)
  1. Si los niños mexicano-americanos aprenden el inglés desde pequeños English corren el riesgo de olvidarse que son mexicanos
  2. Los mexicanos que emigran a los Estados Unidos nunca olvidan su idioma
  3. Los niños de padres mexicanos que emigraron se sienten orgullosos de ser mexicanos
  4. Cuando los mexicanos emigran a los Estados Unidos se olvidan de México y sólo piensan en el dinero

Actitudes hacia la educación en inglés

Pregunta abierta:
¿Por qué prefiere la educación mexicana sobre la educación americana?
¿Prefiere la educación americana a la educación mexicana?

References

Agheyisi, R. and J. A. Fishman (1970). Language Attitude Studies. *Anthropological Linguistics* 12 (5):137-157.

Aguilar, M. (2018). *Language Attitudes Toward Mexican Spanish-accented and standard varieties of English*. M.A. thesis. The University of Texas at El Paso.

Azuela, M. (1958-1960). *Obras completas*. México: Fondo de Cultura Económica. 3 vols.

Bell, J. S. (1997). *Literacy, Culture and Identity*. New York / Bern: Peter Lang.

Bills, G. D. et al. (1995). The geography of language shift: distance from the Mexican border and Spanish language claiming in the United States. *International Journal of the Sociology of Language* 114:9-28.

Blasio, J. L. (1905/1973). *Maximiliano y su corte: memorias de un secretario particular*. Mexico: Editora Nacional.

Bloomfield, L. (1933). *Language*. New York: Henry Holt.

Bratt Paulston, C. and R. G. Tucker (eds.). (1997). *The Early Days of Sociolinguistics: Memories and Reflections*. Dallas: SIL International.

Bustamente, J. (1983). *Uso del idioma e identidad nacional*. Tijuana: El Colegio de la Frontera Norte.

Bustamante, J. (1985). National identity along Mexico's northern border: report of preliminary findings. In L. J. Gibson (ed.). *The U.S.-Mexico Border. Development and the National Economics*, 49-63. Boulder: Westview.

Chomsky, N. (1957). *Syntactic Structures*. The Hague: Mouton.

Chomsky, N. (1965). *Aspects of the Theory of Syntax*. Cambridge. MIT Press.

Comar, S. C. (2105). *The Tigua Indians of Ysleta del Sur. A Borderlands Community*. Ph.D. dissertation. The University of Texas at El Paso.

Fasold, R. (1984). *The Sociolinguistics of Society*. Oxford: Blackwell.

Fasold, R. (1990). *The Sociolinguistics of Language*. Oxford: Blackwell.

Fishman, J. A. (1972). *The Sociology of Language. An Interdisciplinary Social Science Approach to Language in Society*. Rowley, MA: Newbury House Publishers.

Fuentes Flores, C. M. (2001). Los cambios en la estructura intraurbana de Ciudad Juárez, Chihuahua, de monocéntrica a multicéntrica. *Frontera Norte* 13 (25):95-118.

García, M. T. (1975). *Obreros: the Mexican workers of El Paso: 1900-1920*. Ph. D. dissertation. University of California at San Diego.

García, M. T. (1981). *Desert Immigrants. The Mexicans of El Paso, 1889-1920*. New Haven: Yale University Press.

Garciadiego, J. (coord.) (2004 /2016). *Gran historia de México ilustrada IV. De la Reforma a la Revolución, 1857-1920*, 225-262. México: Editorial Planeta.

Giles, H. and P. Johnson (1987). Ethnolinguistic identity theory: A social psychological approach to language maintenance. *International Journal of the Sociology of Language* 63:69-99.

Giles, H.; N. Coupland and J. Coupland (eds.) (1991). Accommodation Theory: Communication, context and consequence. In *Contexts of Accommodation. Developments in Applied Sociolinguistics*, 1-68. Cambridge University Press.

Giles, H. (ed.). (2016). *Communication Accommodation Theory: Negotiating Personal Relationships and Social Identities across Contexts*. Cambridge: University Press.

Gonzales, M. G. (1989). *The Hispanic Elite of the Southwest*. El Paso: University of Texas at El Paso. Southwestern Studies 86.

González de la Vara, M. (2009). *Breve historia de Ciudad Juárez y su región*. Chihuahua: El Colegio de la Frontera Norte.

Gudykunst, W. B. and K. L. Schmidt (1987). Language and ethnic identity: An overview and prologue. *Journal of Language and Social Psychology* 6 (3/4):157-170.

Gumperz, J. (1971). *Language in Social Groups*. Stanford: Stanford University Press.

Gutiérrez, E. (2019). ¿Quién fue 'La Adelita' de la Revolución Mexicana? *El Universal*, 11 de noviembre.

Gutiérrez Casas, L. E. (2009). Ciudad Juárez en los sesenta: la estructura urbana en transición. *Nóesis: Revista de Ciencias Sociales y Humanidades* 18 (36):128-154.

Halla, F. L. (1978). *El Paso Texas and Juárez Mexico: A study of a Bi-Ethnic Community 1846-1881*. Ph. D. dissertation. University of Texas at Austin.

Hamann, B. (1983/1994). *Con Maximiliano en México. Del diario del Príncipe Carl Khoverhüller: 1864-1867*. Mexico: Fondo de Cultura Económica. (Translated from German by Angélica Scherf).

Hamilton, N. (1976). *Ben Dowell, El Paso's first Mayor*. El Paso: University of Texas at El Paso. Southwestern Studies 49.

Harwood, J; H. Giles and R. Y. Bourhis (1994) The genesis of vitality theory: Historical patterns of discoursal dimensions. *International Journal of the Sociology of Language* 108:167-206.

Heller, M. (1984). Language and ethnic identity in a Toronto French language school. *Canadian Ethnic Studies* 16 (2):1-14.

Herzog, L. (1990). Border commuter workers and transfrontier metropolitan structure along the United States-Mexico border. *Journal of Borderland Studies* 5 (2):1-20.

Hidalgo, M. (1983). *Language Use and Language Attitudes in Juárez, Mexico*. Ph. D. dissertation. The University of New Mexico.

Hidalgo, M. (1986). Language contact, language loyalty and language prejudice on the Mexican border. *Language and Society* 15 (2):1992-220.

Hidalgo, M. (1993). The dialectics of language maintenance and language loyalty in Chula Vista, Ca.: A Two-generation study. In A. Roca and J. M. Lipski, (eds). *Spanish in the U. S.: Language Contact and Diversity*, 47-71. Berlin: Mouton de Gruyter.

Hidalgo, M. (Forthcoming). *Mexican Spanish in the Twentieth Century. Stratificaation and Variation.*

Hill, J. E. (1965). El Chamizal: A century-old boundary dispute. *Geographical Review* 55 (4):510-522.

Holmes, J. (1997). Women, language and identity. *Journal of Sociolinguistics*. 1 (2):195-223.

Hughes, A. E. (1914). *The Beginnings of Spanish Settlement in the El Paso District*. Berkeley: University of California Press.

Hymes, D. (1973). Speech and Language: On the origins and foundations of inequality among speakers. *Daedalus* 102 (3):59-85.

Hymes, D. (1974). *Foundations of Sociolinguistics. An Ethnographic Approach*. Philadelphia: University of Pennsylvania Press.

Jaramillo, J.A. (1995). The passive legitimization of Spanish. A sociolinguistic study of a quasi-border: Tucson, Arizona. *International Journal of the Sociology of Language* 114:67-93.

Jessup, P. C. (1973). El Chamizal. *Journal of International Law* 67 (3):423-445.

Knowlton, C. S. (1982). Patterns of accommodation of Mexican-Americans in El Paso, Texas: an analysis of a barrio. In Z. A. Kruszevewski et al. (eds)., *Politics and Society in the Southwest. Ethnicity and Chicano Pluralism*, 215-236. Boulder: Westview.

Leal, L. (1964). Recuerdos de Ciudad Juárez en escritores de la Revolución. *Hispania*. 47 (2):231-241.

Lévi-Strauss, C. (1947/1967). *Les structures élémentaires de la parenté*. Paris/La Haye: de Gruyter et Maison des sciences de l'Homme.

Luckingham, B. (1982). *The Urban Southwest: A profile history of Albuquerque, El Paso, Phoenix, Tucson*. El Paso: Texas Western Press.

Lyons, J. (1970). *Noam Chomsky*. New York: Viking Press.

Márquez, B. (1985). *Power and Politics in a Chicano Barrio*. Lanham, MD: University Press of America.

Martínez, O. (1980). *The Chicanos of El Paso. An Assessment of Progress*. El Paso: University of Texas at El Paso. Southwestern Studies 59.

Martínez, O. (1990). Transnational *fronterizos*. Cross-border linkages in Mexican border society. *Journal of Borderland Studies* 1:70-94.

McLaughlin, W. V. (1962). *First Book of Baptisms of Nuestra Señora de Guadalupe del Paso del Norte*. M. A. thesis. University of Texas at El Paso.

Newmeyer, F. J. (1986). Has there been a Chomskyan Revolution in linguistics? *Language* 1:1-18.

Norton, B. (1997). Language, identity and the ownership of English. *TESOL Quarterly* 31 (3):409-429.

Paz, O. (1950). *El laberinto de la soledad*. Mexico: Cuadernos Americanos.

Pérez Ruiz, M. L. (1991). Los múltiples rostros de la identidad en Ciudad Juárez. *Alteridades* 1 (2):63-73.

Portilla, S. (1997). *Una sociedad en armas. Insurrección antirreeleccionista en México, 1910-1911*. México: El Colegio de México.

Quitarte, M. (1970). *Historiografía sobre el imperio de Maximiliano*. México: Universidad Nacional Autónoma de México.

Ramos, S. (1951). *El perfil del hombre y la cultura en México*. Buenos Aires: Espasa-Calpe.

Reynolds, T. R. (2011). The rise and fall of native communities at the old El Paso del Norte mission. *Southern New Mexico Historical Review* 18:26-32.

Santiago Quijada, G. (2013). *Políticas institucionales y conformación espacial de Ciudad Juárez, 1940-1990*. Cd. Juárez: Universidad Autónoma de Ciudad Juárez.

Saussure, F. de (1915/1945). *Curso de Lingüística General*. Buenos Aires. Losada. Published by C. Balley, A. Sechehaye and A. Riedlinger.

Sonnischen, C. L. (1968). *Pass of the North*. El Paso: Texas Western Press.

Tajfel, H. (1981). *Human Groups and Social Categories*. Cambridge: University Press.

Tajfel, H. (1982). Introduction in *Social Identity and Intergroup Relations*. In his *Social Identity and Intergroup Relations*, 1-10.
Tajfel, H. (ed.). (1982). *Social Identity and Intergroup Relations*. Cambridge / Paris: Cambridge Press / Editions de la Maison des Sciences de l'Homme.
Terrazas, F. (2005). *La voz de los siglos: Cd. Juárez*. Cd. Juárez: Universidad Autónoma del Noreste.
Teschner, R. V. (1995). Beachheads, islands, and conduits. Spanish monolingualism and bilingualism in El Paso, Texas. *International Journal of the Sociology of Language* 114:93-106.
Teschner, R. V.; G. D. Bills, and J. R. Craddock (1975). *Spanish and English of United States Hispanos: A Critical, Annotated, Linguistic Bibliography*. Arlington, VA: Center for Applied Linguistics.
Timmons, W. H. (1990). *El Paso. A Borderlands History*. El Paso: The University of Texas at El Paso.
Valdés, G. (1990). Consideraciones teórico-metodológicas para el estudio del bilingüismo inglés-español en el lado mexicano de la frontera. *Estudios Mexicanos / Mexican Studies* 6 (1):43-66.
Vasconcelos, J. (1935). *Ulises criollo*. México: Editorial Botas.
Weber, D. J. (1982). *The Mexican Frontier 1821-1846. The American Southwest under Mexico*. Albuquerque: The University of New Mexico Press.
Wundt, W. (1912). *An In°troduction to Psychology*. New York: Macmillan.
Wundt, W. (1928). *Elements of Folk Psychology. Outlines of a Psychological History of the Development of Mankind*. London / New York: Macmillan.

Part II
Language use and language attitudes in Juárez, Mexico (1983)

Chapter 1

Theoretical Considerations

One of the major urban complexes straddling the 1,900-mile boundary between Mexico and the United States is the Juárez-El Paso area, a rather complex language setting which involves the use of the two official languages—Spanish and English, their regional and social varieties, and more interestingly, the blending of the two in the vernacular. An understanding of such complexity demands an assessment of the societal values and societal roles of the languages and language varieties utilized in the area.

Juárez is the oldest and largest city along the Mexican side of the border. Both ethnically and linguistically the community is highly homogeneous, inasmuch as the entire population can be considered of Mexican descent and predominantly monolingual in Spanish. The geographic, social and linguistic contacts of the border residents are manifested in two main but opposite directions: (1) with the network of communities in Mexico's interior, and (2) with the immediate vicinity north of the border, El Paso, Texas. In El Paso two major and differentiated ethnolinguistic groups have evolved: Anglo-Americans whose characteristic code is the English language, and Mexican-Americans, who are normally speakers of both Spanish and English. The latter group may be distinguished from Mexicans and Americans by the use of Spanish-English Code-switching, the mixed language variety also known as Spanglish.[1]

The work at hand is based on a corpus of data collected through personal interviews with eighty-five Juárez residents, whose verbal reports on language use and language attitudes are presented here. The study deals primarily with the attitudes of Mexican residents of Juárez toward Spanish, the official language of Mexico; toward English, the official language of the United States; and toward Spanglish, the code emerging from the mixture of the two. Secondarily, this investigation examines the use of the three codes, with an emphasis on the functions of English on the Mexican side of the border. Attitudinal dimensions and the informal use of English in different domains are treated as both dependent and independent variables; their multiple interrelationships with other demographic dimensions, such as social class, education, sex and formal instruction in English, are analyzed herein and interpreted in light of both theoretical assumptions and empirical universal discoveries in the fields of sociolinguistics and language attitudes.

One recurring characteristic of the research on language attitudes is the absence of a continuous theoretical and methodological framework. Cooper and Fishman (1974) attribute this discontinuity to the apparent isolation of sociolinguistics and attitude theorists. "Sociolinguistic investigators' use of attitude as a variable has proceeded largely without reference to issues in the theory and measurement of attitudes, and the procedures and data developed by sociolinguists have been largely ignored by attitude theorists" (p. 5). Despite this dissociation, language attitude remains a major concept in a number of investigations dealing with second language learning (Gardner and Lambert 1972), interethnic communication (Giles 1973; Giles et al. 1977), overt behavior toward language (Solé 1976; Cooper and Fishman 1977), and language policy and language planning (Ryan 1981).

Another significant difficulty in the study of language attitudes is the very definition of such a fragile and subjective state of mind. Cooper and Fishman (1974) have chosen to define language attitude in terms of its referent. They have amplified the referent to include:

language, language behavior, and referents of which language or language behavior is a marker or symbol. Thus, attitudes toward a language (e.g., Hebrew) or towards a feature of a language (e.g., a given phonological variant) or towards language use (e.g., the use of Hebrew for secular purposes) or towards language as a group marker (e.g., Hebrew as a language of Jews) are examples of language attitudes. Conversely, attitudes toward Jews or attitudes toward secular domains are not language attitudes, although they might be reflected by language attitudes (p. 6).

The nature of language attitudes thus has to be assessed in relation to the specific domains in which a language or language variety is utilized, and with consideration of the sociocultural factors contributing to its positive or negative evaluation. Likewise, language attitude can be studied in terms of the behavioral consequences in a speech community, "since almost any attitude, under the right conditions, might affect language behavior or behavior toward language" (Cooper and Fishman 1977:6).

The following sections of this chapter outline several major concepts and discoveries drawn from the study of language attitudes and sociolinguistics. This review will lead to each of the major highlights and assumptions about language attitudes and language use that are explored in this dissertation. Insofar as the studies are disconnected in scope, the topics of discussion have not been arranged according to the order in which they are discussed in my own study, but according to a logical framework that will facilitate the comprehension of the assumptions under which I operate, and the methodology employed when planning the study

1.1. Attitudes toward a second or foreign language

Considerable work has been carried out in the past twenty years regarding the affective aspects of second/foreign language learning. The general assumption is that the learner's positive or negative attitudes toward the target language and its representatives can either enhance or inhibit the acquisition of that particular language. Pioneer studies compiled in Gardner and Lambert (1972) were conducted in such different settings as Montreal, Louisiana, Connecticut, Maine and the Philippines in order to determine what factors contribute to achievement in second language learning. The results of the research indicate that language aptitude and motivation are the most important contributors to achievement. Motivation is then interpreted as having two components—an integrative orientation and an instrumental orientation. Gardner and Lambert define both concepts:

> The notion of integrative motive implies that success in mastering a second language depends on a particular orientation on the part of the learner, reflecting a willingness or a desire to be like representative members of the "other" language community, and to become associated, at least vicariously, with that community. The contrasting form of orientation is referred to as an instrumental orientation toward the language-learning task, one characterized by a desire to gain social recognition or economic advantages through knowledge of a foreign language (p. 14).

Intimately associated with the instrumental and integrative components is another form of orientation to language learning that could come into play. This is "the resentment members of one linguistic group (usually the minority group) can have toward another group whose language or dialect they are forced to learn through social or economic pressure" (p. 15).

Gardner and Lambert suggest, in addition, that learners can also be influenced by their own ethnocentric tendencies or prejudices toward foreign people. Such an attitude would supposedly impede successful language acquisition (p. 16).

These considerations applied to the context of the Mexican border would imply, for example, that Mexican residents of Juárez might claim to learn English due mainly to economic benefits, inasmuch as this language is very useful in certain occupational activities, such as tourism and the assembly industry. It would also be assumed that highly ethnocentric individuals would report low indices in the integrative orientation and higher indices in the instrumental one. Integrative-oriented subjects, on the other hand, would be expected to claim a relatively greater appreciation of representative members of the community where the foreign language (English) is spoken.

1.1.1. Gardner's model

The above mentioned pioneer studies have been followed by a number of investigations proposing several models that would explain the relationship between affective aspects of second language learning and second language achievement. The present stage of research on this particular issue "has resulted in the incorporation of findings from earlier studies into an elaborated model proposed by Gardner" (Oller 1981:15). After a careful examination of the results of empirical studies conducted throughout the world, Gardner (1979) establishes the following four hypotheses: (1) The social milieu provides the basis for attitudes of learners and propagates the cultural beliefs of the community. (2) These beliefs affect the approach to the second language acquisition process and are directly linked to four individual variables: intelligence, language aptitude, motivation and situational anxiety. (3) Intelligence and language aptitude appear to affect the formal language situation while motivation and situational anxiety are more influential on informal language exposure. (4) Both formal language training and informal language experience have direct effects on linguistic and nonlinguistic outcomes. The term linguistic outcomes includes second language knowledge (structural aspects such as grammar or vocabulary) and specific second language skills (i.e., reading, writing, understanding and speaking). Nonlinguistic outcomes, on the other hand, refer to extra-language attributes developed as a function of formal and informal exposure to the second language. Examples of nonlinguistic outcomes are favorable attitudes toward other ethnolinguistic communities and a general appreciation of other cultures and languages (Gardner 1979:195-9).

Among the distinctions proposed by Gardner, one that may be considered essential for my own study refers to how the second language is acquired. The author differentiates between formal language training and informal language experience:

> Formal Language Training refers to that instruction which takes place in the classroom or any other teacher/student context. Informal Language Experience, on the other hand, refers to those situations which permit the student to acquire competence in second language skills without direct instruction. Instances of such experiences would be speaking with members of the other cultural community, watching movies or television, listening to the radio, or reading material in the other language (Gardner 1979:198).

In my own study it is important to distinguish formal from informal language exposure, since in the Juárez setting individuals have the opportunity for both. Formal training in

English is compulsory in Mexican secondary and preparatory schools. Informal language experience takes place in many different ways since Juárez residents have ready access to the native speakers of English living in El Paso, tourists from other American communities visiting the city, and also to the written and spoken media originating in the United States. The informal use of English might well be assumed to be the most important moderator of attitudes toward the three codes spoken in the area: English, Spanish, and Spanglish.

Another concept that this model incorporates is the distinction between additive and subtractive bilingualism first proposed by Lambert (1974). This conceptualization encompasses

> A distinction in terms of the social implications of developing bilingual skills in which bilingualism is viewed as contributing to an individual's growth by offering him access to other cultural communities (additive) or as contributing to his feeling of loss of identity by orienting him away from his own cultural background towards another (imposed) one (subtractive) (Gardner 1979:197).

This differentiation between additive and subtractive bilingualism might be utilized in explaining the nature of bilingualism in a context such as the one encountered in Juárez, as opposed to that encountered in El Paso. One may hypothesize that in Juárez bilingualism is additive whereas in El Paso it tends to be subtractive.

Finally, Gardner's model has been extended in my work to hypothesize that in the Juárez setting the social milieu is a major factor responsible not only for the attitudes toward the second/foreign language (English), but also for the attitudes displayed toward the native tongue of the informants (Spanish) and toward the mixed language variety (Spanglish).

1.2 Evaluations of majority languages and language varieties

In addition to Gardner and Lambert's studies, other significant investigations in the past two decades have linked language, attitude and the prevailing societal values where the language in question is spoken. These investigations have examined the close relationship between the perceived values of a prestigious language or language variety and the accompanying confrontation with another culture and its symbolic representations. Cultural and linguistic confrontation involves perceptions of different ethnolinguistic groups, attitudes toward representatives of those groups and willingness to identify with them.

One line of thought in the study of language attitudes and social values suggests that prestigious languages are favorably viewed by both majority and minority members, and are preferred, at least attitudinally, to low prestige language norms. A second line of thought insinuates that speakers of prestigeless languages and language varieties do not seem to accept the societal values assigned to prestigious languages and therefore overvalue their own linguistic codes (Ryan 1979). The following discussion of the evaluation of majority languages and varieties of languages is intended to pave the way for an understanding of the assumptions in this study with respect to the design of the attitudinal dimensions related to Spanish.

The instrument developed to indirectly measure individuals' reactions toward language varieties is known as the matched-guise technique, originally utilized by Lambert et al. (1960) and Lambert (1967). This procedure consists of a number of speakers reading the same passage of prose in two or more contrasting languages or language varieties.

Listeners are then required to evaluate each of the speech samples in bipolar adjective rating scales which refer to personality traits. The method is utilized in order to explore the listener's more private feelings and to evoke in his mind certain attitudinal reactions that have become associated with the particular group of people who habitually use that language or language variety. The studies undertaken by Lambert and his associates focused on the social significance of linguistic differences; these were used as a means of eliciting the perceived moral traits of the subjects' ethnolinguistic group as opposed to other groups. The authors found that English-Canadians perceived the French-Canadian speaker as being less intelligent, less attractive and less trustworthy when he used French than when he used English. Interestingly, the results also showed that both French and English speakers evaluated the English group more favorably on most traits, even though the voices belonged to the same bilingual speaker.

In a more recent attempt to understand the social importance of language in intergroup relations, Lambert (1979) argues that negative views of the self held by minority members "often promote shifts in values, behavioral styles, and in the case where a different language is involved, socially important shifts away from the use of one's own language or dialect to that of the more prestigious group's language or speech style" (p. 188).

Because differences in speech identify individuals as members of a certain prestigious or prestigeless community, several other studies have been carried on in different settings; ratings similar to Lambert's have been encountered among minority and majority groups. Members of both groups in the United States agree in assigning a higher status to a prestigious standard variety speaker and a lower status to nonstandard speakers. To validate this hypothesis, samples of taped speech of representatives of six American-English dialect groups (Network, Educated White, Southern Educated Black, Southern Mississippi Peer, Howard University Alumni, and New York University Alumni) were played to three groups of college students (one northern Black, one southern white and one southern Black). The results suggested that they unanimously perceived Network speakers as having the most favorable profile of traits. The study also showed a relation between the perceived favorableness of the speakers and their perceived race, i.e., speakers thought of as being white were judged more favorably, as opposed to those perceived as Black (Tucker and Lambert 1969).

The assumption that an individual's speech reveals his social status to members of his community has also been borne out in Labov's study of the social stratification of English in New York City (Labov 1966). This investigation examined a number of phonological variables which included presence or absence of final and preconsonantal /r/ in words such as *car* or *card*, *bare* or *bared*; realization of voiceless and voiced dental fricatives in words such as *thing* and *then*; the height of the vowel in words like *bad* and *bag*; and the realization of the mid-back rounded vowel as in *caught*, *talk*, and *dog* (pp. 50-6). The language usage patterns found by Labov reveal that social and stylistic variation of the aforementioned linguistic features fit together closely, i.e., "a variant that is used most often in formal styles is also the variant that is used most often in all styles by speakers who are ranked higher on an objective socioeconomic scale" (p. 405). The objective combination of both types of variation suggests that most New Yorkers think or feel that particular variants are more correct or more prestigious. This attitude is exhibited in the New Yorkers' response to the subjective evaluation test administered by the researcher. Through this test, the respondents were able to detect certain "incorrect" or stigmatized features of the local speech with great regularity; but when reporting their own individual usage, New Yorkers were very inaccurate, that is, they simply gave their own norms of correctness. The native New Yorker would not admit using a variant pronunciation that he perceived as substandard. According to the researcher, this reaction indicates that New Yorkers consider their own speech in terms of the norms at which they are aiming rather than the norms they actually produce (pp. 476-80). Speakers deny their own speech due to the social pressures exerted on their group at the same time that they express their desires of eluding identification as New Yorkers. This negative attitude toward their own variety is based on the lack of prestige of the community in the eyes of the outsiders. Different reasons move speakers to either downgrade or upgrade the evaluation of their own language or language variety or that spoken by members of other communities. The study reviewed above gives good evidence that people aim at the characteristic pronunciation of the dialect to which they aspire.

Dialects seem thus to be expressive of personal and social motives and aspirations, as is supported by another study conducted by Escobar (1978) in the South American setting. The matched-guise technique was slightly modified in Lima, Peru, in order to prompt the subjective evaluations of Peruvians toward the varieties spoken in both the capital of Peru (Lima) and in the provinces. Twelve voices (nine of them from five distinctive sectors of Lima and three from the provinces) were incorporated into a matrix tape. Each voice was identified as belonging to one of the five sectors of the city or one of the provinces, and as representative of the level of education of the speaker. Five different groups of judges classified the speakers as coming from Lima or outside of Lima and as having low, medium or high levels of education. The judges came from the *élite limeña*, the upper-middle class, the lower-middle class, the lower-working class (all of Lima), and various social groups of the provinces. The results showed that only the lower-middle class subjects showed a high level of accuracy in the recognition of the regional and educational backgrounds of the speakers, whereas the other groups did not demonstrate the same precision. This finding has been interpreted as an indication of concern for prestigious linguistic norms (i.e., the "typical" speech of Lima, the speech of the educated) in the group that identified the provenance of the speakers. Apparently, members of the lower-middle class in Lima strive, for both upward mobility and status, and they convey their aspirations in their evaluative reactions toward speech (Escobar 1978).

The literature on language attitudes provides additional examples of respondents' giving less positive evaluation to their first language or dialect than to a superimposed language or language variety. These favorable evaluational judgements have been found to be associated with different contextual domains. In Egypt, for example, El-Dash and Tucker (1975) investigated the views held by Egyptians of various ages and educational backgrounds toward several of the speech varieties used in the country (Classical Arabic, Colloquial Arabic, Egyptian English, British English and American English). This study also ascertained the perceived suitability of these codes for diverse purposes within Egyptian society. The matched-guise technique was employed to examine the relationship between language and ethnic identity, as well as to examine the prestige, status and perceived utility of one code in relation to another. The authors of this investigation report that the superimposed language, English, is preferred over the native language of the country in the contexts of home and college courses by those individuals with university education. In addition, they indicate that English speakers are considered by most age and educational groups as being more intelligent, and as possessing more leadership ability than speakers of colloquial Arabic. Furthermore, speakers of classical Arabic are rated more favorably than those of colloquial Arabic, and English is felt more suitable for all situations except home. A similar trend has been observed by Carranza and Ryan (1975), who found that Mexican-American-accented English was downgraded relative to standard English more in the school context than in the home context.

The major assumption drawn from the studies discussed above is that superimposed, prestigious, majority languages and language varieties tend to be perceived as possessing superior qualities when compared to prestigeless, minority linguistic codes. In this dissertation, I intend to explore Mexicans' judgements of their own language. The judgmental dimension explored herein is related to the values of correctness of the variety of Spanish spoken in Juárez as compared to that spoken in other important urban centers in Mexico's interior, but especially as compared to the variety of Spanish spoken in the capital of the country.

1.2.1 Other values assigned to languages

The opposite general direction in the study of language attitudes shows that some groups and individuals react favorably to less prestigious language varieties with which they identify and feel solidarity. In the United States, for instance, the matched-guise technique was employed by De la Cerda and Hopper (1975) among Mexican-Americans who evaluated Standard Spanish, Standard English, Tex-Mex Spanish and accented English on ten personality characteristics. These characteristics did not vary for Standard Spanish and Standard English speakers, but they did for Tex-Mex Spanish which was rated higher by those who considered themselves Chicanos. This study suggests that only those subjects identifying with a low-prestige language variety rate it higher than the standard varieties.

In the context of New Mexico similar results were encountered by Hannum (1978). Sixty-four Mexican-American students enrolled in Spanish for native speakers classes rated the personalities and speech of speakers from Argentina, Costa Rica, Mexico, Spain, Puerto Rico and New Mexico. The results indicated that the subjects evaluated the samples of the Spanish of New Mexico as high or higher than that of all the other countries. This positive attitude shows a sense of pride in the subjects' own language variety.

Along the continuing tendency of positive evaluations of language varieties, one more study is worth mentioning. It was conducted among Welshmen and the matched-guise technique was utilized. The subjects were classified into three groups: (1) English-Welsh bilinguals, (2) English speakers of Welsh origin who were learning Welsh and (3) English speakers of Welsh origin who neither knew nor were studying Welsh. These groups listened to the stimulus voices of two male bilinguals reading the same passage once each in Welsh with a South Welsh accent, in Welsh-accented English and in Received Pronunciation (RP) English. This investigation demonstrated that the three groups upgraded the Welsh with South Welsh accent speakers on most traits but also the Welsh-accented English speakers on a considerable number of traits. The RP English speakers were favorably evaluated on only one trait: self-confidence. This study suggests that Welshmen do not appear to value the prestigious out-group's speech patterns but have pride in the code of the in-group (Bourhis et al. 1973).

The different outcomes in the investigation of attitudes toward language varieties hint that there are two main social values accounting for their positive or negative evaluation. A fundamental distinction proposed by Ryan (1979; 1981) is status—the value of a speech variety for social advancement—versus solidarity—the value of a variety for identification with a group. This dichotomy is based on findings which reveal both "majority and minority group preferences for speakers of the standard language with respect to status and competence traits. On the other hand, the nonstandard variety is viewed more favorably on other traits, especially those related to group solidarity" (Ryan 1979:155).

In applying the distinction of status and solidarity proposed by Ryan, I assumed that speakers from the Mexican side of the border would display a rather strong appreciation for their national language, Spanish, since this code is not only the mother tongue, but a necessary vehicle utilized to maintain the ties with the local system as well as the allegiance with Mexico (solidarity). At the same time, Mexicans could be expected to claim a high attitudinal loyalty to Spanish, asserting with this attitude their desires to differentiate themselves from the group of Mexican-Americans residing in El Paso (status).

1.3 Attitudes toward mother tongue

Attitudes toward mother tongue have been linked to a profound need of preserving one's own language, especially in a situation of language contact. The term language loyalty has been proposed to designate "the state of mind in which the language as an intact entity, and in contrast to other languages, assumes a high position in a scale of values, a position in need of being 'defended' " (Weinreich 1968:99).

In response to an impending language shift, language loyalty would raise the consciousness of the population to preserve the threatened mother tongue and would make the language a symbol and a cause. The extent of language loyalty displayed by different communities varies with other sociocultural factors from one contact situation to the next. Sometimes language loyalty is associated with nationalism, but these two phenomena do not necessarily have parallel goals. The Rhaetoromansch, for example, like the Italian Swiss, cultivate the fullest possible loyalty to their respective languages, but they do not aspire to national independence from their common country, Switzerland (Weinreich 1968:100).

The relationship between language loyalty sentiments and nationalism has been addressed by Fishman (1973) who suggests that language has been traditionally regarded as a defining characteristic and as a 'shibboleth' of nationalism. Language is thus a link with the glorious past, with cultural authenticity, and with the sense of identity of a nation. Moreover, national beliefs are language dependent, inasmuch as language is the carrier of all the other notions and symbols advanced by nationalism (pp. 44-54).

One question raised from the very existence of language loyalty sentiments is the connection between attitudes toward the mother tongue and overt behavior toward the mother tongue, as well as the feelings of ethnocentrism. The relationship between language loyalty, ethnocentrism and language use has been assessed within the bilingual English / Chamorro segment of the Guamanian speech community (Riley 1975). A total of 194 surveys were administered at the University of Guam among the students enrolled in English courses. The survey focused on the attitudes of the population toward the use of Chamorro and the maintenance of Guamanian culture and traditions, as well as on the usage of the mother tongue in the community. The results of the study indicated that, overall, the mean knowledge of Chamorro was higher than the mean use of this language, and that, as the reported feelings of ethnocentrism decreased, so did the use rates of the subjects. In brief, the data indicate that subjects show only mildly ethnocentric attitudes or are completely neutral. The author emphasizes, moreover, that language loyalty is predominantly an intellectual activity found most often among those in academic circles.

The study was repeated seven years later after the government and the educational system had all been active in their attempts to enhance the use of Chamorro and to instill in the people a respect for Chamorro culture and traditions. The results were very similar, that is, they suggested that despite the emphasis given to ethnocentric awareness and to the importance of the use of the indigenous language over the past seven years, the population seemed not to have been strongly impressed by the institutional policies (Riley 1980).

In the context of the United States the sentiments of language loyalty have been associated with an active, self-conscious reinforcement of the non-English immigrant languages. Case studies of separate cultural/linguistic groups (Ukrainian, Spanish, French and German) show that these languages have been maintained through religious-ethnic schools, publications, broadcasts, and cultural activities. These efforts, however, have served as a transition to marginal ethnicity and restricted language maintenance. Language loyalty in the United States is stronger among those groups who have maintained greatest psychological distance from the American mainstream, e.g., the Spanish-speaking population in the Southwest. Most non-English immigrant groups have drifted consistently toward Anglicization, maintaining the mother tongue in restricted domains, such as the family, or in a limited number of individuals, e.g., in first-generation speakers, older children or first children. Third generation speakers have generally lost the tongue of their ancestors but have, on the other hand, experienced increases in general esteem and favorable attitudes toward language maintenance (Fishman 1965; 1966).

If the concept of language loyalty is applied to the language setting of the Mexico-United States border, one could presume that a connection between these sentiments and those of ethnocentrism would exist, inasmuch as Spanish is the national language of Mexico and assumes a higher position in the scale of values of its speakers, a position in need of being 'defended'.

1.4 Speech accommodation

When dealing with the values assigned to Spanglish, the mixed language variety characteristic of Mexican-Americans inhabiting El Paso, I have considered the "Theory of Speech Accommodation." This theory proposes a framework to account for the diverse roles of language in intergroup relations. The model describes the sociocultural factors influencing differentiated ethnolinguistic groups and outlines some of the sociopsychological processes and linguistic strategies adopted when those groups come into close contact. The basic postulate of this theory is that under certain conditions a speaker may shift the characteristics of his speech (accent, speed, style, grammar) in order to obtain his listener's approval. Under different social and personal circumstances, the speaker may alter his way of speaking in order to dissociate himself from others and hence accentuate his linguistic differences. A shift toward the speech style of the interlocutor is termed convergence whereas a shift away from the interlocutor's speech is termed divergence. Through speech accommodation and adjustment individuals express positive and negative values, attitudes and intentions toward others (Giles 1973; 1977; Giles et al. 1977).

One experimental study illustrates how a French-Canadian speaker was favorably evaluated by English-Canadians because of his perceived considerateness and effort in bridging the cultural gap even though his English was not natively fluent. In a situation such as this there is reciprocal accommodation or convergence which functions as a stimulus for positive attitudes between members of conflicting groups (Giles et al. 1973). The opposite has also been shown, that is, that speakers tend to diverge in order to stress the differences between themselves and the out-group. Accent divergence among Welsh people learning Welsh was investigated in a language laboratory where subjects were asked questions about their reasons for learning a 'dying language'. The questions were presented verbally by a British-accented speaker who threatened the subjects' feelings of ethnic identity. The subjects replied by broadening their Welsh accents and by introducing Welsh words and phrases in their responses (Bourhis and Giles 1977).

I have considered the "Theory of Speech Accommodation" to be a relevant basis for exploring the possible sources of attitudes and reactions prevailing on the Mexico-United States border between Mexicans and Mexican-Americans. The judgmental dimension explored in this study focuses on the usefulness of Spanish-English Code-switching for general communication in the Juárez-El Paso area. My assumption was that Mexicans from the Mexican side of the border would downgrade the mixed variety of Spanish spoken in El Paso because they perceive it as an impediment to communication.

1.5 Attitudes and behavior

While there exists a good deal of information on attitudes toward languages, very little is known about the interaction between language attitudes and actual language behavior. In this section I will discuss the assumptions underlying such a relationship and the most relevant studies dealing with it. Most research exploring this connection has focused on language proficiency or language achievement, but very few investigations ask to what extent attitude is related to the usage of a given language (Cooper and Fishman 1977:240).

In order to shed light on the connection between language attitudes and language behavior a study by Fishman (1971a) was conducted among 500 New York youngsters of the Puerto Rican community who were sent questionnaires and prepaid return envelopes. The survey focused on the desirability of social contacts with non-Puerto Ricans, attitudes toward being Puerto Rican, attitudes toward being American, observance of everyday Puerto Rican behavior, and use of Spanish and English. Eighty percent of the 500 questionnaires were accompanied by a ten-item commitment scale which explored the desire of the youngsters to actually help strengthen the Spanish language in the community. Those individuals who signed the commitment scale when replying to the mail questionnaire were subsequently sent an invitation to attend an evening of Puerto Rican songs, dances and recitations. Out of all 500 subjects, 375 replied, but 47 did not receive the commitment scale; 53 returned the commitment scale unsigned and, therefore, no invitation was sent; 178 signed the commitment scale but did not reply to invitation; 22 signed the commitment scale and replied negatively to invitation; 49 replied affirmatively but failed to attend the program, and 26 replied 'yes' to invitation and also attended the program. The results of this study show that most subjects agreed on assigning an affective, traditional value to

Spanish in the vernacular culture, but very few were willing to overtly commit themselves to maintain the ties in the community via language.

A different study conducted among Mexican-American students enrolled at the University of Texas at Austin explored the attitudes toward Spanish on three different dimensions: (1) ideological, (2) instrumental and (3) affective, as well as the use of Spanish in the community (Solé 1976). The findings revealed that the students' attitudinal language loyalty was fully verbalized only among the most educated, English proficient and upwardly mobile segment of the group, but their behavioral commitment toward Spanish seemed to be primarily a function of linguistic ability rather than attitudinal orientation toward language.

Within Ireland, the language and demographic data of more than six thousand subjects were collected to assess questions such as the preference of the speakers for Irish, their proficiency in this language, the involvement in Irish activities and use of Irish outside the home. The major question was the effect of language attitudes upon language behavior. The conclusion drawn from this national survey is very similar to that of the studies reviewed above. "Language attitudes in Ireland, while highly structured, internally coherent, and superficially correlated with language usage, do not appear to exert any independent effect on the individual's own language behavior" (Brudner and White 1979:65). Attitudes and behavior are strongly influenced by ability and opportunity to perform and by the degree of support and personal involvement in Irish-related activities.

Finally, a slightly different study (Cooper and Fishman 1977) was carried out in Israel among high school students who were presented with twelve statements, each giving one reason for studying English as a second language. The statements reflected three different types of reasons for studying this language of wider communication: (1) instrumental, (2) integrative and (3) personal/developmental. Second, the subjects were presented with a list of thirty-two means-ends ratings which expressed the degree to which students view a particular language skill (e.g., English speaking, English reading) as contributing to the acquisition of a given goal (e.g., making a good impression on people, being sophisticated, being popular). In addition, the students were administered a battery of tests which measured their English proficiency in reading, writing, speaking and understanding. The students also provided self-reports of their English usage and English proficiency for various purposes, such as speaking to native speakers of English, reading publications in this language, listening to English language nonmusical broadcasts, etc. The results of this study indicated that those students who viewed English as facilitating their attainment of valued goals tended to be more proficient in English and to use it informally more often than those who viewed English as less useful in this regard. The means-ends responses were the only language attitude items which showed a consistent relationship to proficiency and usage. This means that subjects are more motivated to use the language if they perceive that the language serves personal goals and purposes. It is possible, however, that their view of English as valuable for personal ends, is both a result of and a contributor to English proficiency (Cooper and Fishman 1977:272).

All the studies reviewed above confirm that there is not a complete correspondence between language attitudes and language behavior. When the relationship is in fact possible, usage seems to be related to an instrumental view of the language, as can be seen in the study among Israelis. The results of the works carried out among Israelis and Puerto Ricans have led

Fishman to assume that acquiring, using and liking a language are very imperfectly related to each other (Fishman 1977b), except in those populations which are language-politicized and language-ideologized and are, therefore, more conscious and more concerned with both language usage and language behavior (Fishman 1971a:114). In the context of the Mexican border, one could assume that speakers would behave similarly with respect to the language of wider communication (English) with which they are in daily contact, and which is learned as a subject of instruction. That is, one would expect Mexicans to claim low usage of the language and report very positive appreciation, or, on the other hand, to report high usage and a very negative attitude. In order to investigate the relationship between attitudes and behavior in Juárez, the informal use of English will be assessed and quantified.

1.6 Bilingualism and diglossia

Those speech communities where two or more languages or varieties of the same language are used by some speakers under different social circumstances require an analysis of the functions of the distinct codes. Diglossia is the term that was first proposed by Ferguson (1959) to characterize the use of two genetically related languages in the same speech community. One of these two languages is the classical, standardized or literary version of the other regional or colloquial variety. In a community where two such varieties exist the standard language is utilized for all kinds of formalized communication (High function) whereas the everyday familiar variety is used for ordinary conversation (Low function).

The specialization of functions for High and Low situations is one of the most important features of diglossia; consequently, the concept of diglossia has been expanded to mean language choice in specialized domains of interaction (Fishman 1971b; 1971c). Diglossia functions take place in rather large and complex speech communities in which there exist both a range of compartmentalized roles and ready access to these roles. When members of the speech community have access to these roles, they are likely to engage in a series of situations which require the use of one differentiated language or language variety. The selection of the differentiated linguistic code depends upon the particular domain (e.g., the church, the school, the family) and the particular set of domain-appropriate people (priest-parishioner, teacher-student, parent-child) who interact with each other. When the functions of two languages are clearly demarcated and serve distinct purposes in the speech community, a situation of diglossia and bilingualism is encountered (Fishman 1971b). It is possible, however, to find bilingualism without diglossia, that is, competently bilingual individuals in two or more languages but who never have the opportunity to use them in role-playing situations (e.g., a Yoruba speaker in the United States who cannot interact with native speakers of Yoruba and is therefore unable to behave as a Yoruba).

A number of studies illustrate that, as members of a speech community, individuals reflect the sociolinguistic norms of the networks of which they are a part. The individual's bilingualism varies with respect to the particular situation in which he participates. Two experiments conducted among Puerto Rican bilingual youngsters living in New York City measure the normative views of the subjects with respect to bilingual usage (Greenfield 1972). The situationally based instruments utilized in the experiments included a number of hypothetical conversations consisting of a list of persons, places and topics; these conversations were ranked along the dimensions of intimate-distant, private-public and personal-impersonal, respectively. The subjects indicated how much Spanish and English they would be likely to use in each situation. The results obtained indicate that the amount of Spanish and English differs according to domain of interaction. Use of Spanish was claimed in the domains of family, friendship and religion, but not in education and employment. The reverse was true for English usage.

Another attempt to document the functions of English *vis-à-vis* the native tongue was made in India where English has co-existed with several Indian languages for about two centuries. The sample of this study carried out by Parasher (1980) comprised 350 educated bilinguals employed in diverse all-India institutions and organizations in two important cities. The subjects were asked to report on the use of languages in communication in 29 oral and 10 written situations. The data obtained showed that for the bilingual population under study there were certain spheres of activity associated with the native tongue and certain others with English. The native language is the dominant language in the domain of family while English dominates the fields of education, government and employment. Although English is dominant in the domains of friendship and personal transactions, the mother tongue is also used in certain situations in these areas. No language emerges clearly as the dominant one in the domain of neighborhood.

In this dissertation the distinction between diglossia and bilingualism proposed by Fishman (1971b; 1971c) will serve to illustrate the nature of language usage in the community under investigation. An attempt will be made to exemplify the use of English, the foreign language, in contrast with the use of Spanish, the native tongue.

1.7 Summary of theoretical considerations

This dissertation is an attempt to explore a series of linguistic dimensions selected *a priori* but defended on previous research dealing with language attitudes and language use. The data obtained from my own investigation are based on a questionnaire elaborated for the purpose of eliciting information on language attitudes, language use and demographic characteristics of the informants. This questionnaire is spelled out in the second part of Chapter 2, after introducing the reader to the historical, socioeconomic, and linguistic background of Juárez. Chapters 3, 4 and 5 focus directly on and fully analyze and interpret the results of the survey. In the third chapter I examine the role of English in Juárez; I discuss integrative versus instrumental orientation, the connection between language use and language attitudes, the use of the foreign language, English, in specific domains within the city, the effects of the local milieu on attitudes toward English, and the opinions of the subjects about native speakers of English. In Chapter 4 I consider the role of the native language, Spanish; I deal primarily with the notion of superimposed language varieties in the Spanish-speaking world and attitudinal language loyalty in Mexico in general and in Juárez in particular. Additionally, I provide brief examples of disloyal behavior toward Spanish, the mother tongue. The relationship between language loyalty and national ethnocentrism is also analyzed in this chapter.

Chapter 5 explores the evaluation of the subjects related to Spanglish, the values of this language variety, the reported difficulties of communication between Mexicans and Mexican-Americans, and the stereotypes of the latter group. I resort here to the "Theory of Speech Accommodation" and return to the concept of language loyalty. In the last chapter I summarize the most relevant findings of this research and highlight those assumptions which were clearly demonstrated. I close this work with a discussion of three fundamental attitudinal and sociolinguistic issues; (1) usage patterns of English, the foreign language; (2) the relationship between behavior and attitudes toward English; and (3) attitudes toward English, Spanish and Spanglish, the three main codes spoken in the Juárez-El Paso setting. In the last two sections of this dissertation, I discuss its possible theoretical implications and provide suggestions for further research on the Mexican side of the border.

Footnotes

(1) Spanglish, Spanish-English Code-switching, Codeswitching, Pocho, and the phrase "the Spanish spoken in El Paso" will be used interchangeably throughout this dissertation.

Chapter 2

The Study and its Background

Before introducing the methodology employed in this study and the characteristics of the respondents, it is indispensable to present the historical, socioeconomic and cultural/linguistic background of the city of Juárez. Some relevant events and transformations throughout its history are highlighted in the first sections of this chapter. The modifications of both mentality and behavior of the border residents due to the proximity of the United States are discussed herein to facilitate the comprehension of the results presented in the three subsequent chapters. This background information also pinpoints the identical roles of the two official languages—Spanish and English—at the same time that it stresses the distinctive functions of Spanish-English Code-switching. The sections dealing with languages and language varieties aim at defining the functions of these three codes in their own territory as well as outside of their own territory. This brief survey of the social and linguistic milieu will hopefully serve as a basis for appreciating the methodology employed and the sociolinguistic background of the subjects. The questionnaire elaborated for this investigation reflects the socioeconomic and attitudinal setting of the speech community under study. The demographic characteristics of the eighty-five informants are examined in the last sections of this chapter. These demographic characteristics will be constantly utilized as independent variables throughout the dissertation and correlated with all the linguistic dimensions of the following chapters.

2.1 Historical background

With more than six hundred thousand inhabitants, Ciudad Juárez is the largest city along the boundary between Mexico and the United States. Of all the border cities, Juárez is the oldest and most populous center along the Mexican side and one of the fastest-growing cities in Mexico (Martínez 1978:3). Juárez is rather isolated from other important centers in Mexico's interior—333 miles north of Chihuahua City, the capital of its state, Chihuahua, arid 1,300 miles northwest of Mexico City, the capital of the country, but it is very well connected with the United States through the American transportation system.

Juárez and its twin city, El Paso, Texas, share a common life that dates to the 17th century when the two cities were one, known as Paso del Norte. After the Mexican-American War (1846-48), the Treaty of Guadalupe-Hidalgo established the Rio Grande as the boundary between the United States and Mexico and separated the two communities politically, but Juárez and El Paso have remained closely linked by social, economic and cultural forces (Martinez 1980a:l). The two cities enjoyed a peaceful life until the beginning of the 20th century when they were caught up in one of Mexico's major upheavals, the Revolution of 1910-21. This social movement severely disrupted life in both towns and displaced many residents of Mexico who headed toward the northern frontier. El Paso received not only the well-to-do political refugee, but also the hungry peasant who was escaping from poverty (Martínez 1978:42).

The northern frontier played a prominent role in Mexico's revolutionary cause since many leaders were of northern origin. The Battle of Juárez in February 1911, between the major northern caudillo, Francisco Madero, and government forces stands as the first decisive victory of the revolutionaries over federal troops (Martinez 1978:38). In fact, no other city in Mexico played such an essential role in the heroic period from 1910 to 1915 (Leal 1964:241). During the violent decade of the 1910's Juárez endured not only severe economic disruption but also physical destruction (Martinez 1978:55), both of which were glorified in the epic novels of the Mexican Revolution (Leal 1964), the first authentically Mexican literary genre.

The contribution of Juárez to the Mexican revolution enhanced the *juarenses'* democratic outlook (Martinez 1977:89) and their feelings of being part of the Mexican nation inasmuch as the Revolution integrated and linked the vast northern area with the rest of the country. The national conflict, nevertheless, led to strained relations with the United States. Rumors of an organized invasion to recapture the territory lost by Mexico during the Mexican-American War circulated widely in 1915, and open fighting between Juárez and El Paso—and Mexico and the United States— almost occurred in 1916. Several acts of hostility against the United States and its citizens occasioned an American expedition into Mexico in search of another caudillo, Pancho Villa, who had promoted acts of violence and aggression in American territory (Martinez 1978:39).

When the Revolution ended, the relations between Mexico and the United States ameliorated, but Juárez saw its meager resources seriously strained. This led consequently to an accentuated dependence on its neighboring town across the border (Martinez 1978:55). The acceptance of American economic and cultural influences on the part of Juárez residents never set well with the Mexicans from the interior (Martinez 1977: 89). Juárez' recovery since the Revolution has depended on the economic and political maneuvers of both Mexico and the United States inasmuch as its strategic position makes it extremely vulnerable to external and internal forces. Throughout its history Juárez has been either greatly benefited or profoundly injured by the bilateral agreements between the two countries (Martinez 1978: passim).

2.2. Socioeconomic overview

Census data for 1980 show that almost two thirds of the Juárez population was born in this city, whereas the rest came from other regions in Mexico's interior. It is estimated that 68.8% of the population is gainfully employed; of these, the vast majority (88.2%) work in Juárez and 11.8% work in El Paso. The population of Juárez is involved in different activities such as industry (37%), services (27%), commerce (17%), government (7%), transportation (4%), and agriculture (4%) (Census 1980: Tables 2, 3, 5).

Those residents of Juárez who are legally employed in El Paso work in agriculture, construction, trade and services; these individuals are daily commuters who compete for jobs with Mexicans who reside permanently in the United States (Castellanos 1981:193, 175). Almost the entire population of Juárez is, for economic purposes, very much part of American society (Martinez 1978:155). It is estimated that one third of the population of Juárez draw their livelihood from the one hundred and twenty American-owned assembly plants set up on a permanent basis in this locality. These plants were established as part of the Border Industrialization Program implemented by the Mexican Government in the mid-1960's. This program consists of factories which use Mexican labor to assemble and hand-finish materials from the United States and then return the products for market distribution (Martínez 1978:150). This program led to unprecedented levels of foreign dependency

(Martínez 1978:147). As a result of its industrialization Juárez now has an active working class in the two main economic sectors: industry and services. The proximity of the United States, however, and the implementation of development programs such as the one described above have not changed the socioeconomic disparities and contrasts characteristic of a typical Latin American urban class system (Castellanos 1980:128)

2.3. The effects of migration

For Mexicans, Juárez appears as a center of wealth and opportunity (Martínez 1978:6). This city is, in fact, in comparison to other regions of Mexico, a very developed area which has historically attracted thousands of migrants from Mexico's interior (Castellanos 1981:131). Since the 19th century Juárez has been a springboard to cross to the United States in order to work (Martinez 1977:80). Research on migration to the border has shown that the population of Juárez increases when the American economy is prosperous and decreases during recession (Castellanos 1981:143). This objective fact is supported by the responses of 125 informants from a poor neighborhood (Ugalde 1974:20-1) and 360 assembly plant workers (Castellanos 1981:135) interviewed in Juárez. Only small percentages in these two groups would admit that the proximity of the United States exercised an influence on their coming to the border, but well over half of them claimed to have worked legally or illegally in the United States.

The Juárez population is both dependent on and interdependent with El Paso. Daily contact occurs on all social and economic levels, and involves a wide complex of activities such as work, shopping, entertainment, visits to relatives and friends, and commercial transactions (D'Antonio and Form 1965:218). The contact depends on variables such as sex, age, income, individual occupational activity, education, and attitudes toward the United States (Castellanos 1981:154).

Many people from Mexico's interior move to the northern border seeking a higher standard of living and assuming they will be in contact with a more developed culture. Juárez itself does not offer as many opportunities as the hundreds of peasants and transients from the interior assume (Ugalde 1974:16), but residence in Juárez does facilitate the process of permanent immigration to the United States, and helps in commuting daily to El Paso, or in obtaining a visitor permit (Castellanos 1981:135).

The proximity of Juárez to the United States has certainly affected the stability of the local population, since *juarenses* move constantly from the Mexican side to the American side and vice versa, due to different causes such as deportation, termination of seasonal jobs, and family and financial problems, among others. Many of these mobile individuals are able to work legally (and sometimes illegally) in the United States, but when the country faces serious economic crises, they tend to return (or to be deported) to Mexico where they carry out a completely different activity. These legal and illegal commuter workers are a minority that usually competes for unskilled and semi-skilled occupations with Mexican-Americans, not only because they cannot demand as much from their employers as those who reside permanently in the United States (Castellanos 1981:170-9), but also because they demonstrate an exceptional willingness to improvise and take almost any nonspecialized job that pays for their work. This competition has been pointed out as one of the sources of negative attitudes between Mexicans and Mexican-Americans (Stoddard 1978:7,8). In general, the Mexicans from the northern frontier have developed a strong sense of industriousness and individual competition, presumably because they have been contending with Anglo-Americans for more than one hundred years (Solís Garza 1971).

Due to the process of migration and to the proximity of the United States, a different type of Mexican people has evolved in the northern frontier. Migration has affected border residents in values and behavior; they have undergone some modifications in diet, dress, language and interpersonal relationships (Martinez 1977:87; 1978:135). One form of behavior that has been completely modified due to the proximity of the United States is that of consumer habits. Several decades of intense interdependence with El Paso have stimulated Mexicans to buy as much and the same kinds of products that their American neighbors consume (D'Antonio and Form 1965:73; Martinez 1978:123; Castellanos 1981:157-9).

2.4. Cultural controversy

The consumer habits of the border residents have provoked in the past harsh criticism from the interior of Mexico, not only on the level of purchasing per se, but on the level of cultural beliefs, language use and language education. The criticism on cultural issues arose in the 1920's as a result of the economic dependence of Juárez on El Paso and lasted through the 50's. The economic disadvantages of Juárez *vis-à-vis* El Paso and the severe economic crises assaulting Mexico during the years immediately after the Revolution caused continuous charges of "denationalization" against Juárez residents. These accusations were responded to by local leaders and concerned citizens who projected more than usual insight. For almost forty years *juarenses* defended themselves by making clear that the commercial vassalage to El Paso was almost an obligatory condition since Juárez was historically a city very much apart from the Mexican economy (Martínez 1978: passim).

This defense was extended to linguistic issues, but at the same time, in order to combat the problem, influential individuals exhorted their fellow citizens to enhance the language loyalty of their children by educating them on Mexican soil. The leaders failed, however, to pin down the actual linguistic and cultural problems of the residents of Juárez, that is, the inevitable contact with other groups (Mexican-Americans and Anglo-Americans) inhabiting the area. The controversy of the past helped *juarenses* to define and distinguish themselves from those other groups, especially Mexican-Americans. *Juarenses* now feel attached to the national heritage in the face of their economic orientation towards the United States. This affiliation is not only a voluntary decision but the result of the constant pressures from the interior of Mexico to maintain, to a certain extent, the basic linguistic and cultural institutions that exist in other Mexican communities. The 60's and 70's did not witness the controversy on "denationalization," and the accusations from the interior became silent, because now cultural and linguistic penetration from the United States is considered to exist at the national level. Consequently, the entire nation has reacted against the influence of the American culture and the English language, and very recently there has been created a "Commission for the Defense of the National Language" which will deal with both language policy and language planning and will have as a purpose the eradication of English and Anglicisms in Mexico (see 4.4).

2.5. Languages and language varieties

The Juárez-El Paso area has been characterized as highly diverse, both culturally and linguistically. A broad swath extending north and south of the international frontier is assumed to be an area of stable bilingualism. El Paso is inhabited by a sizeable proportion of Anglo-Americans whose major linguistic code is the English language and its standard and nonstandard varieties. Mexican-Americans in El Paso might be speakers of both languages and their respective bilingual dialects. On the Mexican side, Ciudad Juárez is populated by speakers of standard and nonstandard Spanish (Ornstein et al. 1975:393).

Following Stewart (1970:540), English and Spanish are functionally described as legally appropriate languages for all representative political and cultural purposes in their own contexts (English in El Paso and Spanish in Juárez). In their own territories, both languages are utilized by government, education, mass media, religious institutions, and in general, the cultural establishment. The international political frontier has created niches for English and Spanish, so that one language cannot function officially for all culturally and politically representative purposes in the territory of the other, but both have identical functions in their own political contexts. This equality of status makes English and Spanish compete on the international scenario, since both can be used as languages of wider communication, in diplomatic relations, foreign trade and tourism. The two languages are also taught as school subjects in each other's territory and are offered commercially on both sides of the border by a number of language schools and academies.

The mixture of the two official languages occurs primarily in the spoken vernacular and characterizes speakers of Mexican descent residing on the American side of the border (Webb 1980:329, 333). The blending of the two languages has been called Spanglish (Peñalosa 1980:73; Webb 1980:333) or *Pocho* (Peñalosa 1980:73; Ornstein-Galicia 1981). This mixed variety may be English with Spanish, Spanish with English, code-switching, all of those, or a separate code (Peñalosa 1980:73). Although Spanglish or *Pocho* functions mainly in informal-oral intragroup situations, it is minimally utilized for some culturally representative purposes in the speech community where it is spoken; Spanish-English Code-switching has even gained widespread acceptance in very formal situations related to the domain of religion where it is used as a device to establish rapport with the people of the community within the Catholic church (Huerta 1978:21).

Spanglish lacks, nevertheless, some of the attributes which define independent linguistic systems. A comparison of English, Spanish and Spanglish on the basis of the typology proposed by Stewart (1970) is presented in Table 2.1. As can be seen, Spanish and English are recognized on the basis of the presence of four attributes. Both languages are standardized for all types of formalized communication; both are autonomous systems; both are associated with national traditions; and the number of native speakers of the two languages in their respective territories is sufficient to give them vitality.

Table 2.1. Attributes of Spanish, English and Spanglish

Attribute	Spanish	English	Spanglish
Standardization	+	+	−
Autonomy	+	+	−
Historicity	+	+	−
Vitality	+	+	+

Spanglish, on the other hand, lacks three important attributes: standardization, autonomy and historicity, but it certainly possesses one which is as important as the other three: vitality. It is this vitality that makes Spanglish so unique and so influential in the attitudes of both native speakers of 'pure' English and native speakers of 'pure' Spanish, since "the vitality of an ethnolinguistic group is that which makes a group likely to behave as a distinctive and active collective entity in intergroup situations" (Giles et al. 1977:308). While speakers of Spanish and English use their respective official languages in a typical diglossic fashion (High variety for formalized functions and Low variety for everyday conversations), native speakers of Spanglish display a wider and more complex range of functions which have not been fully understood nor fully investigated at the societal level.

2.5.1. English and Spanish outside of their own territories

English in Juárez is used on signs in the street in certain areas of the city and for advertisement in the local spoken and written media. In these domains English is frequently mispronounced or misspelled. Careless translations from Spanish to English are the norm in those establishments visited by English-speaking tourists. Lately, due to the industry's boom, English is used in the American-owned assembly plants, mainly for interaction between Mexican and American executives. English also has lingua franca functions when native speakers of Spanish and speakers of languages other than English interact in this city often visited by tourists from all over the world.

Whereas Juárez is characterized by the absence of a community of native speakers of English, El Paso is distinguished by the presence of a large community of Spanish speakers who comprise more than half of the total population (Martinez 1980b:3). In spite of this, the Spanish language has not achieved a status of equality with English, nor does it carry a prestige function. As a result, the written standard version of Spanish does not serve as a frame of reference for speech usage in formal domains. Spanish in El Paso is not widely utilized for government purposes, but some government and business agencies provide translations of instructions, rules and regulations in this language. Careless translations from English to Spanish are, however, the norm in most private and public agencies. There are also several radio stations that broadcast in Spanish with moderate or high interference from English.

Spanish is not used as the sole medium of instruction in the local schools where the population is predominantly of Mexican descent, but its utilization is expected at least for part of the day in the several programs of English/Spanish bilingual education that have been implemented throughout the city. One study of language use in this community revealed that equal amounts of Spanish and English are used in the domains of work, school, and the environment (Ornstein and Goodman 1979).

The use of Spanish in El Paso has been the object of much controversy in the local newspapers. An investigation carried out by Polizzi (1977) examines the language attitudes of the El Paso community as manifested by individual letter-to-the editor writers during 1974-1976. This work suggests that the El Paso community supported federal, state and local efforts to implement bilingual programs which would require all English-speaking students to take Spanish as part of their curriculum and all Spanish-speaking children to study English as a second language. On the other hand, many individuals expressed opposition to and dissatisfaction with bilingual programs, basing their arguments on the concept that English is the official language in the United States and therefore should be the only one utilized in the schools (Polizzi 1977:60). Strong reactions also surfaced in 1975 when a newly elected Spanish surnamed county clerk dismissed four employees because they were not bilingual. This action provoked a series of protests from individual writers who viewed these dismissals as evidence of a conspiracy by Spanish speakers to gain control over El Paso County. Other no less concerned citizens justified the clerk's decision on the grounds that the large population of native Spanish speakers in El Paso are better served by a bilingual employee. Overall, the study showed that despite the fact that this city's population is approximately equally divided between Anglo-American and Mexican-American groups, the use of Spanish in education and places of employment is not universally accepted (Polizzi 1977:61).

2.5.2. Spanglish in Juárez

As English in Juárez is restricted to certain domains such as tourism, business and industry, the phenomenon of interference, borrowing or continuous code-switching is minimized. Language mixture does occur, of course, but it is limited to lexical borrowing. Lexical borrowing takes place in Juárez as in other parts of the Spanish-speaking world. Language mixture occurs most commonly in the use of nouns of English provenience which alternate with the standard Spanish equivalents (e.g., *parqueo* < parking and *tiquete* < ticket, alternating with *estacionamiento* and *boleto*, respectively). On the other hand, many English lexical items have been modified and adapted to Spanish phonology and morphology, and for many Mexicans they are no longer identified with the original English source: for example, *mofle* (< muffler) and *yonque* (< junk yard) are often found in local newspaper advertisements and in the local telephone directory. Among those border residents who are knowledgeable of English, the insertion of English words and phrases in the Spanish discourse serves numerous minor functions. An almost imperceptible code-switching takes place when individuals want to clarify concepts that appear ambiguous in Spanish, when they need to joke sarcastically or when they desire to express affection or taboo words. This use of English is, however, restricted to informal situations and settings which enhance a relaxed atmosphere and tone of conversation. This sporadic, informal use of English is a style of the young adults under thirty-five who have studied English formally for a number of years. Older people tend to maintain an only-Spanish style, although they do not disapprove of this particular behavior.

Children and youngsters use English in the same way that the young adults do; they also tend to inject English words or phrases in order to provoke laughter, to convey disrespect or disobedience, or to deflate the formality of the adult world. These personal shifts to English by the younger generations are perhaps the result of the more intense penetration of English in Mexico in the past fifteen years. These sudden changes based on personal motivations function as an outlet to the social pressures exerted on the border residents to use only Spanish in all intragroup communication.

2.5.3. Spanglish in El Paso

El Paso is a unique American speech community where Spanish language maintenance is constantly reinforced by the proximity to Mexico and the regular use of the mass media originating in Spanish (Casillas-Scott 1969). At the same time, a considerable percentage of the Mexican-American population is bilingual, at least to the degree of being able to carry on a conversation in either language (Huerta 1978:18). Approximately one-half of the population in El Paso are native speakers of both Spanish and English and function in these two codes in their daily interaction with each other. Switching between these two codes occurs quite commonly as a form of communication among the bilingual population (Huerta 1978:18). Thus, the linguistic repertoire of El Paso residents includes English, Spanish and Code-switching. Use of English exclusively only occurs with Anglo-Americans whereas exclusive use of Spanish generally occurs with monolingual Spanish speakers. The use of 'pure' English or 'pure' Spanish, however, not only restricts a member of the community in his interaction with other bilingual speakers but often engenders a negative attitude on the part of the listener, who may interpret the use of all English as a form of Anglicization, and the use of all Spanish as a pedantic, snobbish sort of behavior (Huerta 1978:18-9).

In spite of the fact that the linguistic repertoire range of Mexicans residing in El Paso is great, Code-switching is the most prevalent and natural style of speech for the Mexican-American population as a whole and the mark of in-group membership and ethnic identity (Huerta 1978:21). Thus, all members of this speech community switch between Spanish and English "although differences exist as to what triggers the switching, as to what cultural/ethnic values are associated with this style of speaking, and as to the extent of the switching done by different population groups" (Huerta 1978:20).

In sum, English and Spanish are official national languages legally protected by the Establishment and with impeccable credentials as languages of culture and tradition. English and Spanish are also in fact the two Western European colonial languages most widely spread throughout the world. Spanglish is evidently at a disadvantage. It is not only a variety which has not gained this universal reputation but one which is associated with ethnic minority groups in a country which has demonstrated a high degree of intolerance with respect to ethnolinguistic diversity.

2.6. Methodology

The questionnaire elaborated for this investigation consists of three main sections: Section 1 was constructed to determine the demographic characteristics of the Subject sample; Section 2 was intended to measure the Subjects' informal use of English and formal exposure to this language; and Section 3 was designed to gauge the respondents' attitudes toward the three linguistic codes spoken in the area, stereotypes of outsiders and evaluations of their city and their country. One open-ended question dealing with attitudes toward education in English is also included at the end of the questionnaire. The complete questionnaire is provided (in English translation) as Appendix I.

The demographic information elicited includes birthplace, age, sex, length of residence in Juárez, parents' occupations, income, residence, property, individual occupational activity in both Juárez and El Paso, formal education in both Mexico and the United States, other places of residence, and activities carried out in El Paso.

Data on English includes information on the formal exposure to this language; the types of courses taken, the location of the schools where English was formally studied, and the number of years of instruction in this language. The informal use of English focuses on exposure to spoken and written English in diverse channels. The informal use of English is a comprised measure based on approximations of functions of this language and its domains. Subjects report how often they speak English, how frequently they listen to the American radio and watch American television, how frequently they go to see American movies and read American books and magazines.

Language attitudes, stereotypes of outsiders, local identity and national ethnocentrism were appraised only by direct statements to which respondents indicate, on a five-point scale, the degree of agreement or disagreement with each of forty items. These forty items can be divided into three groups as follows.

(a) A total of twelve items deals with attitudes toward English and native speakers of this language. Eight statements on English were adapted from Gardner and Lambert (1972: 147-9) to reflect two types of reasons for studying or having studied English: instrumental and integrative. Attitudes toward Americans focus on moral traits of this group as compared to the same moral traits of Mexicans.

(b) Sixteen items examine evaluations of the local variety of Spanish, the national language, the city of Juárez, and the nationalistic sentiments toward Mexico. Four statements on Spanish were created to explore Juárez residents' perceptions of their own variety as compared to other urban varieties of Spanish spoken in the capital of the country and capitals of important states. The evaluations of the local Spanish were complemented with another four items dealing with loyalty to the national language and its maintenance without the mixture of English. Four statements on national ethnocentrism call on respondents to evaluate the stability and independence of Mexico as a nation. Four items on local identity explore the border residents' appreciation of and identification with their city.

(c) Twelve direct questions explore the judgements of Mexicans on the Mexican-American style of communication and stereotypes of this group. The questionnaire contains four statements dealing with the evaluation of correctness, beauty, pleasantness and ethnicity of the Spanish-English Code-switching encountered in El Paso. Parallel to these subjective judgements, the communicative values of Spanglish are ranked through another four direct statements. Finally, Mexican-Americans are also judged on the basis of their retentiveness of Mexican customs and mores.

2.6.1. Data collection

Forty-five males and forty females were conveniently selected from different occupational strata in the city of Juárez. I visited Juárez on two occasions. The first visit took place during December-January 1980-81, and the second during May 1981. During these two visits I went to a variety of establishments such as stores, restaurants, government offices, American assembly plants, small private firms, schools and universities. I personally explained the nature of the project to supervisors and instructors and asked permission to interview volunteers or to make appointments with subjects interested in answering my survey. I also approached a few residents in the two local markets where merchants interact intensively with American and Mexican-American tourists. The criteria utilized to select an informant were: (1) willingness to participate; (2) residence in Juárez over five years; and (3) actual residence in Juárez at the time of the interview.

All the interviews, which lasted from 30 to 60 minutes each, were conducted by me personally. The potential informants were allowed to glance over the questionnaire before they decided to participate. I advised every respondent-to-be about the content of the survey, since from the Mexicans' viewpoint, a few questions were either too 'personal' (income, property) or too 'political' (national ethnocentrism, stereotypes of outsiders). Group interviews were conducted with five students from the University of Texas at El Paso, and eight from the Universidad Autónoma de Ciudad Juárez. In these two cases I was able to monitor the groups, so that the procedures were as close as possible to a personal interview. All interviews were conducted in Spanish, in a semi-formal style determined mainly by the topic of the survey.

2.7. The respondents

Almost half of the informants (46%) interviewed for this study were born in Juárez; a little more than a third (39%) were born somewhere else in Mexico, and a few (14%) were born in El Paso. The ages of the subjects range from 16 to 68 years, with a mean of 27 and a mode of 24. Of the eighty-five informants, slightly more than a fourth (27%) lived somewhere else in Mexico before coming to Juárez. Also, slightly more than a fourth (26%) lived in the United States for short periods of time, and less than half have never lived anywhere else but Juárez. The years of residence in this city averaged 20.6 with a mode of 19. This means that the majority of the subjects have resided in Juárez almost all their lives, and more than half of them have lived either in the interior of Mexico, or in the United States (El Paso or elsewhere).

The type of activities carried out in El Paso by this sample of Juárez residents includes shopping, business, entertainment, visits to relatives and friends, work, and education. Briefly stated, more than three fourths (81%) of the eighty-five subjects surveyed carry out at least one of these activities in El Paso, whereas the rest (19%) reported that they never go to El Paso. This 19% includes very young individuals who have not obtained a visitor permit or who still depend on their families for financial support. More than three fourths (77%) of the respondents claimed to go shopping in El Paso, many of them as often as 2 or 3 times per week. Almost half of the subjects (48%) have relatives and friends in El Paso whom they visit approximately 2 or 3 times per month or occasionally. Many of these informants reported that they shop either after or before visiting their relatives and/or friends; that is, when they visit El Paso, they tend to do more than one errand. Also, nearly half of the entire sample (45%) carry out commercial transactions in El Paso or have jobs in Juárez that are somehow related to business firms in El Paso. Individuals involved in work-related activities tend to cross the border more frequently than those who only shop or visit; some claim to go daily or 2 or 3 times per week. Daily commuters are normally students (7%) and Green-Card holders (8%) employed in El Paso. Those individuals who visit El Paso sporadically (less often than 2 or 3 times per month) typically go for entertainment. The information collected in this part of the survey validates the statement proposed in section 2.1: Juárez residents are closely linked to El Paso by social, cultural, and economic forces.

2.7.1 Socioeconomic characteristics

Subjects' occupations cover a varied range which includes unemployed individuals (1%), unskilled workers (2%), semiskilled workers (19%), skilled workers (11%), skilled white-collar workers (34%), administrative personnel (12%), professionals (13%), entrepreneurs (1%) and housewives (2%). (Occupation was not determined for an additional 6%.) The majority of the subjects (92%) are employed in Juárez whereas the rest (8%) work in El Paso. All of the El Paso workers hold semiskilled or skilled white-collar occupations.

Income, father's occupation, and the neighborhood of residence in Juárez were considered the three variables determining socioeconomic status.[1] Whereas income and residential area provide objective bases to determine economic status, father's occupation offers a subjective scale founded on a hierarchical social prestige. This prestige is undoubtedly a distinctive feature in social and interpersonal relations in urban communities throughout Mexico. The subjects were divided into groups (six each for income and residential area, and eight for the father's occupation), as seen in Table 2.2. The scale numbers assigned to each subject for each of these three variables were transformed into z-scores and summed. The z-scores changed the raw scores to reflect the relationship of every subject to the mean and the standard deviation of fellow subjects. By utilizing this standardized statistical device, I obtained z-scores between 6.32 and -4.75. With this procedure each informant has an individual score for socioeconomic status (SES) which is utilized for all correlations with other variables. The z-scores of all eighty-five subjects were further redistributed in six social groups as presented in Table 2.3.

Table 2.2 Percentage of respondents by income, residential area, and father's occupation

	Monthly income in U.S. dollars	(%)		Residential Area	(%)		Father's occupation	(%)
1.	$80-$160	8	1.	Lower-lower	11	1.	Unskilled	19
2.	$161-$240	28	2.	Lower-working	15	2.	Semi-skilled	18
3.	$241-$480	33	3.	Lower-middle	32	3.	Skilled	22
4.	$481-$880	16	4.	Middle-middle	28	4.	White-collar	8
5.	$880-$1,600	10	5.	Upper-middle	6	5.	Administrative	8
6.	$1,600 or more	7	6.	Upper-upper	8	6.	Government	8
						7.	Administrative	8
						8.	Entrepreneurs	7

Table 2.3 Distribution of Informants by Social Class

GROUP

```
I.
   1. I*****                                    z-scores from -4.75 to -3.292
   2. I******************************           z-scores from -2.94 to -1.04
   3. I***********                              z-scores from -0.74 to 0.03
   4. I*****************                        z-scores from -0.31 to 1.91
   5. I**********                               z-scores from 2.16 to 4.17
   6. I**********                               z-scores from 4.62 to 6.32
      I
      I............I............I............I............I............I
      0           10           20           30           40           50
```

FREQUENCY

Group Percentages:

1. Lower-lower class = 7%   2. Lower-working class = 34%
3. Lower-middle class = 13%   4. Middle-middle class = 22%
5. Upper-middle class = 12%   6. Upper-upper class = 12%

2.7.2. Education

This sample represents a group of individuals who are involved in characteristic activities of the city of Juárez and who receive the range of incomes typical of their occupations: workers from the American assembly plants, white-collar workers employed in small and large private companies and tourism, merchants, civil servants, administrative personnel, independent professionals, and executives. Proportionately speaking, however, the middle classes are overrepresented whereas the lower classes are underrepresented. This sample includes, nevertheless, individuals of all strata, and reflects the extremes of wealth and poverty characteristic of Mexico.

      Juárez residents are normally educated in Mexico, but they also have access to the American school system. Approximately one fifth (21%) of the subjects have been exposed to elementary, secondary, or college education in the United States (in El Paso or elsewhere). For this reason, I have summed the number of years of formal education in Mexico and the number of years of formal education in the United States for every subject and considered one whole number as that representing total education. With this procedure the respondents have been divided into seven educational groups whose percentages are shown in Table 2.4.

Table 2.4 Percentage of respondents by education

Rank	Formal education	%
1	Less than elementary education	2
2	Elementary education completed	11
3	Went beyond elementary school but did not finish secondary school (9 years in the Mexican school system)	5
4	Secondary school completed, or a 9-year program known as *comercio* completed	17
5	Preparatory school completed (11 or 12 years in the Mexican school program) or high school in the American school system	15
6	Preparatory school or High School plus one or several years of college	37
7	College completed, including those with some graduate study	13

Inasmuch as secondary-school attendance is not compulsory in Mexico, and because secondary, preparatory and college fees are charged beyond the sixth grade, one-half of the subjects (50%)—the first five groups—did not have access to a college education, whereas the other half in groups 6 and 7 had some college education or hold a college degree. The education of the subjects clearly reflects their socioeconomic background, i.e., almost half of them (46%) are distributed in the middle-middle, upper-middle, and upper-upper classes, whereas the rest (54%) lies in the opposite extreme of the scale (see Table 2.3). Total education and SES are, in fact, significantly correlated at 0.512 ($p < .001$).

2.7.3 Formal exposure to English

Almost two thirds (61%) of the respondents surveyed in this study have been exposed in Mexican secondary and preparatory schools to the mandatory English courses offered for three hours per week. Almost one half of these two thirds have complemented this instruction with intensive English as a second language courses in language academies in both Juárez and El Paso. They have been enrolled in this type of course for short periods of time that fluctuate from one month to one year. In addition, one out of six subjects (16%) studied English in commercial schools which train students for services and clerical positions.

One out of every five persons in this sample had been exposed to English as a medium of instruction in American schools (at the primary, secondary or higher education level). Fully 4% had graduated from a college in the United States, and another 7% were currently enrolled at The University of Texas at El Paso at the time of this interview. An additional 5% had graduated from high school in El Paso or elsewhere in the United States, while a further 4% had attended elementary school, middle high school, or high school from two to four years in El Paso but had failed to complete any of the programs.

One pattern that emerges from these data is that the majority of the Juárez residents tend to study English at the beginning of their adult years. The data also reveal that border residents take advantage of all the programs of English study available in the two cities.

In addition, the data obtained in this survey show that the total number of years of formal instruction in English in both Mexico and the United States are significantly correlated with SES (r =.622, p <.001) and with total education (r =.691, p <.001). Formal exposure to this language of wider communication therefore seems to be the result of socioeconomic background and formal education (in either of the two countries).

2.8 Summary and Implications

This chapter is divided into two major parts. The first part discusses the evolution of Juárez from a small frontier settlement into one of the major urban industrialized centers in modern Mexico, highlighting the close relationship between Juárez and its twin American city, El Paso, Texas. Great emphasis is given to the economic dependence of Juárez on El Paso and on the United States in general, at the same time that the political and cultural ties to Mexico are accentuated. Due to its strategic position as a border city, Juárez is considered here as a community which is closely linked to both the Mexican and the American systems. The historical migratory pattern to the northern frontier is proposed as one of the most significant contributors in the social evolution of the border residents and in the transformation of their mentality, lifestyle, and behavior.

The sociolinguistic background of the Juárez-El Paso area is provided in this second chapter in order to illustrate the social functions of the three main linguistic codes (Spanish, English and Spanglish) utilized in the two urban complexes. The fact that the international political frontier serves as an effective demarcator of the two official languages is stressed. It is also highlighted that the two languages encroach on each other's territory predominantly at the informal and vernacular domains.

The second part of Chapter 2 presents the methodology utilized for the study and the sociodemographic characteristics of the subject sample. The methodology employed for this investigation is based on the socioeconomic and sociolinguistic background of the community discussed at length in the first part. The subject sample selected covers diverse and representative occupational and socioeconomic strata of the city of Juárez. The eighty-five residents of Juárez have in common their permanent residence in this city, their contacts with both the Mexican and the American systems, and a relative economic stability in their community. The overview provided in this chapter will facilitate the comprehension of the results presented in Chapters 3, 4 and 5, which focus directly on language attitudes and language use, and which allude constantly to the demographic characteristics of the subject sample.

In this study, the most relevant demographic dimensions to language use and language attitudes turn out to be: (1). Socioeconomic Status (SES); (2) Education; (3) Formal Instruction in English; and (4) Sex. These dimensions are treated as independent variables. One linguistic dimension and two attitudinal dimensions are treated, too, as independent variables; they are: (1) English Use (or the Use of English); (2) Language Loyalty; and (3) Local Identity. The attitudinal dimensions which are treated as dependent variables only are the following: (1) Attitudes toward English; (2) Beliefs about Americans; (3) Local versus National Spanish; (4) National Ethnocentrism; (5) Inherent Values of Spanglish; (6) Communicative Values of Spanglish; and (7) Beliefs about Mexican-Americans. The complex interrelationships between these variables are explored in the following chapters.[2]

Footnotes

(1) Lic. Luis García de la Rosa, Director of Desarrollo Socioeconómico, Municipio de Ciudad Juárez, advised me to measure social class by considering income, residence and father's occupation. He also provided the scales utilized for the first two variables. The scales for income correspond to 1980-1981 and were originally specified in Mexican currency. I converted Mexican currency to American currency for the reader's convenience. I must also make clear that the figures for income do not correspond to reality anymore, since salaries have been raised by at least 40%, and in addition, the Mexican peso has been devaluated by at least 500%. In spite of these changes, income has always been an important indicator of socioeconomic status in Juárez.

(2) Throughout the following chapters the names of all the independent and dependent variables will be capitalized when I refer to the variable itself (e.g., Language Loyalty); when I deal with the concept, I will use lower-case letters (e.g., language loyalty). All the attitudinal variables consist of four items which are presented with their corresponding response percentages. The scale definitions are sometimes ordered from the lowest score (1 = Strongly disagree) to the highest (5 = Strongly agree), or from the highest (5 = Strongly agree) to the lowest (1 = Strongly disagree). The format (1 = Strongly agree and 5 = Strongly disagree) is also utilized; thus, in each variable the reader must refer to the particular layout of the table in order to better understand the response percentages.

Chapter 3

English in Juárez

As discussed in the previous chapter, the majority of Juárez residents have access to formal exposure to the English language. English is not only a compulsory subject in Mexican secondary and preparatory schools, but it is also offered in language schools and academies in both Juárez and El Paso. These language schools often advertise their services by stressing the advantages of bilingualism along the Mexico-United States border. Announcements in the spoken media frequently report popular statistics such as these: "Two out of three jobs are taken by those who speak two languages," or "The person who speaks two languages is worth two persons." Written announcements emphasize the instrumental value of English in statements such as: "Put your $$$ where your mouth is" or "Mi$$ing $omething? Learn another language."

The setting of the Mexico-United States border certainly appears ideal for the acquisition of a second language. Competence in English is limited, nevertheless, to a small number of individuals who are bilingual in varying degrees. The eighty-five subjects interviewed for this study described their proficiency in English as Excellent, Good, Adequate, Poor or None. The first two categories define a speaker who performs well in all four skills (listening, speaking, reading and writing). One third (33%) of all the respondents rated themselves Excellent or Good; one-half of these same respondents claimed to be almost as fluent as a native speaker of English, mainly in their speaking and reading abilities. This small proportion of subjects considered themselves highly bilingual and claimed to function properly in an only-English setting. Adequate describes a speaker whose knowledge of English is moderate in comprehension skills (listening and reading); one-half (50%) of the entire sample selected Adequate as the most appropriate category. Slightly less than a fifth (17%) of the subjects rated themselves as Poor or None. Poor defines a speaker who knows a few words and phrases without being able to use them in context, whereas None is considered absolutely monolingual.

It is apparent that the majority of the Juárez residents have been exposed to the formal study of English. As a rule, the majority have also had informal exposure to this language through the American media and contact with native speakers of English. Along the Mexican side of the border, English has traditionally been used in those establishments created to give service to the English-speaking tourist, such as restaurants, hotels, shops and supermarkets. With the industrial boom in the mid 1960's, English became more important and necessary in the city of Juárez. At present it is utilized not only in tourism but also in the fields of technology, management and administration, as required by more than one hundred American-owned plants.

Mexicans do not seem opposed to studying English at school, or to having ready access to the English media originating in the United States, or to being in direct contact with native speakers of English. The English language and its concomitants are generally not perceived as a harm but as a benefit. Moreover, for the migrants from Mexico's interior, the proximity to another culture and another language is one of the major attractions in the Mexican border cities.

This chapter assesses the societal functions of English in Juárez: its informal use in different domains, the values assigned by Mexicans to this language of wider communication, the major factors accounting for the prediction of attitudes toward English, the relationship between attitudes and use, and the effects of the local milieu on attitudes toward English. This chapter also attempts to interpret the results of the survey in the light of findings and assumptions drawn from numerous investigations dealing with attitudes toward English as a second and as a foreign language.

3.1. The informal use of English

The informal use of English in Juárez takes place not only when Mexicans interact with Americans in the tourist sectors of the city or in the American assembly plants, but also when they listen to, read or write this language by themselves. The eighty-five subjects interviewed for this study reported how frequently they speak with native English speakers, how frequently they use the American spoken and written media, and how often they may involve themselves in writing English. A total of seven different ways of practicing English were included in the questionnaire, each with a specification of frequency ranging from 0 (=never) to 4 (=daily). Table 3.1 provides the response percentages for the seven types of informal use of English, each of which is discussed separately in the following pages.

Table 3.1 Response Percentages: The Informal Use of English in Juárez

Frequency	Speaking with Mexicans	Speaking with Americans	Radio	TV	Movies	Reading	Writing
Never (= 0)	75	15	15	11	37	50	73
Sporadically (= 1)	7	32	13	13	38	23	6
2 or 3 times per month (= 2)	1	5	6	5	24	8	0
2 or 3 times per week (= 3)	9	22	11	18	1	6	12
Daily (= 4)	10	26	61	54	0	13	9
Frequency in %	100	100	100	100	100	100	100

Speaking with native speakers of Spanish
The use of English with native speakers of this language contrasts significantly with the use of English among native speakers of Spanish. As shown in Column 1, the majority of the subjects claimed not to speak English with other Spanish speakers: friends, relatives and fellow workers in either Juárez or El Paso. The use of English with other Mexicans and many times with Mexican-Americans is therefore an exceptional, incongruent form of behavior whose parameters deserve a more cautious and exhaustive study. Only one fourth (25%) of the entire sample reported ever using English with native speakers of Spanish. This sporadic, informal usage pattern was discussed in section 2.5.2.

Speaking with native speakers of English
In Column 2 it is seen that almost all the residents of Juárez interviewed for this study (85%) claimed to speak English with Americans: tourists wandering the streets of the city or clients visiting the establishments where they work. Those who use English with

considerable regularity (at least several times per week) total 48%. These individuals tend to occupy contact or managerial positions in tourism or in the American assembly plants, locales which compel use of English with native speakers of this language. The students enrolled at The University of Texas at El Paso and a few individuals employed in sales in El Paso also use English more frequently than those who work in places in Juárez not visited by Americans (public offices, schools, small companies situated outside the sectors where Americans are normally encountered). Only 15% of the informants claimed to never speak English with Americans. Those who claimed to speak English sporadically (32%) or 2 or 3 times per month (5%) are usually involved in casual encounters with American tourists or visitors asking for directions. Most people claimed to enjoy this informal interaction with native speakers of English (or speakers of other foreign languages who use English as a lingua franca) because this is the best opportunity to use the language in a natural context.

Radio
Among the most common ways to use English passively, Juárez residents encounter the American media available to them. As shown in Column 3 of Table 3.1, the vast majority of respondents listen to radio broadcasts in English. Only those who reported Good or Excellent knowledge of English claimed to be able to understand the weather and the news which creep into music programs every 30 or 60 minutes. Most informants, however, reported that they listen to American radio because of the quality of the music programs or because they tune in to English programs by pure chance. The radio does not seem to be intentionally utilized to learn or to practice English. American television, on the other hand, has a stronger appeal to the border residents.

Television
Column 4 of Table 3.1 shows that more than half of the entire sample (54%) watch American television programs on a daily basis. And another fifth (23%) watch American programs at least several times per month. Small groups of subjects watch American television sporadically (13%) or not at all (11%). Those respondents with a little knowledge of English commented that they watch only those programs with a special interest to them. Sports programs are among the favorites of aficionados who understand the rules of the game but need not understand all the spoken explanations. Television series and movies without subtitles are among the most frequently seen by the entire family, and those who are more fluent in English in a household are almost obliged to translate simultaneously to the rest. In contrast with American radio, American television is considered one of the most useful devices to learn English. Youngsters who have studied English formally tend to expose themselves intensively to American television, and many develop an extraordinary ability for simultaneous English/Spanish translation, due mainly to this practice of watching television when the entire family is together.

Movies
American television has certainly had a strong impact on the habits of border Mexicans. Watching American movies broadcast on television has apparently caused a decrease in the number of people who attend movies in English. As seen in Column 5, more than a third (37%) of the respondents never attend American movies, and more than a third (36%) go to see movies only sporadically. Almost a fourth (24%) of all the informants reported watching

movies 2 or 3 times per month. All the informants who watch American movies claimed to do so in Mexican theatres where they can read Spanish subtitles. As with American radio, American films are fully understood only by those who are highly proficient in English. The majority of the movie-goers claimed to rely on the subtitles when watching an English language movie; only a few individuals reported that they use American films as a foreign language learning device, attempting to process the spoken English at the same time that they read in Spanish.

Reading
Whereas the great majority of the border residents have access to the American spoken media, the American written media are limited to 50% of the population. One-half of all the subjects interviewed for this study claimed that they never read magazines, books or newspapers in English. Almost a fourth of the entire sample (23%) read English only sporadically. These informants often read by necessity or chance, when they try to understand instructions in El Paso stores, instructions for cleaning products or toys and games and other American goods purchased in El Paso. Employees in the American assembly plants are sometimes required to have a minimum knowledge of reading in English, since they have to handle merchandise from the United States, and the instructions on boxes and packages are written in English. More than a fourth (27%) of the subjects in the sample claimed to read English books and magazines habitually. These respondents are typically the students enrolled at The University of Texas at El Paso and the local colleges, whose textbooks and other assignments tend to be in English. As is the case in their selection of American products and television programs, Juárez residents select books and magazines according to their personal taste and need, and the variety of topics appears unlimited. Some patterns of reading habits were encountered among those who claimed to read daily or 2 or 3 times per week. Habitual readers reported reading books and magazines related to cars and mechanics; fashion and cosmetics; plants and gardening; nutrition, diet and physical fitness; adventures and romance; world affairs and politics; administration and economy; English and American literature; psychology and parapsychology. Habitual readers are those who are extremely fluent in English or those who have developed reading skills in this language. Reading in English is in fact the only ability truly emphasized in Mexican programs of English as a foreign language.

Writing
Writing in English is even more restricted than reading, as shown in Column 7. Almost three fourths (73%) of the informants never write in English. Only 6% of the respondents write sporadically; slightly more than a tenth (12%) claimed to write 2 or 3 times per week; and slightly less than a tenth (9%) write every day. Daily English writers are typically students who have to do homework assignments for their school subjects. Writing is also practiced by those few individuals who need to communicate to the United States (less frequently than daily) through business or personal letters.

As presented in this section, the informal use of English is a comprised measure based on approximations of spoken and written functions of the language and its domains. I must stress, however, that the Juárez population uses Spanish, not English, for all High and Low purposes as discussed in section 2.5. The functions of Spanish in some specific domains are thus the same as those encountered for English—e.g., people also use the written and spoken media originating in Mexico, but as befits a study of this sort, I have not quantitatively contrasted the use of English as opposed to the use of Spanish in such settings. It is possible, however, to make generalizations about the use of the English media within the environmental framework of Juárez.

A study carried out by Castellanos and López (1981) in this locality reports that 83% of all television programs broadcast in Juárez in 1978 originated in the United States. In contrast, only 36% of all movies exhibited in Juárez theatres the same year had been filmed in the United States; 40% had been produced in Mexico and 24% were of diverse provenance (Castellanos and López 1981:71, 74). The succinct data of this investigation together with the usage patterns reported in Column 4 of Table 3.1 suggest that the massive use of American television in Juárez is determined, to a certain extent, by the availability and diversity of programs in English. The consumption of American movies is, on the other hand, more moderate by virtue of the fact that Mexican films do compete in quality and quantity with American productions. The accessibility of the English mass media is not the only circumstance contributing to the informal use of English. The educational opportunity and the socioeconomic background of the individual are also relevant factors influencing English use.

3.2. Predictors of English Use

The informal use of English in Juárez is positively and significantly correlated to SES ($r = .543$, $p < .001$), number of years of Formal Exposure to English ($r = .621$, $p < .001$), and total number of years of formal Education ($r = .390$, $p < .001$).[1] The first two variables are sources of variance in the multiple regression analysis presented in Table 3.2. As seen in this table, two main variables account for the Use of English: Socioeconomic Status, which accounts for almost 30% of the variance, and number of years of Formal Exposure to English, which accounts for 13%. These two demographic variables in combination make a multiple regression coefficient of 0.65, and account for a total variance of almost 43%.[2]

Table 3.3 shows the correspondence between Socioeconomic Status and the informal Use of English. The scattergram shows that more than half of all the subjects (49 out of 85) use English with mid-frequency; mid-frequency is the general usage pattern of all six social groups. This considerable proportion of individuals normally listen to the radio, watch television or speak with Americans. The tendency of the lower working class of the assembly plants is to use English passively through radio and television, and occasionally, to speak with Americans or to read by chance. On the other hand, the tendency of the two upper classes is to use English in all the aforementioned contexts in addition to reading, writing and speaking English—very sporadically—with native speakers of Spanish. High English usage is not at all exclusive of the two upper classes; the scattergram shows that there are a few subjects with more than 20 points in the middle and lower social strata.

Table 3.2 Multiple Regression Analysis: The Informal Use of English

Step	Variables entered in the equation	R	R^2	ΔR^2	r	F
1	SES	0.543	0.295	0.295	0.543	6.68
2	Formal exposure to English	0.653	0.426	0.130	0.621	18.21

3.3. Diglossia and bilingualism

The functions of English as opposed to the functions of Spanish are clearly demarcated at least at the level of personal interaction. Typically, residents of Juárez use Spanish for communication with Mexicans, whereas they tend to use English with Americans. The more proficient they are in the latter language, the more they use it in interaction with native speakers of English. The use of English in Juárez takes place in a series of domain-appropriate locales such as the hotels, restaurants, night clubs and shops in the tourist areas of the city visited by Americans. These establishments are situated immediately across the international bridges in the areas marked 1, 2, 3 and 5, in Map 1. A similar language usage pattern has been observed in the extensive industrial zone in area 4 where the majority of the American assembly plants are concentrated. In all these locales, a particular set of domain-appropriate people interact with each other—American tourist with Mexican resident, American client with Mexican clerk, American executive with Mexican executive.

The description of the use of English and Spanish in Juárez makes clear that residents of this city have access to clearly differentiated social and linguistic repertoires which are utilized when they engage in interaction with either native speakers of English or native speakers of Spanish. Whereas Spanish functions for all public and private domains for intragroup purposes in the speech community, English is restricted to intergroup communication for tourist-type and business-type transactions with Americans.

Functionally differentiated sociolinguistic roles of this sort have been characterized as both diglossic and bilingual (Fishman 1971b; 1971c). It is apparent that the use of English in Juárez is severely restricted in both the institutional and intimate domains but culturally approved in business firms where the presence of Americans is the norm. One exception to the primarily-Spanish rule for public interaction among native speakers of Spanish might involve a situation in which a "secret" language is needed (Valdés 1981:12). Juárez is thus a speech community in which both diglossia and bilingualism are widespread in certain specific contexts. It must be borne in mind however, that diglossia has been defined as a characterization of the social allocation of different languages or language varieties, whereas bilingualism stands as the characterization of individual linguistic versatility. That is, bilingualism may exist with or without diglossia (Fishman 1967; 1970a:102). In the context of the Mexican border, bilingualism with diglossia is plausible when border residents engage in verbal interplay with native speakers of English; bilingualism without diglossia may also be encountered when bilingual border residents utilize English for individual practice, such as listening to American radio, watching American television or reading American magazines or books.

Table 3.3 Scattergram: Socioeconomic Status by English Use

```
6│                           2
5│              3       3
4│     2     2  2         2     2
3│              3    2
2│  2        3 2    3 4    4 3
1│                 2
 └──────────────────────────────────
 0     5    10   15   20   25   30
```

Socioeconomic status (down): 6. Upper-upper; 5. Upper-middle; 4. Middle-middle; 3. Lower-middle; 2. Lower-working; 1. Lower-lower
English Use (across): 0-10 = Low; 11-19 = Middle; 20-28 = High; Total score = 28

3.4. Attitudes toward English

The Mexican side of the border provides a very useful scene for the study of attitudes toward English. English is not only a compulsory subject from the seventh grade onwards, but also a basic requirement for numerous college programs. English is indispensable, of course, for those individuals who want to pursue their education in the United States. Closely associated with these academic incentives are economic ones, inasmuch as English is an explicit job requirement for many attractive positions offered not only in Juárez but in the interior of Mexico. In the Juárez setting one can expect, therefore, that Mexicans will be strongly oriented toward learning English due to its evident instrumentality. One might also expect that Mexican residents of this border city will display a low integrative motivation to learn the language spoken in the United States, inasmuch as this language may carry connotations of cultural and economic imperialism.

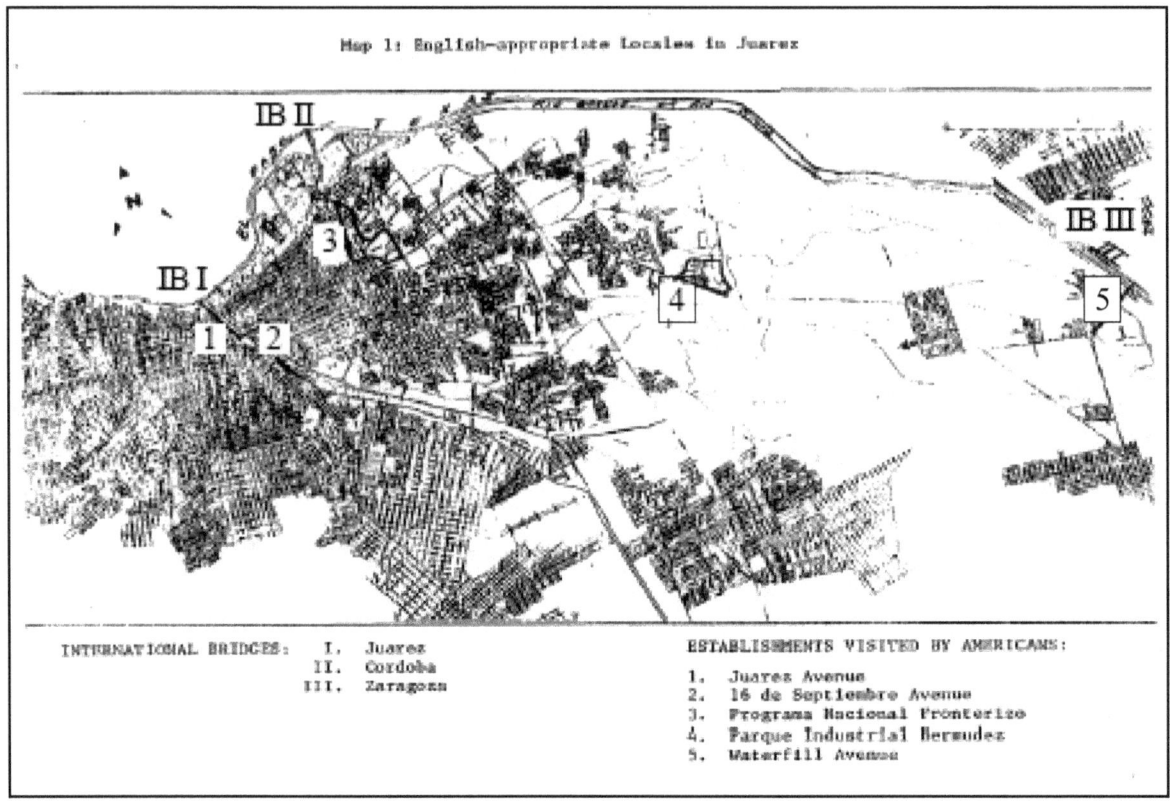

Some of the questions addressed in this section are: To what extent are *juarenses* motivated to study English for instrumental incentives and to what extent do they feel integratively or anti-integratively oriented? What are their attitudes toward native speakers of English and how do these attitudes affect their evaluation of English? In order to explore both instrumental and integrative orientation toward English, eight items were adapted from Lambert and Gardner (1972:148-9). The items and the results are presented in Table 3.4. This table is divided into two main parts: the first one presents those questionnaire items dealing with the integrative orientation toward English, whereas the second one focuses on its instrumental values.

3.4.1. Integrative orientation

As seen in Table 3.4, almost three fourths (71%) of the informants interviewed for this study somewhat agreed or strongly agreed that they studied English because they wanted to understand the American people and their way of life. This considerable majority of subjects was so positive about English that they failed to remember that their first exposure was not a matter of personal choice but rather a result of educational opportunity. What most subjects probably tried to convey was their subsequent motivation to learn English after the initial exposure took place.

Equally positive were the responses of the subjects to the question exploring the usefulness of English for making friends among native speakers of English. Fully 75% of the entire sample somewhat or strongly agreed with the statement in Item 2. The overwhelming majority of the respondents (90%) also rated English as highly valuable for communication with and understanding of people from abroad. The highly positive evaluation of English as a language of wider communication, as a means to gain friends among Americans, and as a means to understand the American culture, contrasts significantly with its evaluation as a means to assimilate to such a way of life. Two thirds of the subjects (67%) somewhat disagreed or strongly disagreed with the statement expressed in Item 4, whereas small proportions of respondents were uncertain (12%), somewhat agreed (7%), or strongly agreed (14%).

Table 3.4 Response Percentages: Attitudes Toward English in Juárez

I. Items: Integrative Orientation	1	2	3	4	5
1. I study/studied English because I want/ed to understand the American people and their way of life	15	9	5	17	54
2. English will enable me to gain good friends among Americans	12	9	4	20	55
3. English will allow me to meet and converse with interesting and different people	4	2	4	11	79
4. Knowing English will enable me to think and behave as Americans do	51	16	12	7	14
II. Items: Instrumental Orientation	1	2	3	4	5
5. I need English in the El Paso-Juárez area to get a good job	12	2	6	21	59
6. I need English to keep the job I have	46	8	9	12	21
7. I need English for interrelationships with people in the El Paso-Juárez area	11	7	5	20	57
8. English will make me a better educated person	81	7	6	5	1
Scale: 1=Strongly disagree; 2=Somewhat disagree; 3=Uncertain; 4=Somewhat agree; 5=Strongly agree					

The response percentages on integrative orientation reflect a desire to become associated with representative members of the American community. These results should be no surprise if one analyzes the lingua franca functions of English along the Mexican side of the border and, in general, its communicative values. The positive judgement of the integrative values of English means perhaps that Mexicans do want to communicate with Americans and feel that the only effective way to achieve such communication is through the English language.

3.4.2. Instrumental orientation

The questionnaire items dealing with instrumental orientation explore the subjects' evaluations of English for the job market, as a means for social interaction in the area, and as an educational resource. The second part of Table 3.4 shows that more than three fourths (80%) of the informants strongly agreed or somewhat agreed with the statement proposing the usefulness of English for a well-paid job. The remaining 20% of the subjects divided their opinions among the other three options.

One third (33%) of all the informants confirmed that they need English to maintain their current positions, whereas 9% did not know if English was a *sine qua non* condition to keep their jobs, and more than one half (54%) claimed not to need English in the positions they held at the moment of the interview. Those who claimed to need English are individuals who work in tourism or in the American assembly plants.

The evaluation of English as a means for social interaction was also highly positive. More than three fourths of all the subjects (77%) agreed or strongly agreed that English was necessary to establish rapport with people in certain areas in both Juárez and El Paso. The response percentages for Item 8 show a striking difference when compared with all the others, including items 1 through 3 in the first part of Table 3.4. The overwhelming majority of the subjects (81%) strongly disagreed with the statement extolling the value of English for general education.

Overall, the evaluations of English for its integrative values are slightly higher than those reported for its instrumentality. The results demonstrate that although most people perceive English as a potential tool to get a good job, only one third actually claim that they need this language to maintain their positions. Most people recognize, however, that communication is facilitated if they know English, and that this language is an instrument contributing to the acquisition of a given goal, e.g., making better business deals with Americans, serving the English-speaking clientele more efficiently and therefore making higher profits.

The results for Items 6 and 8 also suggest that a good proportion of Juárez residents are perhaps unwilling or unable to acknowledge the relative but genuine importance of English for education and for the maintenance of their current positions. These two responses are not at all random, but meaningfully interconnected in the context of Mexico where the vast majority of people do not have access to higher education in their own language, much less in English. It seems then that English is not generally perceived as indispensable or vital for education or for upward mobility in Juárez society, even though many border residents do make efforts to pursue education in this language. My own hunch is that the values of formal education in Mexico go beyond language and are linked to personal pride. English may thus be judged as superfluous when people feel confident about their skills, their training and their education in certain fields.

3.4.3. The values of English

Taken as separate variables, attitudes toward the integrative values of English have a higher mean (x=3.65) than attitudes toward instrumentality (x=3.15) on the five-point scale. When considered as different measures, attitudes toward integrativeness and attitudes toward instrumentality correlate insignificantly (below the .05 level) with several other demographic and linguistic dimensions. In order to validate the presupposition that these two orientations do not contrast significantly, a further test was applied to the eight questionnaire items dealing with attitudes toward English. The scores in each of the eight variables were correlated among themselves. The result is the eight-correlation coefficient matrix presented in Table 3.5 in which columns 1 through 4 correspond to the integrative orientation items and columns 5 through 8 represent the instrumental orientation items.

If the six coefficients in the upper-left triangle are summed and the mean compared to that obtained by adding the six correlation coefficients in the lower-right triangle, the results turn out very similar. The mean of the correlation coefficient for integrativeness is slightly higher (x=2.54) than the mean of the correlation coefficient for instrumentality (x=2.32). The difference between the two measures is not therefore significantly contrastive to consider them as separate variables.[3]

Table 3.5 Correlation Coefficient Matrix: Eight Items on Attitudes Toward English

	Integrativeness				Instrumentality			
	1	2	3	4	5	6	7	8
1	–	0.415	0.073	0.338	0.272	0.109	0.119	-0.158
2		–	0.192	0.335	0.218	0.084	0.262	0.158
3			–	0.172	0.216	0.372	0.048	0.246
4				–	0.397	0.144	0.374	0.177
5					–	0.326	0.217	0.211
6						–	0.233	0.266
7							–	0.138
8								–
N = 85								

The absence of contrast between instrumentality and integrativeness in this work is noticeably different from those results consistently reported in the literature on attitudes toward English. The conclusions reached in most studies conducted in settings where this language is either a second or a foreign language are rather uniform in pointing out the dissimilar motivations of the subjects toward learning English (see section 3.7 for a thorough discussion).

It seems then from this particular finding that the values of English are perceived as equally instrumental and integrative. According to Lambert and Gardner (1972:132) an integrative orientation is justified in most social groups in order to sustain the long-term motivation needed for the extremely demanding task of second-language learning. Without a sincere and personal interest in the other people's language, the process of acquisition would become futile. Mexicans may also have an instrumental motivation to learn English, inasmuch as the language does contribute to success in Mexican society even though it may not be absolutely vital and indispensable. The foregoing data show that the integrative and instrumental values of English are balanced in the Mexican border setting.

3.5. Beliefs about Anglo-Americans

Bound up with the attitudes toward the language spoken in a given community are the attitudes toward its representative members. Gardner and Lambert (1972) assume that the association between the language itself and the group of speakers "may have been established through direct experience with members of the group or indirectly through attitudes picked up from important people in one's social environment who in turn may have had little or no direct experience with the group in question" (p. 98). In the context of the Mexican border, people may or may not interact directly with native speakers of English. The popular opinion that Mexicans have about the citizens of the United States varies from person to person, and depends primarily, as pointed out by Gardner and Lambert, on their experiences. In order to assess the attitudes of Mexicans toward native speakers of English, four questionnaire items were created. The statements and the results are presented in Table 3.6.

Table 3.6 Response Percentages: Beliefs about Americans

Items	1	2	3	4	5
1. Americans are more sincere than Mexicans	11	6	53	7	24
2. Mexicans are more fun-loving and creative than Americans	39	8	28	8	17
3. Mexicans are more organized and efficient than Americans	25	9	22	15	28
4. American education is better and more disciplined than Mexican education	8	17	37	11	24
Scale: 1=Strongly agree; 2=Somewhat agree; 3=Uncertain; 4=Rather disagree; 5=Strongly disagree					

Item 1 in this table shows that more than one-half (53%) of the respondents did not commit themselves to make a judgement about the moral trait of sincerity; almost one third of the sample (31%) rated Mexicans higher than Americans; and slightly less than a fifth (17%) rated Mexicans as less sincere than Americans.

With respect to item 2, nearly half of all the subjects (47%) believe that Mexicans enjoy life more and are more creative than Americans; a little more than one fourth (28%) expressed uncertainty on this statement, and exactly one fourth of all the respondents (25%) favored Americans over Mexicans.

On the issue of organization and efficiency, Americans are rated slightly higher than Mexicans, with almost one-half of the entire sample expressing a positive evaluation of this particular trait. A little more than a third (34%), however, rated Mexicans as more efficient and organized than Americans, whereas more than a fifth (22%) were uncertain about the Item 3 proposition.

The opinions of Mexicans about the quality of American education versus the quality of Mexican education are equally divided. More than a third (37%) were uncertain; one fourth (25%) of all the informants ranked American education as better than Mexican education; and slightly more than a third (35%) considered Mexican education of higher quality.

Attitudes toward Anglo-Americans are inversely and weakly correlated to SES ($r = .217$, $p < .025$), total Education ($r = -.165$, $p < .05$), and English Use ($r = .158$, $p < .05$). These low correlations mean that some individuals in the lower-lower and lower-working strata, with fewer years of formal education and low and mid scores in English use, tended to be slightly more negative when judging their American neighbors. The group of subjects interviewed for this study did not verbalize positive or negative evaluations of Anglo-Americans. Similarly, attitudes toward Anglo-Americans and nationalistic sentiments toward Mexico were neither displayed nor interconnected. The relationship between Attitudes toward Anglo-Americans and National Ethnocentrism is in fact irrelevantly correlated at .040.

In an earlier exploratory study carried out by Castellanos (1981) among 360 assembly plant workers, it was found that approximately 48% of all informants claimed to look up to the goods available in the United States, the high standard of living of Americans and employment benefits offered in the United States (p. 208). At the same time, this group of workers (percentages are unspecified) expressed open resentment against Americans because their experiences across the border were characterized by conflicts. Most of the disagreements and offenses reported by the author have to do with poor treatment in the United States, poor wages for the Mexican employees; and in general, deficient work conditions (pp. 199-200).

In the present study, attitudes toward the group of speakers of English and attitudes toward the language spoken in the United States are seen imperfectly related to each other ($r = .063$). Attitudes toward Americans along the Mexican side of the border appear associated with either economic exploitation, as demonstrated by Castellanos, or to the frequent and unavoidable clashes that occur on a daily basis between Mexican residents of Juárez and the United States border authorities, as suggested by Martinez (1978:156).

Even though the daily impersonal relations with Americans in the Juárez-El Paso area are sometimes colored by tension, anger and dissatisfaction, the attitudes toward the English language seem to remain unaffected. It is thus possible to argue along with Fishman (1977a:119) that English has gained a neutral ethnic and ideological status due to modernization, urbanization, technological development, and habits of consumption.

Generally speaking, the people of the northern frontier do not seem to be radically opposed to being in contact with native speakers of English. They are, on the other hand, fully aware of the consequences of their association with Americans: they have voluntarily assimilated more from their neighbors than their neighbors have assimilated from them. On this particular issue, American researchers have observed that, whereas Americans of the area seem inflexibly ethnocentric and fail to internalize Mexican culture and language,

Mexicans have looked to the United States as a source of different values and ideas, in addition to the economic advantages and technological benefits derived from the proximity to the superpower (D'Antonio and Form 1965:218-9; Stoddard 1969:481).

In sum, the statistically irrelevant correlation between Attitudes toward Americans and Attitudes toward English, and Attitudes toward Americans and National Ethnocentrism invalidate the two assumptions proposed in section 1.1: (1) The appreciation of representative members of the American community would be strongly correlated to an integrative orientation toward English, and (2) highly ethnocentric individuals would display negative opinions about the citizens of the United States. On the whole, it seems that as long as they remain in Mexico, Mexicans do not feel seriously threatened by the United States and its citizens.

3.6. Predictors of attitudes toward English

When attitudes toward the integrative values of English and attitudes toward the instrumental values of this language are considered as one single variable, the best predictors of attitudes toward English are English Use and Local Identity. Both variables are significantly correlated with attitudes toward English, the first one correlating at .410 ($p < .001$) and the second one at .383 ($p. < .001$). Table 3.7 shows the multiple regression analysis. English Use and Local Identity in combination make a multiple regression coefficient of almost 0.55. The first variable accounts for almost 12% of the variance, and the second one for almost 13%. This analysis demonstrates that English Use and Attitudes toward English are not only related to each other, but the former predicts the latter.

There is only one possible causal relationship that explains attitudes toward English. Those who have had the opportunity to learn English as an additional language are consequently capable of using it. No single individual who claimed to know English dislikes it or fails to use it. Once English is learned—and even if it is not learned well, it is used. In this community people are committed to use English when they know it, and they cannot afford to dislike it because they have made personal efforts and economic investments in order to learn it. Moreover, English is seen as a worthy component of the linguistic and cultural repertoire of Juárez by those who feel stronger identification with their city.

Table 3.7 Multiple Regression Analysis: Attitudes toward English in Juárez

Step	Variables entered in the equation	R	R^2	ΔR^2	r	F
1	English Use	0.410	0.116	0.116	0.410	14.94
2	Formal exposure to English	0.546	0.298	0.126	0.383	14.46

3.6.1 Local Identity as a predictor of attitudes toward English

Local Identity is the variable created to explore the subjective appreciation and degree of attachment to the border on the basis of its mixed culture and the lifestyle in the city.

Table 3.8. Response Percentages: Local Identity

Items	1	2	3	4	5
1. I find it difficult to live in this area where two such different cultures exist	4	2	7	7	80
2. I am *juarense* and I feel proud of it	51	26	7	5	11
3. Despite the problems of delinquency and family disintegration the border is to me the best part of Mexico	60	16	9	5	10
4. The border has the advantage that people are able to get acquainted with another culture	77	14	7	1	1
Scale: 1=Strongly agree; 2=Somewhat agree; 3=Uncertain; 4=Rather disagree; 5=Strongly disagree					

Table 3.8 shows that the great majority of the subjects interviewed are consistently positive when evaluating the city of Juárez. On the whole, more than three fourths of all the informants strongly agree or somewhat agree with items 2, 3 and 4, which deal with local pride, social adjustment and cultural advantages of the border. More than three fourths of all the subjects do not believe that life on the border is difficult due to the clash of two different cultures.

This positive view of the border predicts attitudes toward English as seen in Table 3.8 This connection might appear paradoxical to those who believe that border residents are highly ethnocentric. This relationship, however, has to be understood in light of local values and local behavior. The Mexican border has always been considered a milieu of social maladjustment and uprooting, inasmuch as the dynamics and lifestyle in the area differ considerably from those in the typical *provincia*. The major contrast has to do with the anti-traditional, anti-conventional behavior of the border residents, who appear too liberal in the eyes of the typical Mexican *provinciano*. The border residents are migrants from all over Mexico who have not only imported a variety of values, linguistic characteristics and lifestyles, but who are easily influenced by innovations of all sorts. The city of Juárez is host, for example, to an unusually large number of political and religious groups which do not exist in other Mexican cities of the size of Juárez. In addition, the English language and the American mass culture are strikingly noticeable to those who are not native residents.

Many migrants from Mexico's interior find this collage impossible to digest. Those informants with low scores in local identity claimed that life on the border was "shocking," "exasperating," difficult to assimilate. The poor, unskilled, unemployed migrant from the interior is thus likely to go through a cultural shock, at the same time that he/she experiences identity crises, anomic feelings and social uprooting in his own country. The migrant has to adjust himself to the life on the border in order to take advantage of the opportunities that the city provides. Those who survive the painful process of dislocation begin identifying with Juárez and finally come to appreciate it because of its not being "typically" Mexican.

The prediction of Attitudes toward English by Local Identity seems therefore associated with the more profound assimilation to border life, inasmuch as the contact with American mass culture and the English language is a very important part of the local milieu. Over the years the native residents have accepted English because of the evident material and cultural benefits derived by contact with the United States. The people of the border have realized that the acceptance of English causes less of a conflict than its rejection. Liking English and using English are not at all a threat to the people residing along the Mexican border, because bilingualism is for them additive, not subtractive. Border residents learn this language of wider communication without relinquishing Spanish, and they can be comfortably bilingual as long as they feel that they are using two languages for two different purposes, and as long as they maintain the two languages apart.

3.7. Attitudes toward English in other settings

The spread of English around the world has been attributed to the political ascendency, colonial domination, and economic hegemony of the English-speaking world. Due to its status as a language of power, English is used internally for official and semi-official purposes in many non-English mother-tongue nations, especially in Africa and Asia. Several of the Asian and African countries have not reached an agreement as to which of the many native tongues will serve as the official language; as a result, many of these former Anglophone colonies have retained English as a fully official or co-official language. In Europe and Latin America, where most countries have adopted a common national language, many efforts have been made to teach English as a foreign language, substituting in this way for French as the "first" foreign language. Studies concerning the spread of English indicate that English is clearly the major link-language with the world due to its lingua franca functions and its worldwide use in diplomacy, education and media (Conrad and Fishman 1977). "English is used by some persons in virtually every country of the world" (Conrad and Fishman 1977:6). Inasmuch as English has become the most prestigious and useful language on a worldwide basis, almost any cultural setting is valuable to study attitudes toward English.

Gardner and Lambert (1972:121-30) selected the context of the Philippines because of the societal, economic and personal importance of English as a second language. In that country where more than sixty native tongues are spoken, English is currently the most prestigious language of all. Proficiency in English determines Philippino upward mobility and future. The setting was thus ideal to test one of the authors' major hypotheses, namely that the integrative motive plays a substantial role in the acquisition of a second language. In order to validate this hypothesis, 103 senior high school students residing in Manila were administered a series of tests on proficiency and attitudes. The results of the study showed that those "students who approach the study of English with an instrumental outlook are clearly more successful in developing proficiency in this language than those who fail to adopt this orientation" (p. 130). Learning a language of universal recognition is of vital importance for the Philippino inasmuch as English is the language of instruction and business, and therefore, becomes an endorsement of the culture. Those who are integratively-oriented are more likely to develop oral-aural features of second language proficiency. In spite of the fact that the Philippines are ethnocentric in outlook, they also develop an integrative orientation toward English and hold favorable attitudes toward Americans.

In another post-colonial country, India, a study on attitudes toward English was conducted in Bombay by Lukmani (1972). Sixty female high school students who were native speakers of Marathi served as the subjects; they belonged to a non-Westernized section of Bombay society and had been studying English as a second language for approximately seven years. The author hypothesized that (a) the Marathi speakers would be more instrumentally than integratively oriented; (b) those with higher integrative motivation scores would be more proficient in English and (c) subjects would rate their group membership higher than English-speaking Indian people on given traits. The study revealed that the subjects were more oriented to learn English for instrumental reasons than for integrative reasons. Their instrumental motivation was in turn significantly correlated with English proficiency scores. The Marathi speakers also showed little desire to identify with English-speaking Indians, even though they regarded the English community as being more successful, more modern and more independent. Apparently, these subjects desired to use English as a means of entry into the reference group but only as a tool with which to understand and cope with the demands of modern life.

A related line of research on attitudes toward English and toward the vernaculars was undertaken in Rhodesia by Hofman (1977). His study reached more than three hundred African students and more than one hundred students of European descent. Attitudes toward the main languages spoken in Rhodesia were categorized into four types: sentimentalism, value, instrumentalism and communication. Under this general scheme, the speakers of English differed in their views from the speakers of African languages. Shona, the strongest vernacular in this country, is generally appreciated by both groups because it is needed for self-expression, literary enjoyment, interracial communication, and national identity. On the other hand, English is perceived by Africans as an imposed language by the dominant group and therefore, they can only see it as an instrument for education, better jobs, upward mobility, and wider communication. The non-African speakers prefer English not only for these instrumental and the communicative values but also for its sentimental and value attributes.

English is no longer seen as a sign of colonialism in Israel, a country which was formerly under British rule. The current trend in Israel is to stress this language of wider communication, but presumably not at the expense of Hebrew (Nadel and Fishman 1977). In order to assess attitudes, usage and proficiency with respect to English, 65 high school students were selected for an intensive survey conducted in Jerusalem by Cooper and Fishman (1977). This group of subjects most frequently chose instrumental reasons as being the most important ones to learn English. This basically instrumental view of the language proved to be correlated to both English proficiency and usage. The subjects also exhibited very positive attitudes toward Americans, who were evaluated about as highly as native-born Israelis and even more highly than other immigrant groups. Their positive views of Americans, however, are largely irrelevant with respect to their attitudes toward English. In the United States, where English is fully official, several investigations have also demonstrated that there exists a difference between the instrumental and integrative orientation toward this language of wider communication.

A study conducted by Oller, Hudson and Liu (1977) among 44 Chinese students attending American universities, showed that subjects were primarily instrumentally motivated since reasons like "getting training in my fields" were judged more important than reasons like "getting to know Americans" (p. 8). The same instrumental orientation was evidenced in other sections of the study dealing with reasons for learning English (e.g., fulfilling school requirements). Overall, subjects were not particularly integratively oriented toward Americans since they rated their own group higher on several important desirable personal traits.

One study among Mexican immigrants learning English in Albuquerque (Oller, Baca and Vigil 1977) and another among Mexican and Mexican-American students attending college in El Paso (Probst Muro 1982) also explore the instrumental versus the integrative motive. Both works report similar findings, i.e., Mexican individuals living and/or studying in the milieu where the language is spoken typically claim instrumental reasons to learn English. The subjects surveyed by Oller et al. seem, nevertheless, to develop ill feelings against Americans as they gain proficiency in English—that is, as they begin to feel closer to the group of native speakers—whereas those subjects studied by Probst Muro appeared to have somewhat positive feelings toward citizens of the United States, regardless of their proficiency.

All the investigations carried out in countries of the Third World and the study undertaken in Israel clearly demonstrate that non-English speakers are definitely more motivated to learn English due to its universal instrumental values. Likewise, speakers of foreign languages living in the United States seem to be more inclined to prefer English because of its instrumentality. The results of my own survey reported in section 3.5 reveal, nevertheless, an unusual equality in value and importance between the two forms of orientation towards English; this finding evidently contradicts the general trend in the evaluation of English. Furthermore, most studies reviewed in this section show that attitudes toward native speakers of English are not consistently connected with attitudes toward the language, the exception being the investigation by Oller, Baca and Vigil (1977) among recent Mexican migrants in New Mexico. The relationship between attitudes toward the language and attitudes toward the group of speakers in my own study turned out insignificant, as in the majority of the aforementioned investigations.

3.8. Attitudes toward education in English

The only open-ended question included in this survey is one related to the values of education in English. This issue was discussed at length with those informants who had been exposed to the American school system. Approximately one fifth (21%) of all the informants surveyed in this study claimed to have had exposure to English as a medium of instruction at elementary, secondary or college levels in the United States. All the subjects who had attended or were attending American schools at the time of the interview had also had experiences in the Mexican school system in at least two of the three educational levels. These individuals were, consequently, capable of comparing both systems and willing to verbalize their reasons for attending schools in the United States. These major motivations seem to be related to: (1) the acquisition of the English language in a formal context and in the country where the language is spoken, and (2) training in a professional field.

Border residents study English in American schools because they perceive both the instrumental and the integrative values of this language of wider communication. Those who attended elementary or secondary schools in the U.S. were expecting to acquire a nearly perfect command of the English language at the same time that they were completing one of the school programs. The acquisition of English at puberty or prior to puberty was the major goal of those who planned their education: their parents. Individuals who perceive American elementary or secondary education as highly valuable appear to be more integratively-oriented, since reasons like "speaking English like a native speaker" or "getting to know the American system at an early age" were frequently mentioned. In contrast, those who seek college education in the United States perceive English as secondary to professional skills, and for them the language becomes more of a means than an end in itself. College students approach the study of English with an instrumental outlook and their primary objective is usually a professional degree.

Similarly, one of the major findings of the study conducted by Probst Muro (1982) was that the group of Mexicans from Juárez (and Mexican-Americans from El Paso) enrolled at The University of Texas at El Paso, displayed a stronger motivation to learn English due to practical reasons (e.g., to study at an American university, to get a job in the United States) than due to their desires for integration (p. 24). It is apparent that, with respect to education in English, border residents make decisions in opposite directions; they seem, on the whole, to be motivated by the desire to communicate with their American neighbors as well as by the undeniable values of English in the job market.

Individuals who reported previous or current attendance at American schools typically belong to the upper-upper, upper-middle, middle-middle, and lower-middle social strata. With the small sample surveyed it was impossible to determine, nevertheless, which segment of the population within these four strata is more likely to prefer the elementary educational level in the United States, as opposed to secondary or college levels. The informants themselves cited a series of intervening variables that influence the selection of education in English, to wit: family pressures, vocational inclinations, having relatives in the United States, prospects of future residence in El Paso (or elsewhere in the United States), desires of exploring the "other" culture, etc. In contrast, border residents seem to remain in Mexican schools if they do not feel parental pressure, if they do not have relatives in El Paso, if they do not consider emigrating to the United States, or if the careers they are planning on studying are not as readily available in American colleges (e.g., Medicine or Law).

3.9. Conclusions

(a) One of the goals of this chapter was to determine the domains in which English is used on the Mexican side of the border, as well as the characteristics of the individuals who use English more frequently and more intensively. The findings of this investigation conform to several hypotheses proposed by Fishman and his associates in *The Spread of English* (1977):

(1) The vast majority of people learning English today in the developing countries are learning it in secondary schools as a subject of instruction (Conrad and Fishman 1977:14, 17, 25).

(2) The most important factors which promote the spread of English as an additional language are related to the degree of urbanization and educational development of the collectivities (Fishman et al. 1977:80-1). This is certainly the case of the Mexican border, in which industry, school and the urban setting have disseminated this language of wider communication.

(3) English as an additional language is more often characterized by contextual specificity than most native tongues (Fishman 1977a:109). This is also the case on the Mexican side of the border, where English is typically utilized in such specific contexts as tourism and the assembly industry.

(4) Languages of wider communication are more often heard than read, more spoken than written, more used at the level of comprehension than that of production (Fishman 1977a:109). This assumption is validated in section 3.1.

(5) The use of English in some countries (e.g., Israel) is associated with socioeconomic status (Nadel and Fishman 1977:146). This finding is similar to that reported in section 3.2, Table 3.3.

There is no doubt that English is simply an additional language that helps Juárez residents to communicate in those contexts in which, for personal, social, and economic reasons they need and want to communicate; this language is learned primarily by individuals who take advantage of the opportunities available to them. English in Juárez presents many similarities with diverse universal contexts, but what makes its use unique is the overwhelming effect on language attitudes, given the extent to which English is used, its availability and its omnipresence in the form of mass media.

Another important objective of this chapter was to examine the attitudes of border residents with respect to English. The sample surveyed for this study displayed both an instrumental and an integrative orientation toward this language of wider communication. This particular finding differs considerably from those reported in other settings where English is either a second or a foreign language. This finding provides the basis for a further assumption: the Mexican border setting fosters a healthy mixture of integrative and instrumental attitudes toward English.

In the context of the Mexican border English has lost its connotations of an imperialist language. For the present generation of *juarenses*, English does not appear as a threat to their identity, due perhaps to its use and prestige in the international political arena in the last two decades and to its alleged neutral ethnic and ideological status as proposed by Fishman (1977a:119). That English is not a threat to border Mexicans is also supported by the fact that the best single predictors of attitudes toward English are English Use and Local Identity. The data on English Use and Attitudes toward English reveal that acquiring, using and liking English as an additional language are actually related to each other. This finding contradicts the hypothesis that knowledge, use and attitude toward language are imperfectly (if at all) related (Fishman 1977b). When the people of the northern frontier know English, they tend to use it, and the more they use it the more they find it valuable.

Footnotes

(1) The criteria utilized to thoroughly discuss a correlation are $p < .001$ and $p < .01$. Three sets of variables (National Ethnocentrism and Language Loyalty, Beliefs about Americans and SES, and Beliefs about Mexican-Americans and SES) falling below this statistical level of significance are superficially approached. Since National Ethnocentrism, Beliefs about Anglo-Americans and Beliefs about Mexican-Americans were ex professo created for this study, I decided to present correlations that were practically significant for the understanding of the attitudinal border setting.

(2) The criterion utilized for this multiple regression analysis and all subsequent analyses has been a coefficient of at least 0.54 and a variance of at least 6%. All coefficients falling below this criterion were not discussed at all in this study.

(3) This analysis was suggested by Dr. John W. Oller in his Seminar on Second Language Acquisition, The University of New Mexico, Summer 1981.

Chapter 4

Spanish in Juárez

This chapter is intended to provide a general overview of the Spanish spoken in Juárez from an attitudinal vantage point. The introductory section discusses the characteristics of formal and informal northern Mexican Spanish and, by the same token, the features of the varieties of Spanish spoken in Juárez, as identified by this writer. The following sections deal with the eighty-five informants' evaluations of the local variety as compared to other varieties of Mexican Spanish. Great emphasis is given to educated border residents' attitudes and the origins of these attitudes. In addition, this chapter is devoted to exploring the informants' feelings of language loyalty, and the possible sources of the reported strong attachments to Spanish, the national language of Mexico and the mother tongue of all the inhabitants of Juárez. Finally, the last sections outline the principles enunciated by a new official organism, the National Board for the Defense of the Spanish Language, regarding language policy in Mexico and in Juárez.

4.1. The Spanish of the northern frontier

Most research dealing with the Spanish spoken in Mexico focuses on the Spanish of Mexico City, the capital of the country. Due to Mexico City's cultural prestige and due to the convergence of diverse regional varieties of Spanish in the Mexican capital, the speech of this metropolis has been extensively studied in different aspects of phonology, morphology, syntax and vocabulary (Lope Blanch 1972:9). Other studies have been carried out in areas of the High Central Plains neighboring the Mexican capital, e.g., in the states of Guanajuato, San Luis Potosi, Puebla, Tlaxcala and Michoacán. Similarly, the Southeastern Coast along the Gulf of Mexico, where the states of Veracruz, Tabasco and Chiapas are located, has been the subject of several dialectological investigations (Davies 1971).

In spite of the fact that the northern part of Mexico was recognized as one of five separate dialect zones as early as 1938 (Henríquez Ureña 1938:334), the variety of Spanish spoken in the northern areas has been traditionally neglected. The dialectological division of Mexico as proposed by Henríquez Ureña was seriously questioned forty years later by Lope Blanch (1970; 1971). In the earlier article Lope Blanch argues that there do not exist valid and complete phonological, morphological and syntactic data to support Henríquez Ureña's division. In his article of 1971, he proposes from 17 to 19 different dialect zones based on the usage of lexical items which are common throughout the country. In the North of Mexico, he distinguishes four varieties: (1) the *bajacaliforniano septentrional* in the northern part of the Baja California Peninsula; (2) the northwestern variety in the states of Sonora and Sinaloa; (3) the *chihuahuense* dialect in the state of Chihuahua, where Juárez is located; and (4) the northeastern variety in the states of Nuevo León and Tamaulipas.

In contrast with other small and large Mexican communities in the High Central Plains and the Southeastern Coast, no community in the desert area of Mexico has been generally described in a comprehensive study such as that of Peter Boyd-Bowman's *El habla de Guanajuato* (1960). At present, a description of northern Mexican Spanish appears to be an extremely difficult task because the geographical dialect variation is great. The vast northern zone of Mexico covers an area from the Baja California Peninsula along the Pacific Ocean, to the state of Tamaulipas along the Northeastern Coast of the Gulf of Mexico. In addition, the entire area is characterized not only by massive migration from other regions of Mexico, but also by its high degree of urbanization and industrialization, especially in the most populous centers.

There are, however, certain dialect features which seem to be, as a whole, characteristic of the northern regions: 1. The articulation of affricate /č/ as fricative [š], as in *noche, coche, muchacho*. 2. The aspiration of /s/ in intervocalic position, as in *nosotros, pasamos* and, less frequently, the aspiration of /s/ in final position as in *dijimos, pudimos*. 3. The loss of intervocalic /y/, as in *gallina, botella, chiquillo*. 4. The pronunciation of bilabial /f/ as velar [x], or as an aspirated [h], before the diphthongs *-ue, -ui*, as in *fuera, fuimos*.

This combination of features, though individually found elsewhere in the Spanish-speaking world, may well represent the *norteño* dialect, and may enable Mexicans from the central and southern areas to identify the typical uneducated or somewhat educated *norteño*.[1]

All these features have been documented in other varieties of Peninsular and American Spanish. Lapesa considers the *fricativization* of /č/ and the aspiration of /s/ in final position as originally Andalusian phenomena (Lapesa 1959:328, 349). The loss of intervocalic /y/ and the velarization of bilabial /f/ are typical of many other Peninsular and Spanish American dialects (Lapesa 1959:356, 362), whereas the aspiration of /s/ in intervocalic position has been documented in only a few regions, e.g., in the Dominican Republic (Henríquez Ureña 1940:147; Jiménez 1975:77).

The unique intonation of the northern people, which differs dramatically from that encountered in the center or the south, along with the phonological characteristics discussed above, unmistakably single out the *norteño* speaker even to a naive ear. The northern intonation is distinguished by its sharp rise of pitch in the final vocalic segments of a sentence and by the elongation of stressed vowels at the end of yes-no questions, information questions, exclamations, and even affirmative and negative statements revealing insistency, urgency, anger or clarification.

This writer's residence in northern Mexico and experience with native northern Mexicans from different states of the region have, revealed that the people from the northern part of Mexico are very proud of their *norteño* way of speaking. Their speech is often perceived as rude, impolite and tactless by those Mexicans who inhabit central and southern Mexico, and they are often accused of talking too loudly and of lacking a flowery, delicate speech style. Northern Mexicans are convinced, nonetheless, that in their speech they convey those moral traits that differentiate them from other Mexicans; they believe that their way of speaking reflects the inherent virtues of frankness, directness and naturalness; they also believe in doing and saying things the northern way (*a lo norteño*) and in speaking with northern self-assurance (*con aplomo norteño*).

Given that the urban industrialized centers in northern Mexico have consistently received a wide conglomerate of immigrants from rural and semi-rural communities, the speech of large northern cities such as Juárez is distinguished by the presence of dialect features as well as by the existence of various levels of stylistic usage associated with a fixed academic standard. The intense contact and mobility of speakers of different geographical, social and educational backgrounds in the urban setting makes it, nonetheless, impossible to single out the "typical" speech of particular northern communities. The vernacular speech of Juárez, for example, is easily recognized by residents of the capital of the state,

Chihuahua, but remains indistinguishable from that of other communities for persons in the interior of Mexico. Whereas dialect features of the northern region are more frequently found in Juárez among recent migrants of limited education, the standard characteristics are normally encountered among the lifelong border resident of greater education. The educated native *juarense* is less likely to omit intervocalic /y/ or to produce the affricate /č/ as [š], the intervocalic /s/ as [h], and so on. Certain dialect features can be observed, however, among young, educated speakers. Thus, for example, those under twenty-five years of age are currently shifting in the direction of the original northern dialect, especially in the use of fricative [š] instead of affricate /č/.

Along with phonological variables, there can be found in Juárez a number of nonstandard forms in morphology and syntax. In the traditional Hispanic purist, the use of *haiga* instead of *haya*, the use of *duérmanos* instead of *durmamos*, or the use of *dijistes* instead of *dijiste* would provoke a swift judgement about the lack of correctness of the vernacular speech of the community. All these nonstandard phonological, morphological and syntactic characteristics carry a negative social prestige only when individuals from lower social strata attempt to occupy higher positions in Mexican society. When speakers of lower social class remain in lower positions, the speakers in middle or upper classes just perceive all these nonstandard features as the expected characteristic speech of the northern peasant[2]. The formal variety of Spanish spoken in Juárez is tied, however, to the conservative, written tradition of the schooled Spanish of educated Mexicans. The use of the standard variety of Spanish for all types of formalized communication has thus served to clearly distinguish the values assigned to the formal and colloquial versions of Spanish. The formal version of Spanish spoken in Juárez approximates a general Mexican standard norm utilized in urban formal domains throughout the country, and the mastery of such version is perceived as desirable and as one of the keys to upward mobility in Mexican society. Through the national mass media, the inhabitants of the northern frontier are in daily contact with the most prestigious variety of Spanish spoken in Mexico, that is, the Spanish of Mexico City, which has been considered for centuries a very important and "superior" variety of Mexican Spanish and regarded as equivalent to the national "official" norm (Lope Blanch 1972:9).

4.1.1. Local versus national Spanish

Part of the questionnaire prepared for this study was designed to gauge the respondents' evaluation of their own local variety when compared to other varieties of Spanish spoken in important urban centers in Mexico's interior: Mexico City, Guadalajara and Chihuahua. Mexico City, the capital of the country, was chosen for comparison with Juárez because of its reputation as a center of cultural diffusion in Latin America. Guadalajara (Jalisco) is currently the second largest and second oldest colonial Mexican city. Chihuahua, the capital of the state of Chihuahua, is not one of the largest urban centers in Mexico, but it is politically more important than Juárez. The geographic proximity and the common background of Juárez and Chihuahua often incite inhabitants of the two communities to compare their speech varieties and lifestyles. Mexico City, Guadalajara and Chihuahua have in common that, as compared to Juárez, they have less direct and less intense contact with the official language of the United States (English) and the language variety spoken in the American Southwest (Spanglish).

Four questionnaire items explore the attitudes toward these varieties of Spanish held by the eighty-five informants residing in Juárez. These direct questions and the response percentages are presented in Table 4.1. As seen in Item 1 in this table, almost half of the respondents (45%) rated the Spanish of Juárez as being as correct as that spoken in Mexico City. Also, slightly less than half (47%) of the subjects evaluated their own variety as less correct than that spoken in the capital of the country. When the same question was reversed in Item 4, the results were virtually the same: 46% confirmed that the Spanish spoken in Juárez was as correct as that spoken in the Mexican capital, and 51% rated their own variety as being less correct than the Mexico City variety.

Those informants who believe that the Spanish spoken in Juárez is as correct as that spoken in the capital of the country also tend to believe that the variety of Spanish spoken in smaller cities is as correct as that spoken in Juárez. Almost half of the entire sample (41%) consider the Spanish spoken in Guadalajara as correct as that spoken in Juárez; and more than half (57%) feel that the Spanish of Chihuahua is as correct as that spoken in Juárez. On the other hand, sizeable percentages of respondents were unable to make a judgement about the speech of the speech of Guadalajara (18%) and Chihuahua (13%). They reported that they had never had any contact with native residents of these two state capitals. Almost one third (31%) of the sample rated the speech of Guadalajara as being more correct than their own variety (see Item 2), whereas only a fifth (18%) perceive the Spanish spoken in Chihuahua City as being more correct than the speech of Juárez (see Item 3). The results show that border residents hold favorable opinions about the varieties of Spanish spoken in the center whose political influence is undeniable. They are definitely more impressed with the Spanish of Mexico City than with that of Guadalajara, and they do not have very high regard for the speech of Chihuahua City.

Table 4.1 Response Percentages: Local Versus National Spanish

Items	0	1	2	3	4	5
1. The Spanish spoken in Mexico City is more correct than that spoken in Juárez	1	5	0	45	12	35
2. The Spanish spoken in Juárez is more correct than that spoken in other important cities of Mexico, e.g., Guadalajara	18	14	17	41	2	2
3. The Spanish spoken in Juárez is more correct than that spoken in the capital of the state, Chihuahua	13	5	13	57	9	2
4. The Spanish spoken in Juárez is more correct than that spoken in Mexico City	1	39	12	46	0	2
Scale: 0=Did not know, 1=Strongly disagree; 2=Rather agree; 3=They are the same; 4=Somewhat agree; 5=Strongly agree						

The tendency to evaluate the Spanish spoken in Juárez as less correct than other national varieties is characteristic of young, college-educated, bilingual adults coming from upper-upper, upper-middle and middle-middle class backgrounds. In this sample, SES is in fact significantly correlated with a negative attitude toward the Spanish spoken in Juárez ($r = -.473$, $p < .001$). Formal Education ($r = -.463$, $p < .001$), number of years of Formal Exposure to English ($r = .530$, $p < .001$), and the informal Use of English ($r = -.380$, $p < .001$) are also negatively and significantly correlated with attitudes toward the local variety of Spanish. As seen in the equation in Table 4.2, the most important predictors of attitudes toward local Spanish are SES, which accounts for 22% of the variance, and formal education, which accounts for almost 7%. These two variables in combination make a modest multiple regression coefficient of almost 0.54. This means that those individuals in the upper and middle social strata are most impressed with the status of the capital city vis-à-vis la *provincia* (as the rest of the country is pejoratively denominated).

Table 4.2 Multiple Regression Analysis: Local versus National Spanish

Step	Variables entered in the equation	R	R^2	ΔR^2	r	F
1	SES	0.473	0.224	0.224	-0.473	7.24
2	Education	0.538	0.290	0.066	-0.463	8.10

4.1.2. The capital versus the province

Most young, educated speakers from Juárez believe that their local variety lacks preeminence because it did not evolve in the capital of the country. This belief arises from the unquestionable acceptability of the Spanish spoken in Mexico City. Mexico City's linguistic prestige emerges in turn from the fact that this metropolis has been since colonial times an economically prosperous capital in Latin America and an important center of cultural diffusion. As a result, its Spanish was not only recognized as the "purest and most elegant" in Mexico but was regarded as having a high status amongst the varieties spoken in the Spanish-American colonies (Lapesa 1959:155; Lope Blanch 1972:30).

Evaluating the speech of the capital city as "better" than that spoken in the provinces is not just a typical Mexican attitude, but a universal tendency emanating from the prestige of those language varieties supported by the government, the educational system, and the media (Fishman 1970a:19). The ascendancy of such standard language varieties over local and regional forms has also been attributed to their use in commerce and politics and the presence of the central power in the capital (Giles and Powesland 1975:11-2). This internal linguistic colonialism is true of some of the most important capitals of the Spanish-speaking world. For example, the speech of Lima, the capital of Peru, has been considered the linguistic norm for the rest of the country and compared with the so-called "vulgar," incorrect, careless Spanish spoken in the periphery (Escobar 1978:139, 143). The speech of Bogota, the capital of Colombia, is also proposed as the linguistic model of that country, and therefore, its norm is to be emulated in the provinces (Malmberg 1966:137).

The layman in the street is not aware that his perceptions of correctness and prestige have been conditioned by general beliefs about the political and cultural control of the Hispanic capitals. It is consequently not at all surprising to discover that serious linguistic investigations concerned with subjective evaluations of local versus national varieties have reported that Spanish speakers rate the variety spoken in the capital city as "better" than the local and regional varieties. Thus, for example, 65% of 236 Peruvians from different regions of the country ranked the Spanish spoken in Lima as the best Spanish (Wölck 1972:195, 209). The same general attitude was encountered among educated subjects from San Juan, Argentina, who believe that one of the features spoken in Buenos Aires—multiple vibrant /r/, is "better" than the local feature—fricative assibilated [ɹ] (Sanou de los Ríos 1981:4-5, 13).

The perceptions of linguistic correctness in most Spanish-speaking countries are therefore associated with concepts of centralized, administrative, political and economic power (Escobar 1976:55; 1978:162). Furthermore, the political and economic hegemony of the capital has influenced researchers to undertake linguistic investigations in which the speech of the capital cities is strongly emphasized. Given that the varieties of Spanish spoken in the capital cities are considered more important than all the others, many descriptive studies propose the speech of the capital as the linguistic norm, that is, as an abstract or "average" representation accepted and shared by the majority of the speakers. This concept of linguistic norm consequently presupposes the positive evaluation of such a model on the part of the speakers and the acceptance of linguistic homogeneity as a desideratum (Escobar 1978:143).

4.1.3. The effects of education and social class

Not only the political and cultural position of the capital city *vis-à-vis* la *provincia* but also the beliefs transmitted through the educational system have influenced young educated *juarenses* to rate their own speech variety as being less correct than that of Mexico City and important state capitals. The beliefs about correctness have to do with the prescriptive doctrine of purism which proposes the rejection of language mixture. Language mixture was attitudinally rejected by subjects who enjoyed for a longer period of time the benefits of formal education and whose speech norms are seemingly closer to the national standard. These educated individuals were questioned further. Their consensus was that the Spanish vernacular spoken in Juárez, and to a certain extent the Spanish utilized by the local media, too readily incorporates English borrowings instead of taking full advantage of the resources of the native tongue. These subjects were able to give many concrete examples of English borrowings that they disapproved of. The education of these subjects, and their exposure to both formal Spanish and formal English, have made them cognizant of local anglicized terms which have not been accepted by general standard norms throughout Mexico or throughout the Spanish-speaking world (see Table 4.3).

It has been suggested that in most literate societies, educated speakers become more sensitive to the conservative, standardized forces of educational agencies in which attitudes toward language purity prevail and act as a deterrent to the free development of the language (Weinreich 1968:87-8). Education has thus helped this group of Juárez residents maintain a relatively conservative, standardized Spanish variety; they therefore tend to avoid English terms that can be easily substituted by standard Spanish words. This is not, however, a rule which is applicable all the time in all social settings. Even highly educated border residents do use English words sporadically, and they seem generally aware of this use. Their education, nevertheless, supports to a certain extent the norms of the mother tongue against unchecked English borrowings that have not acquired a communicative value in their community.

Inasmuch as the school is the agency which fosters the traditional aim of language purity in most Spanish-speaking countries (Guitarte and Torres 1974:358), the doctrine of purism has effectively impinged upon attitudes towards the local vernacular; this variety is thus regarded as "impure" and "incorrect" by a cadre of well-read and relatively sophisticated individuals who hold a college degree or have some college education. Highly educated border residents claim that their vernacular cannot be correct because they are able to recognize the gap between their spoken language and the general standard written language learned at school. The common opinion is that the literary language is "pure". One of the persons interviewed made the following revealing, if somewhat extreme, statement:

> *Nadie habla correctamente porque la lengua correcta sólo existe en los libros y en los libros no se mezcla el español con el inglés.*

Intimately related with the prestige of the literary language is that of formal spoken Spanish. Educated informants are generally capable of making a distinction between their Spanish in formal domains, in which language mixture is not allowed, and their informal colloquial variety. As a result, the informal Spanish spoken in Juárez is considered "incorrect." As expressed by one insightful informant, their colloquial Spanish resembles a sloppy shirt as opposed to their formal Spanish, which is perceived as a rather fancy suit.

Those subjects with more years of formal education responded faster to the series of items dealing with correctness (cited in Table 4.1). The term "correctness" was, in addition, familiar to all of them. In contrast, less educated individuals had difficulties understanding the items on this issue. Moreover, most of the relatively uneducated individuals were unable to cite specific examples of differences between the local speech and that of other urban communities in Mexico's interior. The statement by Labov (1966) about the sensitivity of educated speakers is applicable to the situation of my own informants: "Direct questions will tap the reactions of only a handful of exceptionally articulate middle-class speakers" (p. 406).

Formal education thus appears to be a determining factor not only on the formation of attitudes toward language varieties but also on the accurate report of such attitudes. This proposition is ascertained by Cohen (1974), who conducted a study on attitudes toward varieties of Spanish among Mexican immigrants residing in Redwood City, California. The purpose of Cohen's investigation was to explore the formation of language attitudes among eighty-one families with limited formal education and linguistic sophistication. Trends in the data suggest that men more than women, and families at a higher socioeconomic status more than those at a lower level, were more knowledgeable about varieties of Spanish and more willing to express an opinion about the "best" variety of spoken Spanish.

The judgement of educated speakers residing in Juárez is largely based on attitudes learned at school, inasmuch as traditional education in most Spanish-speaking countries has been intransigent with regard to linguistic diversity. The school has propagated erroneous concepts of correctness, making people believe that there exist two types of Spanish: the good, which exists supposedly codified in the speech of educated individuals, and the bad, which is regarded as popular, vulgar, local, regional and the like. The traditional school in most Spanish-speaking countries has failed to educate speakers in the recognition and acceptance of linguistic diversity.

Spanish-speaking countries have been allied, in addition, to language academies whose primary task has been the stabilization and uniformization of linguistic usage. These institutions have significantly contributed to the dissemination of knowledge about the Spanish language and culture, but they have at the same time divulged their reluctance to accept the "popular" and local variations in pronunciation, morphology and syntax (Guitarte and Torres 1974:355-7). Those Spanish-speaking countries most concerned with the defense and unity of the national language have historically supported language academies. Mexico is one which has been distinguished as a pioneer in its allegiance with these institutions since the 19s century (Guitarte and Torres 1974:324-6).

Both the schools and the language academies have propagated attitudes of language purity throughout the Spanish-speaking world. These agencies cooperate with other official and semi-official organisms representing the status quo. Language purity is a value defended on behalf of language unity (Guitarte and Torres 1974:360). Language purity and language unity are thus values projected by influential members of the Spanish-speaking society when they evaluate the local speech of the peripheral communities (Rosenblat 1965).

The speech of these peripheral communities is often characterized by a wide range of variety in phonology, morphology, syntax and vocabulary (Rosenblat.1965; 1967:113-134), but representative members of the status quo frequently regard it with contempt. The origin of this disdain among educated native speakers of Spanish seems to be rooted in the awareness of an "ideal" linguistic norm based on the literary language. In contrast, the awareness of such a linguistic norm among uneducated Spanish speakers is very limited, since their speech follows more spontaneously the regional linguistic patterns. The educated speaker of Spanish is more easily influenced by the prestige of the written language, which is supposedly represented in the "cultured" speech of the capital city (Escobar et al. 1975:48-9)

The prescriptive doctrine of purism, the intolerant judgement of linguistic diversity, the spread of concepts of prestige associated with the capital cities, and the reinforcement of all these attitudes in the homes of the majority of the educated informants may help explain the negative evaluation of their local variety. A very small percentage of insightful informants was able to perceive, nonetheless, that middle class speakers from Mexico City use as many English borrowings as border residents do. The observations of this minority have been corroborated by serious research undertaken in the Mexican capital. Lope Blanch (1977) reports in fact that educated individuals residing in Mexico City habitually use a number of Anglicisms related to dress, meals, cars and sports. It has also been reported that lower-middle-class speakers from Mexico City use English borrowings with the desire to imitate middle-class speakers who in turn emulate the upper-class speakers (Alarcón 1978:101-3). The values assigned to English borrowings in the Mexican capital and on the Mexican border are, therefore, significantly contrastive: whereas speakers from Mexico City may feel that English borrowings carry a positive social prestige, the inhabitants of Juárez perceive certain anglicized forms as strongly stigmatized.

4.1.4. The effects of the border

Although it is not a source of variance in this particular study, the informal Use of English is also negatively correlated with attitudes towards the Spanish spoken in Juárez ($r = -.382$, $p < .001$). This effect of English seems to be peculiar to the sociolinguistic setting of the northern frontier. The negative evaluation of the local variety is based on the perception of objectively identifiable lexical borrowings from English. As elsewhere in the Spanish-speaking world, the local and written media in Juárez use excessive lexical terminology of English provenience instead of providing translations and accommodations to Spanish. In addition, in the informal everyday speech of both the educated and the uneducated, Anglicisms are almost inevitable. English borrowings normally alternate with more "acceptable" Spanish terms and educated border residents try to resist the foreign lexical items which, in their opinion, can be easily substituted by the corresponding translation in the mother tongue. Thus, on the Mexican side of the border, as elsewhere in the Spanish-speaking world, the acceptability of Anglicisms is a common issue about which everyone feels qualified to pass judgement (Guitarte and Torres 1974:360-1).

There exist, however, some common objections among educated border residents, who are reluctant to accept certain words which were incorporated into the informal local variety through contact with Mexican-Americans. These stigmatized terms were reported in the American Southwest as part of the Spanish vernacular as early as 1917 (cf. Espinosa 1972; see also Bowen 1972). Some of the borrowed nouns are related to the domestic domain, parts of cars or objects of everyday use. A few examples are presented in Table 4.3. The acceptance of these lexical items was discussed mostly with those informants who rated the Spanish of Juárez as incorrect due to its contact with English

Table 4.3 Some English Borrowings Used in Juárez

Stigmatized	Popular version	English source	Accepted version	Reported in the U.S. Southwest
No	Boiler	Boiler	Boiler	Espinosa, p. 102
No	Lonche	Lunch	Lonche	Espinosa, p. 111
No	Lonchera	Lunch box	Lonchera	Bowen, p. 118
No	Lonchería	Lunch (place)	Lonchería	Bowen, p. 118
Ambivalent	Troca	Truck	Troca or camioneta	Espinosa, p. 111 Bowen, p. 118
Yes	Breca	Brake	Freno	Espinosa, p. 110
Yes	Quequi	Cake	Pastel	Espinosa, p. 110 Bowen, p. 116
Yes	Escrín or esprín	Door (screen)	Tela de alambre	Espinosa, p. 110 Bowen, p. 116
Yes	Mapiar	To mop	Trapear	Bowen, p. 118
Yes	Ploga	Plug	Bujía	Bowen, p. 117
Yes	Sinc	Sink	Fregadero	Espinosa, p. 111 Bowen, p. 117

There are other nouns of English origin accepted without inhibitions in the written and spoken media, e.g., *yonque* (< junk) with the meaning 'auto salvage' and *mofle* (< muffler); these terms are even included in the local telephone directory, and although many informants were able to give 'standard' equivalents (*silenciador* for mofle and *deshuesadero* for *yonque*), they claimed to prefer the English borrowings since the Spanish version is not as widespread in Juárez and lacks, in fact, the communicative value of the English borrowing.

It is apparent that the Mexican side of the border is assaulted by conflicting attitudes. This is due, perhaps, to the different influences dominating the area: on the one hand there is the influx of migrants from Mexico's interior who daily enrich the local vernacular with characteristics of their own dialects; on the other, the contact with Americans and Mexican-Americans offers new terminology that is accepted if it acquires a communicative value and rejected if a "good" Spanish term is more appealing. The ongoing struggle of acceptance and rejection of English borrowings seems to be a pan-Hispanic phenomenon. The crisis of the border resembles other situations of language contact in the Spanish-speaking world, where "Anglicisms are considered one of the greatest threats to the denaturalization and fragmentation of the Spanish language" (Guitarte and Torres 1974:359).

The proximity of the English language and the traditional belief that the Spanish language has to be pure to be correct have attitudinally overshadowed the dialect features characteristic of the Spanish spoken in northern Mexico. Border Mexicans generally overlook the nonstandard phonological features of their own variety which have been discussed in the introduction of this chapter. Furthermore, educated border Mexicans do not condemn the use of the morphological and syntactic forms which differ considerably from their own speech (e.g., the use of *haiga* instead of *haya*, the use of *duérmanos* instead of *durmamos*, etc.). While they realize that such forms are not utilized in the written language, they do not censure their use, because most of these nonstandard features are perceived as "typically Mexican," that is, they are seen as belonging to the vernacular spoken by the majority of the uneducated individuals throughout Mexico. When making a judgement on correctness, educated border Mexicans concentrate their attention on the amount of mixture that Spanish might have with English. If it sounds all Spanish, it is acceptable. If it sounds "typically Mexican," it is also acceptable. It seems that linguistic acceptability has also ethnicity-related values in this Mexican border city. The more Mexican it sounds the more acceptable it appears. De-ethnicized language is perceived by the same token, as unacceptable (see sections 5.1.1. through 5.2.).

To sum up, the attitudes of educated border Mexicans toward their own variety have to be understood by a series of intertwined factors, such as their disadvantageous position with respect to the capital city, the traditional intolerant attitude of linguistic purity in the Spanish-speaking world, and the effects of the informal use of English on the Mexican side of the border. The negative attitudes of this group of educated *juarenses* stem from self-criticism, inasmuch as they realize that their role on the international frontier should be one of representing a valued culture with which they deeply and legitimately identify.

4.2. Spanish as the national language

The attitudes toward the local vernacular spoken in Juárez have to be distinguished from the sentiments that border residents have toward the national language, inasmuch as the national language is the most acceptable standard throughout the country. The standard national language is, in addition, a unifying force which fosters an identity transcending the local communities. Although regional differences exist in Mexico, Mexicans feel united as a nation because they share a common tongue. This common tongue also stimulates sentiments of allegiance with the rest of the Spanish-speaking world.

In her examination of language policy in Mexico from colonial times to the present Heath (1972) states that after their independence from Spain, the developing countries of Latin America faced the urgent problem of nationhood and nationalistic struggle for an authentic identity. The choice for a national standard language was of crucial significance because its designation would be linked to national unity and national identity. In the linguistically fragmented Latin American countries, the political decision-makers selected Spanish as the national language because of its ties with technological and political modernization (Heath 1972:190-1).

Mexico's process of selecting a standard code extended over the entire colonial period, and none of the educational systems implemented during that time enforced the masses' acceptance of the official language. The leaders of independent Mexico assumed that Spanish would be the nation's standard language. Before Spanish was proclaimed as the national language, several attempts were made to recognize officially the indigenous languages spoken in Mexico. The policy makers of the late 19th century suggested that the Mexican nation should create territorial divisions on the basis of native tongues, but the concept of "little nations" was perceived as a threat and as an obstacle to national unity, and its implementation was never possible (Heath 1972:191).

Spanish was perceived as the means to foster the national identity, but leaders refused to accept the variety of Spanish spoken in Spain as the national code. These nationalistic sentiments prevailing in Mexico after Independence led decision-makers to announce in the late 19th Century an official choice of Mexican Spanish. The variety of Spanish spoken in Mexico thus became legitimate and its speech norms began to be codified with regard to certain rules of spelling, pronunciation, grammar and vocabulary choice (Heath 1972:192). Throughout the 20th century, Mexican Spanish has been the basic instrument for the cultural incorporation of the indigenous populations of the country and the key to maintaining the national ideal of solidarity (Heath 1972: passim).

In the northern frontier of Mexico, as in the rest of the country, Spanish is accepted as fully official, and loyalty to the national language is linked to national loyalty. Some indigenous communities in Mexico maintain, nevertheless, a relatively strong allegiance to their native idioms, inasmuch as the indigenous tongues are still related to intragroup interests and values (Heath 1972:198-9; Hill and Hill 1980). Most Spanish-speaking Mexicans attribute a great symbolic value to the native indigenous tongues, but this value seems to be rooted in the romantic past of Mexico rather than in the present. The affective link to the indigenous languages is only moderately validated by northern Mexicans, since they feel more strongly affiliated to their country because of the actual value assigned to the national language. For the vast majority of the people of the northern part of Mexico, Spanish is the language that identifies them as Mexicans. Furthermore, the northerners have amalgamated the notion of being Mexican with the speaking of Spanish. Folk terms utilized among uneducated speakers in this area of the country suggest that people perceive the close association between their language and their ethnic identity: "we speak Mexican" is often a substitution for "we speak Spanish."

4.2.1. Language loyalty in Juárez

The following sections of this chapter analyze the border residents' feelings toward Mexican Spanish. The questionnaire items elaborated for this study attempt to explore how people from Juárez feel about maintaining their language as it is presumably maintained in the rest of the country, i.e., without the mixture of English. The questions do not call on respondents to claim a behavioral commitment to their language; they are intended rather to elicit an opinion justified upon personal, emotional grounds. The four direct questions and the response percentages on language loyalty are presented in Table 4.4.

Attitudinal language loyalty among Mexican residents of Juárez is rather high. Table 4.4 shows that there exists a relatively strong agreement among the respondents in relation to their attachments to Spanish. The vast majority of the informants (83%) claim that Spanish should be preserved on the Mexican side of the border as it has been preserved in the interior of Mexico. Almost two thirds of the entire sample (62%) strongly agree or somewhat agree with the statement that border residents have the ability to speak their mother tongue as other Mexicans from the interior. Slightly more than half (51%) of the respondents deny that language mixture takes place in their community, and the same percentage believe that they as individual speakers do not mix the two languages. The response percentages on Item 1 show some contrast with those in Items 2 through 4. Whereas in Item 1, the majority of the informants claim that the Spanish of Juárez should be preserved as in the interior of Mexico, a considerable percentage of informants believe that border Mexicans do not speak as well as Mexicans from the interior (30%), that language mixture does occur in the community (42%), and that the speakers themselves do in fact blend Spanish with English (47%). Those individuals who do perceive language mixture in Juárez, or who do admit that they may occasionally mix Spanish with English, tend to be the same ones who do not overtly condemn the variety of Spanish spoken in El Paso, In contrast, those subjects who do not perceive language mixture in Juárez, that is, the bare majority of the respondents, tend to be the same ones who reject more strongly the variety of Spanish spoken in El Paso. Attitudinal language loyalty is in fact significantly correlated to a rejection of Spanglish because of its lack of communicative values ($r = .455$, $p < .001$), and because of its lack of beauty, pleasantness, correctness, and ethnicity ($r = .386$, $p < .001$). Language Loyalty is, in addition, a significant source of variance in the prediction of attitudes toward Spanglish (documented in Tables 5.2 and 5.4 in Chapter 5).

Table 4.4 Response Percentages: Language Loyalty in Juárez

Items	1	2	3	4	5
1. It is very important for border Mexicans to maintain the Spanish language just like other Mexicans	2	8	6	8	75
2. Border Mexicans are able to speak just like other Mexicans although sometimes they know English	12	18	8	23	39
3. In Juárez people mix the two languages when speaking	42	9	6	9	33
4. I speak sometimes mixing the two languages	37	14	1	12	35
Scale: 1=Strongly disagree; 2=Rather disagree; 3=Uncertain; 4=Somewhat agree; 5=Strongly agree					

The sociodemographic and linguistic characteristics of the subjects with high scores in Language Loyalty are very diverse: they are scattered in all six socioeconomic groups, they are either males or females, and their use of English varies from low to high. When claiming attitudinal language loyalty to Mexican Spanish, the simple assertion "I'm Mexican" was more important than socioeconomic status, education, bilingualism, sex, age, or local identity. Language loyalty seems to be a patent and unobstructed attitude which most border Mexicans are willing to externalize at the slightest provocation. The people from the northern frontier appear to have a subjective need for ethnic identity assertion. When confirming their loyalty to Spanish, they are implying that they want to be differentiated from the out-group, Mexican-Americans. Language loyalty has in fact been defined as a subjective state of mind which produces an attempt at preserving the threatened language when language shift is on the threshold (Weinreich 1968:99). The subjective defensive position assumed by a considerable percentage of border Mexicans is not incidental, but the result of the border setting, in which constant interaction with speakers of Spanglish is perceived as a threat to ethnolinguistic "purity."

4.2.2. The values of Mexican Spanish

The inhabitants of the northern frontier have a number of reasons to remain loyal to the official language spoken in Mexico. Spanish has undisputed supremacy in both formal and informal domains throughout the country, and its functions on the Mexican side of the border are identical to those encountered in all the major urban communities of the interior where the population is predominantly Spanish-speaking. In addition to the communicative values of Spanish, border Mexicans have great regard for their mother tongue for its sentimental value, inasmuch as the mother tongue not only serves as a means of communication but also evokes high symbolic values, expressions and references related to the emotional sphere (Fishman 1977c:25).

On the Mexican side of the border Spanish is also highly valued for its own functional range as a language that can be used for economic, educational and political advancement throughout Mexico. The proposition that a mother tongue carries instrumental values was confirmed by Seckback and Cooper (1977), who investigated the preference of English as against Hebrew in an urban neighborhood in Jerusalem. The respondents in this study were all English-speaking immigrant women living in Israel voluntarily. The majority of the subjects displayed strong, positive attachments to their native language; they perceived English as a link to their original countries and did not wish to relinquish its use in favor of Hebrew, the official language of Israel. They were unwilling to forego English usage because this language has remained useful in their host country for economics, education and tourism.

Individuals and communities thus manifest sentimental and instrumental attachments to their native language, especially when that language is a potentially powerful unifying force for a national population (Kelman 1972:194). Border Mexicans perceive their common language as a major sentimental and instrumental link to Mexico. In the city of Juárez as well as in the rest of the country, Spanish is seen as offering advantages of different sorts. Speaking "well," knowing "correct" Spanish, and using the national language without mixture are undoubtedly effective vehicles for achieving personal, social and economic goals in Mexican society. If an individual fails to learn English but remains on the Mexican side of the border, he can work his way up by cultivating his mother tongue through formal education. Preserving the national standard code on the Mexican side of the border as it is preserved in the rest of the country may be the guarantee of unity and solidarity with the political, cultural, and economic national system. A knowledge of standard Mexican Spanish is in fact essential for the attainment of important positions in the government. Those who lack the ability to use rhetorical formal Mexican Spanish when campaigning for a public position may well be doomed to failure.

The allegiance to the language which is both the mother tongue and the national language is rooted in the sociocultural order as well as in the economic system (Williams 1979:58). This common language not only strengthens sentimental and instrumental attachments but also contributes to the reinforcement of the two processes (Kelman 1972:196). The roles that language plays in a unified national system may help explain why border Mexicans of all socioeconomic strata perceive the national standard as deserving of their loyalty and concern, at least at the attitudinal level. Moreover, border Mexicans may have a more powerful reason to claim subjective loyalty to the national language than Mexicans from the interior: they may feel more threatened by the intrusion of a foreign language in their own linguistic code and by the mixture of the mother tongue and the foreign language.

4.3. Language loyalty and national ethnocentrism

The informants surveyed for this study had the opportunity to express their feelings and opinions about their own country. The questionnaire items utilized in this survey to explore ethnocentric tendencies are based on popular and often controversial beliefs that Mexicans have about Mexico. Since the 19th century Mexicans have been concerned with freeing themselves from colonialist attitudes and external influences. They therefore believe that Mexico should be independent when making transcendental decisions in both internal affairs and foreign policy. Many Mexicans also tend to think of Mexico as the "best" country of Latin America, because it has achieved a relative political stability which protects them from a military dictatorial government. At the same time Mexicans think that Mexico has remained culturally authentic despite the proximity of the United States and that Mexico is no longer at the mercy of the United States as it was before the Revolution of 1910-21.

The common denominator of these items—which are presented in Table 4.5 in the same order as mentioned above—is the assumption that some individuals share this series of positive nationalistic concepts as a means of identifying themselves with their country. The vast majority (83%) of the informants interviewed in Juárez believe that it is important for Mexico to be an independent country; a considerable percentage (71%) perceive Mexico as the most stable country in Latin America; three out of five (59%) believe that Mexican culture has not been negatively influenced by the proximity of the United States; and almost two thirds (62%) do not accept as true that Mexico is at the mercy of the superpower. In brief, a positive affect toward Mexico was displayed by the great majority of the individuals interviewed for this study.

Table 4.5 Response Percentage: National Ethnocentrism

Items	1	2	3	4	5
1. I think that the most important thing for Mexico is to be an independent country	6	7	4	12	71
2. Mexico is not a perfect country, but it is the most stable in Latin America	7	8	14	19	52
3. The proximity of the United States has damaged Mexican culture	53	6	12	17	12
4. It is certain that Mexico is very far from Heaven and very close to the United States	49	13	15	9	11
Scale: 1=Strongly disagree; 2=Somewhat disagree; 3=Uncertain; 4=Somewhat agree; 5=Strongly agree					

Only three linguistic variables correlate weakly with national ethnocentrism: Language Loyalty ($r = .175$, $p < 4.05$), English Use ($r = .168$, $p < .05$), and Attitudes toward English ($r = .180$, $p < .05$). The first positive correlation merely suggests that a small percentage of subjects who claim high attitudinal language loyalty believe more strongly that Mexico needs to be independent, that it is in fact politically stable, and that it is free from the "damaging" American influence. The sentiments of Language Loyalty and National Ethnocentrism—discussed in section 1.3—have been explained as (1) phenomena that are not necessarily associated (Weinreich 1968; Riley 1975, 1980) or as (2) dimensions which are deeply connected in some modern states where language safeguards the values of authenticity of a speech community (Fishman 1973).

The data of this study merely suggest that Juárez may lend itself to support the second assumption. The second linguistic variable which is somewhat related to National Ethnocentrism is English Use. The negative correlation between these two dimensions means that a small percentage of individuals with low scores in English Use, have high scores in National Ethnocentrism. A low use of English—which is in turn determined by SES, Education and Formal Instruction in English—seems moderately related to ethnocentric tendencies. Likewise, poor attitudes toward English—which are in turn predicted by English Use and Local Identity—seem modestly linked to an over-evaluation of Mexico as independent, authentic and stable. These trends in the data hint that the Mexican side of the border provides the milieu where the connection between language loyalty and other linguistic and attitudinal dimensions can be more profoundly explored.

4.4. Spanish language loyalty policy in Mexico

The loyalty to the national standard language utilized in Mexico, the correctness of a number of urban varieties of Spanish spoken in the country, and the autochthonous expression of cultural values are all issues that seriously concern at present the central authorities of Mexico. This preoccupation emanates from the accelerated encroachment of the English language into the linguistic system of Mexican Spanish. According to the central government, the geographic proximity of Mexico to the United States, its position *vis-à-vis* the superpower and the intense exchange of commercial and technological transactions between the two neighbors have entailed a situation of insidious contact between Spanish and English. This continuous extensive relationship of the two countries is considered culturally and linguistically detrimental to the Mexican people (Secretaría de Educación Pública 1982:12-3).

The acceptance of English at the public level in commerce, industry, and mass media has become apparent in the past fifteen years. As a result, an official organism, the National Board for the Defense of the Spanish Language (Comisión Nacional para la Defensa del Idioma Español), emerged in the midst of intellectual laxity, spiritual indifference, and serious economic crises encompassing a number of devaluations and an exorbitant foreign debt without historical precedents. The main goal of this official organism is the protection of Spanish from the onslaught of English, inasmuch as this language has presumably deformed and derogated the national standard language (Secretaría de Educación Pública 1982:15). By utilizing language as a force in the enhancement of national loyalty, the central authorities of Mexico intend to reactivate a dormant national consciousness and infirm ethnic identity. The Intersecretarial Board for the Defense of the Spanish Language was legally established in Mexico by the Presidential Decree of August 11, 1981.

The sub-commissions of the National Board will deal with eight different language-related policies: (1) Legal matters concerning the use of the Spanish language in different public domains throughout the country. (2) Promotion of correct usage through the spoken media. (3) Elaboration of linguistic norms for the written media. The norms suggested will be based on standard Mexican Spanish. This will include a program of publications through which the general public will cultivate the standard language. (4) Advisement to users of the Spanish language in the areas of publicity and propaganda. (5) Revision of educational programs directly related to teaching the national standard language. (6) Standardization and codification of neologisms and foreign terms. Also, linguistic investigations which will promote the defense and dissemination of the national standard language. (7) Promotion of preferential use of the national language in services such as tourism. (8) Organization of local committees in those communities distinguished as "disaster" areas: (a) the three largest Mexican metropolises (Mexico City, Guadalajara and Monterrey), (b) tourist centers, and (c) border cities (Secretaría de Educación Pública 1982:15-8).

In order to achieve its goals, this recently created national board is motivating institutions and individuals who may contribute to delineate the principles for effective language planning. Since the national language policy has already been defined, language planning will be implemented in the direction of a new standard of Mexican Spanish. At present, however, the role of the government is one of creating an atmosphere favorable to changes in the direction of an acceptable standard in the fields of industry, commerce, mass media, storefront signs, and the like. In the future, language planning will focus on linguistic change, an area where judgement must be exercised in the form of choices among available linguistic forms. In spite of the fact that the main goal of this official organism is the establishment of a new normative criterion for speakers of Mexican Spanish, the Board for the Defense of the Spanish Language seems to recognize that there are powerful forces that escape governmental regulations. One of these forces is the vitality and diversity of the language spoken throughout the country, a force which is not easily counteracted in any speech community. The National Board for the Defense of the Spanish Language is thus not only laying the foundations for a new standard, but it is also intending to define the roles of the regional varieties of Mexican Spanish and the numerous indigenous languages that are still spoken throughout Mexico. Whether the effects of government planning in this field will be permanent and thoroughgoing, or only motivational as they are at present, remains to be seen[3].

4.4.1. Language Policy in Juárez

Under the general guidelines proposed by the National Board for the Defense of the Spanish Language, the municipal committees have designed the following strategies: (a) To promote the autochthonous values of the Mexican people through the standard language; (b) to create awareness about the intrinsic values of Mexican Spanish and its association with the nation's interests; and (c) to involve the active participation of community members. The immediate goal of the municipal committees is the emotional motivation and the creation of language sensitivity in the local community. Changing the language habits, language attitudes and language preferences of the target population is the long-term objective of the language policy proposed by the state. With this general outline in mind, the local authorities of Juárez have implemented several cultural programs directed toward the improvement of the spoken language. These programs are intended to educate the border residents in the appreciation of their own culture at the same time that the 'correct' standard language is utilized in the transmission of national values. The series of activities directed to the masses include the diffusion of Mexican films, Mexican books and Spanish classical theatre. In addition, a new public library has recently been built in the center of the most populous neighborhoods toward the West side of Juárez. The library has been equipped to serve principally the youngsters and the children residing in the area.

As a part of the local campaign on behalf of the standard language, language planners are utilizing the spoken and written media and the schoolteachers at the elementary, secondary and preparatory levels in order to persuade the public to prefer the standard usage of Mexican Spanish[4]. Finally, community members seem to be participating in the general endeavors to restore standard Mexican Spanish at the public level. Directors and owners of large business firms are offering material rewards to those concerned citizens who locate English words, Anglicisms or spelling mistakes in the local written media. Although the language loyalty campaign has not gained the desired momentum, individuals, private firms and educational institutions have responded positively to what is perceived as a social benefit: the protection of the national standard language.[5]

It is obvious that the state is resorting to a systematic mass persuasion effort in order to unify the Mexican people under the ideal of the national standard. In his examination of universal language contact situations, Weinreich (1968:101-2) observes that language loyalty is sometimes based on manipulation. In cases like this, language loyalty may be fostered by utilizing the standardized pure language as a symbol of group integrity (Weinreich 1968:100, 102),

> Ordinarily, it is true, when a mother-tongue community exposed to contact splits on the point of loyalty to its language, the more loyal sector will resort to exhortation of the less loyal. But occasionally, leaders with more than usual insight will attempt to enhance the language loyalty of their fellow speakers by methodic organized means.

4.4.2. Language disloyalty: A consequence of modernity?

Language problems such as the one affecting Mexico at present usually receive the attention of both linguists and nonlinguists. According to Neustupný (1974) there are two extreme approaches to language problems. The first approach is known as the policy approach, and the second one as the cultivation approach. The first treatment pattern covers problems like selection of the national language, standardization, literacy, orthography, and problems of selection of codes. The cultivation approach is characterized by interests in questions of correctness, efficiency, linguistic levels fulfilling specialized functions, problems of style and constraints on communication capacity. "While the policy approach appeals to administration, the cultivation approach addresses the public in general, and intellectuals in particular" (p. 391).

Having implemented the policy approach in the late 19th Century (cf. Heath 1972), Mexico is at present concerned with resolving its language problems through the cultivation approach. The National Board for the Defense of the Spanish Language attempts to reestablish Mexican Spanish in all commercial advertising and in the spoken language of the young people. The cultivation approach is also being implemented in order to functionally differentiate the national language, Spanish, from the foreign language, English. It is also expected that the cultivation approach will help to narrow the gap between the spoken variety and the written variety of Mexican Spanish.

Language problems and language policies can be interpreted in terms of the attitudes prevailing in the sociocultural system. According to Ryan (1981), the primary attitudinal goal of the cultivation approach is to enhance the status of a highly prestigious language or language variety in need of being enriched. "This policy is typically called for when proponents consider that their language has fallen into neglect or that it could earn greater respect from its speakers as well as from the outside world if it were more stylistically differentiated" (p. 4).

Under Ryan's interpretation of the cultivation approach and through the information provided by the Secretaría de Educación Pública, it can be inferred that the local and national authorities have taken into consideration the indifference of the general public toward the mixture of Spanish and English that is occurring throughout the country. The National Board for the Defense of the Spanish Language intends to make people aware of the excellence, expressiveness and efficiency of the national standard code. The values of the literary language therefore have to be heightened in order to prevent the decline of the national language.

Mexico's policy approach described in detailed historical perspective in the study by Heath (1972) was aimed at maintaining the various indigenous languages as vernaculars, but spreading the knowledge of Spanish as a vehicle for literacy and national integration. In broad outline, on the question of whether modern nationhood is to be established in one dominant language or in more, Mexico occupies a position somewhat intermediate between two very advanced countries; Switzerland and the United States (Pap 1979:204). In like manner, Mexico's current cultivation approach has been sketched along the lines of speech communities encountered in relatively developed countries such as Japan, where functional stratification of language varieties exists, and where problems of nonliterary style and expression come under discussion (Neustupnŷ 1972:40-4). The problem of language mixture that Mexico is currently facing is the direct result of modernity and contact with a highly developed and highly industrialized country. Mexico itself is rapidly becoming industrialized and urbanized and is therefore treating its language problems as a modern nation.

4.5. Conclusions

This chapter aimed at exploring the attitudes of Mexican residents of Juárez toward the Spanish spoken in this locality as compared to other national varieties; it also explored sentiments of language loyalty and the relationship between language loyalty and national ethnocentrism. In addition, this chapter discussed language policy in Mexico in general and in Juárez in particular from the viewpoint of the National Board for the Defense of the Spanish Language. The three most important questions addressed by this governmentally sponsored and governmentally directed organism were dealt with by this writer a few months before it was officially announced. These questions focused on attitudes toward correctness, language loyalty and national ethnocentrism.

(a) With regard to the notions of correctness, the findings of this chapter reveal that two demographic variables are the major factors accounting for negative attitudes toward the Spanish spoken in Juárez: they are Socioeconomic Status and Formal Education. In addition, the Use of English on the Mexican side of the border is an important direct contributor to negative attitudes toward local Spanish. Concerning other varieties of Spanish spoken in Mexico, educated speakers prove to distinguish and report the minor differences between the local variety, other urban varieties and the most respectable form of Mexican Spanish. The unquestionable prestige of the variety of Spanish spoken in Mexico City—which is, according to the layman and according to some linguists, equivalent to the national standard—has provoked an undervaluation of the Spanish spoken in Juárez. It was pointed out in this chapter that the negative attitudes of young, educated border residents toward the Spanish spoken in Juárez are partially the result of general attitudes and opinions toward local and regional varieties throughout the Hispanic world, and partially the effects of formal education and socioeconomic status.

In contrast, uneducated border residents prove to be "dialect-deaf" when they are questioned directly about varieties of Spanish. The majority of the informants with less than preparatory school completed claimed to perceive a uniformity of speech within Mexico. This perception is based on the fact that differences between geographical dialects are not so noticeable as to impede communication. On the whole, uneducated border Mexicans did not display concern for the issue of correctness nor were they able to judge a specific variety as being more prestigious than another. It is necessary to stress, however, that the reliability of direct items exploring language attitudes has been seriously questioned by more than one investigator. Cohen (1974) argues that "there is an inherent weakness in asking people their language attitudes directly" (p. 33), especially when the researcher wants to "derive meaningful responses about abstract notions such as 'best language variety from people with limited education and linguistic sophistication" (p. 49). Cohen found in his study among Mexican immigrants, as I found in my own, that considerable percentages of informants had to be grouped under the category "don't know." He thus proposes that in order to reduce this category among subjects with limited formal education, the researcher should utilize more dissimulative means to assess language attitudes. He puts forward for consideration the matched-guise technique, which was discussed in the first chapter of this dissertation. The findings on attitudes toward correctness among uneducated Juárez residents endorse Cohen's methodological suggestions.

(b) With respect to the inquiries on language loyalty, the results of this chapter reveal that a substantial proportion of the respondents displayed a positive attitude toward the national standard when they were questioned directly. Border Mexicans seem to be emotionally concerned with maintaining their Spanish as Mexicans from the interior do, regardless of their bilingualism. Whereas attitudinal language loyalty is very strong among the people of Juárez, their use of Spanish betrays their attitudes, inasmuch as English conspicuously intrudes in their daily informal speech in the form of brand names, business names, parts of cars and the like. The specific setting of language contact in the northern frontier of Mexico hinders all individual and social endeavors to maintain all Spanish all the time under all circumstances.

Language Loyalty appears not to be directly or indirectly connected to any demographic or linguistic dimensions utilized in this study, but exclusively to a rejection of Spanish-English code-switching. Attitudinal language loyalty twice turned out to be a predictor of negative attitudes toward the style of communication of individuals of Mexican descent living in El Paso. This chapter proposes that border Mexicans claim attachments to the national standard due to its communicative, sentimental, and instrumental values. Mexican Spanish is perceived by border Mexicans as the guarantee of linguistic and ethnic continuity with their country, at the same time that it facilitates the attainment of material goods, public positions, social prestige and upward mobility in Mexican society.

(c) This chapter also reports a very weak connection between values of language loyalty and the perception of Mexico as independent, stable and genuinely autochthonous. This weak relationship may confirm that language loyalty represents an independent subjective need for ethnic distinctiveness and not necessarily a positive nationalistic view of Mexico. This assumption might be either validated or discarded with a larger sample of subjects and with more reliable attitudinal measures.

(d) In addition to exploring attitudes toward correctness, language loyalty and national ethnocentrism, this chapter sheds light on language policy in Mexico and in Juárez, and outlines the different language-related issues that the National Board for the Defense of the Spanish Language is setting forth at present. The institutional creation of this protective program and its organization through municipal committees in cities such as Juárez supports the major assumption of this chapter: the Mexican side of the border is the locus in which there exists a great deal of preoccupation with language correctness, language loyalty and linguistic and cultural authenticity.

Footnotes

(1) The identification of features stems from extensive travel and prolonged residence in the northern area of Mexico.

(2) Impressions gained through direct observation of the community under study and through 20 hours of tape-recorded informal conversations with 11 native residents of Juárez and 8 migrants from rural and semi-rural communities in northern Mexico.

(3) Impressions gained at the Simposio sobre la política lingüística de México, sponsored by the National Board for the Defense of the Spanish Language and held in Mexico City at the Museo Nacional de Antropología e Historia on 19-21 August, 1982. The papers of the participants have been published by this organism. See Comisión Nacional para la Defensa del Idioma Español, Tomos 8, 9 and 10.

(4) Information provided by the current Mayor of Juárez in tape-recorded interview of May 26, 1982.

(5) Impressions gained through the Cd. Juárez mass media between January 1982 and January 1983.

Chapter 5

The Mexican-American Connection

The Spanish spoken in El Paso and the Spanish spoken in Juárez have common roots, Northern Mexican Spanish. This chapter stresses the point that, despite this common origin, the Spanish spoken in El Paso has evolved into a different variety, and it is viewed as such by Mexicans residing in Juárez. The major factor contributing to this radical change of El Paso Spanish has been the absence of cultural and political institutions protecting it. Although Spanish is sometimes utilized in bilingual education programs, this language is not pervasive in the domains of government or media inasmuch as English, the official language of the United States serves all these purposes. As a result, Spanish has been restricted in its communicative functions and relegated to the status of a vernacular with minimal literary and official use. The Spanish spoken by individuals of Mexican descent residing in El Paso is characterized—as pointed out in Chapter I—by a noticeable mixture with the English language. This mixture, known as Code-switching, is defined as a particular style of communication of the bilingual population in which alternating stretches of Spanish and English are utilized.

In the following sections of this chapter, I will discuss the attitudes of the eighty-five informants interviewed in Juárez toward the Mexican-American style of communication. Mexicans' judgements about Code-switching are assessed by means of two dimensions: (1) its inherent values and (2) its communicative values. The evaluation of English-Spanish Code-switching is complemented with (3) an evaluation of Mexican-American values, mores and customs. The results of this chapter are interpreted in the light of (1) general assumptions regarding judgements of inherent values of languages and language varieties, (2) general propositions about language use, language attitudes and sex, and (3) the "Theory of Speech Accommodation," a model attempting to account for certain kinds of speech diversity which occur in interpersonal encounters.

5.1. The inherent values of Spanish-English Code-switching

The items created to explore how Mexican residents of Juárez feel about the beauty, pleasantness, correctness and ethnicity of the mixed language variety spoken in El Paso are presented with the response percentages in Table 5.1. The results of Table 5.1 reveal rather clearly that this variety of Spanish is held in low esteem by most Juárez residents. This low opinion of the inherent values of the Spanish spoken in El Paso is also apparent in the spontaneous comments offered by approximately one-half of the informants. Table 5.1 shows that the majority of the subjects (82%) strongly disagreed with the statement that the Spanish spoken in El Paso is more correct than that spoken in Juárez. Judgements about correctness are based on a perceived lack of formality, on a perceived striking influence of the English language, or on a combination of these two factors. The following opinions illustrate the issue:

> *Como toda la educación es en inglés, el español se deteriora hasta que se habla muy mal, o se pierde por completo.*

En El Paso la gente no puede decir en español lo que quiere decir. Muchas veces falta el vocabulario que se aprende en la escuela.

El español de El Paso se parece al de Juárez en algunas cosas, pero en otras es totalmente distinto. La mayor diferencia es que la gente no puede terminar lo que quiere decir y tiene que meter el inglés. No puede ser correcto lo que se habla tan mezclado.

Table 5.1 Response Percentages: Inherent Values of Spanglish

Items	1	2	3	4	5
1. The Spanish spoken in El Paso is more correct than the Spanish spoken in Juárez	82	0	13	0	2
2. The Mexicans from El Paso should imitate the Mexicans from Juárez when they speak Spanish	12	14	14	11	49
3. It sounds very pretty when the Mexicans from El Paso change from English to Spanish and from Spanish to English	65	9	13	5	8
4. It bothers me when the Mexicans from El Paso speak English and Spanish at the same time	27	16	2	13	48
Scale: 1=Strongly disagree; 2=Somewhat disagree; 3=Uncertain; 4=Rather agree; 5=Strongly agree					

With respect to Item 3, almost two thirds (60%) of the informants strongly agreed or somewhat agreed that the Mexicans of El Paso should imitate the Spanish of Mexicans from Juárez. Many informants were able to externalize their feelings on this issue. The most representative judgements have to do with ethnic identity, for example:

Si los de El Paso quieren llamarse mexicanos entonces deberían de hablar como los de Juárez.

No es que los de Juárez hablen muy bien, pero hablan más como mexicanos, y por esto los de El Paso deberían imitarlos.

Los de El Paso deberían hablar como los de Juárez. Juárez es el modelo más cercano a la manera de hablar de los mexicanos.

Three fourths (74%) of the entire sample disagreed with the statement that it sounds pretty when people change from Spanish to English and from English to Spanish. Finally, almost two thirds (61%) confessed that it annoys them to hear Spanish-English Code-switching.

Those few subjects who strongly agreed, somewhat agreed with or were uncertain about Item 3 were mostly male subjects. Also, those who strongly disagreed or rather disagreed with Item 4 were predominantly male subjects.

5.1.1. Predictors of the inherent values of Spanish-English Code-switching

One demographic variable and one attitudinal variable are positively and significantly correlated with the subjective evaluation of the Spanish spoken in El Paso: Sex ($r = .334$, $p < .01$) and Language Loyalty ($r = .455$, $p < .001$). The first correlation indicates that women more than men overtly reject the mixed language variety spoken in El Paso, principally because of its perceived lack of beauty and pleasantness. The second correlation hints that those subjects (males and females) who claim a strong attitudinal loyalty to Spanish rate El Paso Spanish very poorly. The multiple regression analysis in Table 5.2 shows the percentage of variance and the regression coefficient accounting for the prediction of the inherent values of Spanish-English Code-switching. The results of Table 5.2 make it possible to argue that there exist two major reasons underlying the rejection of Code-switching. One of them, as suggest ed in Step 1, is the sex of the informant.

Table 5.2 Multiple Regression Analysis: The Inherent Values of Spanglish

Step	Variables entered in the equation	R	R^2	ΔR^2	r	F
1	Sex	0.344	0.106	0.106	0.344	16.38
2	Language Loyalty	0.605	0.366	0.232	0.455	29.78

The upbringing of an individual as either male or female seems to impinge upon his/her feelings toward the Spanish spoken in El Paso. The second reason in Step 2 is the loyalty to the national language of Mexico and the mother tongue of all the informants, which may have to do with a deep emotional involvement with Spanish or with ethnocentric tendencies. Inasmuch as Language Loyalty and Sex turn out to be the most important factors accounting for attitudes toward El Paso Spanish, the following two sections will discuss the relationship between the Inherent Values of Spanish-English Code-switching and its two predictors.

5.1.2. Language and the rejection of Spanish-English Code-Switching

The justification for the strong relationship between Language Loyalty and the rejection of the Inherent Values of Spanish-English Code-switching may reside in border residents' sentimental ties to their mother tongue, which they perceive as being menaced by the out-group, Mexican-Americans. Weinreich (1968:77-8) argues in fact that most individuals, if not all, develop a "prerational" attachment to the language of childhood, which is generally the language in which individuals receive fundamental training. These attachments make a person rationalize that his native language is richer, more subtle and more expressive than others. Language loyalty thus seems to satisfy or justify a person's feeling of self-worth and belonging. Moreover, Taylor and Simard (1975) claim that in a language contact setting this concept of language loyalty "would seem to be a specific form of ethnocentrism which is of special significance because of the fundamental and highly visible association between a group of persons and the language they speak" (p. 246). The distinct connection between language loyalty and the poor evaluation of El Paso Spanish can only be explained in terms of ethnocentric tendencies prevailing on the Mexican side of the border.

5.1.3. Sex and the rejection of Spanish-English Code-switching

The second-best predictor of attitudes towards the inherent attributes of correctness, beauty, pleasantness, and ethnicity of the Spanish spoken in El Paso is a demographic rather than an attitudinal variable. In this study, Sex is also significantly correlated with value judgements ($r = .344$, $p < .01$), and it is also a source of variance in the multiple regression analysis presented in Table 5.2. Table 5.3 reveals that both males and females display similar response patterns to Items 1 and 2. By contrast, their responses to Items 3 and 4 exhibit rather discrepant reactions. Whereas the overwhelming majority of females (88%) were unable to admit that Spanish-English Code-switching sounds pretty, barely more than half of the male informants (58%) reported a similar judgement. Furthermore, while 19% of the males acknowledged a relative aesthetic value in Spanish-English Code-switching, only 2% of the females did so. By the same token, slightly more than half of all males (54%) but less than a fifth (15%) of all females claimed not to be at all annoyed by this style of communication. In brief, it seems that while almost all women would reject Spanish-English Code-switching, only one out of two men would rate the Spanish spoken in El Paso as ugly and unpleasant.

Table 5.3 Response Percentages by Sex: The Inherent Values of Spanish-English Code-switching

Items	Female/Male	1	2	3	4	5
1. The Spanish spoken in El Paso is more correct than the Spanish spoken in Juárez	F M	75 87	18 9	5 2	0 0	1 2
2. The Mexicans from El Paso should imitate the Mexicans from Juárez when they speak Spanish	F M	10 13	15 10	17 16	10 9	48 49
3. It sounds very pretty when the Mexicans from El Paso change from English to Spanish and from Spanish to English	F M	75 51	13 7	8 20	1 6	1 13
4. It bothers me when the Mexicans from El Paso talk English and Spanish at the same time	F M	10 40	5 14	2 4	13 16	65 24
Scale: 1=Strongly disagree; 2=Somewhat disagree; 3=Uncertain; 4=Rather agree; 5=Strongly agree						

The connection between language and sex has been researched in diverse related aspects such as differences between males' and females' phonology, morphology, grammar, semantics, speech events and in general, the verbal repertoire. Sex has been proposed as one of the many social factors that impinge on language use, and therefore, a parameter that relates to a number of concrete linguistic variables (Thorne and Henley 1975:10). One stereotype with empirical support is that women's speech is more correct, more proper and more careful than the speech of men.

> The most detailed evidence that women use more correct speech forms is at the phonological level. This difference is also the best documented of all the linguistic differences between the sexes. Where there are phonological variants (e.g., -ing vs. -in; or pronunciation or absence of postvocalic -r), women, compared with men of the same social class, age and level of education, more often choose the form closer to the prestige, or correct way of talking (Thorne and Henley 1975:17).

This pattern has been found in different universal settings such as New England, New York City, Norwich (Great Britain), and Bahía Blanca (Argentina). In New England, Fischer (1958) studied the pronunciation of -*ing* verb endings in interviews with 12 boys and 12 girls. He found that a significantly greater number of girls used –*ing* more frequently. In this community -*ing* seemed to be associated with female speech and the -*in* pronunciation with male speech. In like manner, Labov (1966:288) discovered that among lower-middle class New York informants, women tend to use fewer stigmatized forms than men: women usually pronounce final *r* while men are likely to omit it; women also tend to use less frequently the voiceless stop [t] in words such as *fourth*, *think*, etc. Strikingly similar appear to be the results reported by Fontanella de Weinberg (1973), who studied the social variation of Spanish /s/ in final position. She reports that Argentinian women of diverse socioeconomic backgrounds regularly override men in the use of the prestigious pronunciation of final -s, even if they are speaking informally. On the other hand, men tend to omit final -s even when they are using their most formal speech style.

Labov (1972:301-4) also reports that whereas women use the most advanced forms in their own casual speech (raising tense short *a*), they shift their speech to the standard forms more sharply in formal settings (showing a modal value [ae]). The preference for standard linguistic forms among women is presumably due to their greater sensitivity to the so-called correct patterns. Moreover, when evaluating the prestigeless speech of New York City women tend to project overt hostility. "The terms New Yorkers apply to the speech of the city give some indication of the violence of their rejection. 'It's terrible.' 'Distorted.' 'Terribly careless.' 'Sloppy.'" (Labov 1966:499). This attitude is more typical of the women respondents; only a minority of men expressed themselves negatively about New York City speech.

In urban British English, Trudgill (1972) discovered the same type of sex differentiation. His study confirms that women use and report linguistic forms normally associated with the prestige standard more frequently than men. In exploring the reasons why women adhere more closely to prestigious speech norms, Trudgill offers several possible explanations: (1) Women are more status-conscious than men and are therefore more aware of the social significance of linguistic variables. (2) Since women are not as likely as men to be rated by their work or occupation, other signals of status such as speech become more significant. (3) Women might be more concerned with appearance than men and avoid, consequently, the "rough" language used by lower socioeconomic groups' nonstandard speech may carry connotations of masculinity

Rejection of nonstandard linguistic forms among women is obviously one of the most consistent discoveries in studies dealing with the sexual differentiation of language. These findings reveal a uniform intersection of females' speech and contexts of formality, values of social prestige, greater sensitivity to correct linguistic forms, and actual "careful" usage of language. These studies also suggest that women's linguistic behavior can be both extremely innovative and extremely conservative.

In my own study, border Mexican women displayed more categorically than males their overt rejection of the Spanish spoken in El Paso, a language variety which is not strictly tied to a fixed written standard. When expressing value judgements women utilized the same kind of supplementary remarks reported by Labov's (1966) female informants. Mexican women over-emphasized the ugliness, unpleasantness and incorrectness of the Spanish spoken in El Paso in repeated statements such as: "Se oye muy feo." "Espantoso," "Me molesta." "Me cae mal." "Nadie debería de hablar así." In contrast, most male informants did not claim feeling annoyed by constant Code-switching and did not consider this variety extremely ugly or unpleasant. The evaluation of one male informant summarizes the judgement of most males:

No me molesta que la gente cambie del inglés al español, no me suena mal, no me suena feo, pero se oye diferente.

Mexican women seem to associate the mixture of Spanish and English with the extreme informality of the language spoken in the street. Although Mexican women are normally the promoters of bilingualism in their own children, they are at the same time the guardians of purity of language. Whereas they make efforts to formally expose themselves and their children to both Spanish and English, they also tend to correct their offspring when language mixture threatens their speech. Women seem to perceive the mixture of Spanish and English as a dysfunctional, anomalous code which does not fulfill any legal, prestigious role on either side of the border.

One out of two Mexican males also perceives a linguistic discontinuity in the Spanish spoken in El Paso, but their judgements about this style of communication are more moderate than those of women. This mild subjective acceptance of language mixture has to do with the fact that male border residents have greater occupational and geographical mobility than women, and consequently they come more into contact with the Spanish spoken north of the border. Men are more likely than women to work in or to relate their work to occupational domains which do not require a great deal of formality in language, physical appearance, and behavior: construction, transportation, auto mechanics, repair and maintenance services, street sales, security services and the like, are definitely male activities in both Juárez and El Paso. On the other hand, working women are confined to the assembly line, the office, the shop, and the bank, all these locales which do demand a relatively higher degree of formality in language, physical appearance and behavior. Women are also less likely than men to emigrate to the United States when seeking new job opportunities. Sexual division of labor is thus one of the major factors accounting for language discrepancies between males and females (Thorne and Henley 1975:14).

5.1.4. The origin of linguistic value judgements

Given the sociolinguistic complexity of the border milieu, the outcomes of this investigation invariably turn out to be linked to a number of assumptions which have been researched throughout the world; the examples of diverse universal contexts discussed in this dissertation provide apparent sociolinguistic phenomena which are similar to those encountered in the border setting. Thus, based on the assumption that the Mexican side of the border resembles other language contact situations, I assume that the possible origin of the majority rejection of Spanish-English Code-switching is not incidental. What is then the source of negative judgements about the correctness, pleasantness and beauty of nonstandard languages and language varieties?

In order to demonstrate that judgements about the correctness, adequacy, and aesthetics of nonstandard languages and language varieties are equally unsound, Trudgill and Giles (1979) have critically discussed empirical sociolinguistic research carried out both under experimental conditions and in the speech community itself. In addition, the authors have developed an experiment based on the evaluation of the aesthetic merits of a number of varieties of the English language.

After interpreting the body of data that emerges from empirical studies dealing with urban dialects, Trudgill and Giles demonstrate that the true nature of value judgements is that they are not linguistic judgements but social judgements. In English, for example, multiple negation, absence of third person singular -*s*, and presence of -*s* on other grammatical persons are all widely considered to be "wrong" (p. 170). The data presented in a number of studies (e.g., Labov 1972a; Wolfram 1969) show that they are most typical of working- or lower-class speech; as a result,

> grammatical forms which are most typical of working-class dialects have low status, because of their association with groups who have low prestige in our society. This low status leads to the belief that these forms are "bad" and they are therefore judged to be "wrong." Evaluations of this type are therefore clearly social judgements about the status of speakers who use particular forms rather than objective linguistic judgements about the correctness of the forms themselves (Trudgill and Giles 1979:170).

Another area in which value judgements about language tend to be made is that of aesthetic judgements; this is so because "there is still a widespread feeling that some dialects and, in particular, some accents are much 'nicer,' 'more pleasant' or 'more beautiful' than others" (Trudgill and Giles 1979:173). The aesthetic argument is often used by those who claim that there may be nothing "wrong" about the accent, but such accent may be very "ugly" (p. 173-4). Trudgill and Giles (1979) attempt to demonstrate, too, that aesthetic judgements, just like judgements concerned with correctness, have no place in the objective evaluation of spoken language. Although there is scarce documentary evidence to state that there exist languages and varieties of languages with superior aesthetic qualities, "this is an area where many linguists are prepared, at least informally, to make as many value judgements as laymen" (p. 173-4).

In explaining the reasons for this widespread phenomenon Trudgill and Giles offer two opposing approaches. The first approach (known as the "inherent value hypothesis") "maintains that some linguistic varieties have become accepted as standards or have acquired prestige simply because they are the most attractive" (p. 174). The second view (the "imposed norm hypothesis") proposes that a dialect or accent is not elevated to a position of prestige because it is inherently the most pleasing form of that language, but because it has gained consensual validity due to cultural norms and due also to a perceived association with the status of the social group which happens to speak in that manner.

The authors argue, nonetheless, against both hypotheses. The "inherent value hypothesis" is discarded because the general public is subjected to cultural norms which are strong and pervasive. Against this hypothesis they cite nasalization, a linguistic component commonly associated with "unpleasant" Australian accents of English, but a feature of many "nice" Received Pronunciation speakers (p. 177). The competing view, although seemingly sound, is also discarded on the basis of two experiments whose purpose was to determine whether people who had virtually no knowledge of French and Greek would be able to differentiate on aesthetic and prestige dimensions, the various forms of French spoken in Quebec and two varieties of Greek spoken in Greece. The results of these two investigations indicated that the Welsh judges of the French-Canadian varieties were totally unable to distinguish them on aesthetic grounds (Giles, Bourhis and Davies, 1974). Likewise, none of the British subjects who rated the Greek dialects showed signs of agreement on the relative aesthetic merits of the two types of Greek (Giles, Bourhis, Trudgill and Lewis 1974). These two experiments nullify the "imposed norm hypothesis" because the validity of cultural norms and the prestige of a group of speakers are not universal. Additionally, both hypotheses are invalidated by another experiment involving evaluations of five accents of one language, English. The subjects, coming from diverse regions of the English-speaking world, were unable to assign uniform aesthetic and prestige merits to all the varieties because their connotations change from place to place.

Trudgill and Giles (1979) therefore propose a more flexible hypothesis accounting for the relativity of linguistic value judgements: "…aesthetic judgements of linguistic varieties are the result of a complex of *social connotations* that these varieties have for particular listeners…"Connotations of this type are by no means only a question of prestige or lack of it, and, crucially, they can and do vary within cultures" (p. 180). This "hypothesis of social consnotations" may account for the relationship between the aesthetic merits of different languages and the connotations that they evoke in the minds of members of a particular group. Under this conceptual framework, if social connotations of a language variety are not known to an individual, he will not be capable of ranking it aesthetically relative to other varieties. "Aesthetic judgements about language, that is, are just as much social judgements as those concerned with correctness" (p. 181).

The "hypothesis of social connotations" would thus make clear that Mexicans' evaluations of Spanish-English Code-switching are not accidental, but rather the result of a complex of social, cultural and ethnic associations between the language and its speakers; Mexican nationals relate the variety of Spanish spoken in El Paso with the status of Mexican immigrants residing in the United States. The general belief prevailing in Mexico since the late 19th century when masses of Mexicans emigrated to the United States, is that emigration North of the border is a denigrating process which involves not only economic exploitation but also the loss of the national language and cultural values. Thus, when Mexicans evaluate the variety of Spanish spoken by their countrymen in the United States, they partially base their judgements on the latter's low socioethnic status.

The hypothesis of "social connotations" would also make clear why many attitudes and beliefs held in Mexico regarding the use of Spanish-English Code-switching in the United States are also encountered in Mexican-American communities. In East Austin (Texas), Elías-Olivares (1976) conducted a study for which ninety-three persons of different ages and occupations were interviewed and data elicited on varied issues. The investigator was able to detect negative attitudes toward the mixture of Spanish and English. Some members of this community, including teachers, described "good Spanish" as the avoidance of Anglicisms, and believed that those who code-switch between Spanish and English speak *mocho, revuelto*—a cut-off, mutilated kind of Spanish (p. 152).

The same adjective *mocho* ("incomplete") was utilized by many of my own informants from Juárez belonging to the lower-middle and the lower-working class. With the word *mocho* they wanted to express the idea that Mexicans residing in El Paso typically do not finish their utterances when they speak in Spanish. Not only the Spanish spoken in El Paso, but the Spanish spoken in the American Southwest in general, is perceived as lacking native-like fluency and articulateness.

Most Mexicans are aware that a difference exists between their own speech and that of Mexicans residing in the United States. A few of my informants claimed that Mexicans in the United States evidently go through a personal struggle when they try to communicate entirely in Spanish. Some opinions illustrate the issue:

> *La gente de allá batalla mucho para hablar el español, o no puede terminar lo que quiere decir, o lo dice todo **revuelto**.*

> *Se les hace difícil hablar el español, sobre todo cuando nacen allá, o cuando se van desde niños.*

> *Los adultos nunca pierden el español, pero a los niños y a los jóvenes se les dificulta hablarlo o lo hablan **mocho**.*

Due to the cultural pressures exerted in both Mexico and the United States against Mexican-Americans, many of them have lost confidence in their own native abilities; this insecurity stands out when they involve themselves in verbal exchange with Mexican nationals. Elias-Olivares' (1976) older informants expressed their feelings of discomfort when talking to people from Mexico, who speak, according to them, a "better," more "formal," more "perfect" Spanish (p. 152). Not all Mexicans overlook, however, the complex nature of individual attitudes and feelings involved in verbal interplay. There are a few who claim to adjust their speech in order to accommodate to Mexican-Americans' Spanish. This is the opinion of a merchant working in the market place:

> *Yo hablo muy rápido, como hablamos nosotros aquí, pero si me doy cuenta de que los de El Paso no me entienden, entonces les hablo despacio, o trato de usar las palabras que ellos usan.*

Although there may be occasional individual acceptance of Mexican-Americans' speech style, still, the majority of the people south of the border deprecate the mixture of Spanish and English. This variety of Spanish spoken in the American Southwest may draw forth not only one particular reaction, but a multiplicity of biased meanings which are conveyed through values of correctness, beauty, pleasantness and ethnicity. These reactions are the result—as pointed out by the proponents of the "hypothesis of social connotations"—"of a complex of social, cultural, regional, political and personal associations and prejudices" (Trudgill and Giles, p. 187). This statement is corroborated by Peñalosa (1980): "Attitudes toward code switching are undoubtedly influenced by one's attitudes toward the sociocultural position and political economic deprivation of the Chicano population" (p. 185). I would venture to conclude in this section that the community that I have investigated is not at all unique in its appreciation of the variety of Spanish spoken in El Paso or in the American Southwest in general. The belief that Mexicans residing in the United States are no longer part of the Mexican mainstream is widespread throughout the country, and its beginnings must be traced to the mid-19th century when Mexico lost in war the Southwestern states that now belong to the United States.

5.2 The communicative values of Spanglish

The second set of items was created in order to explore how Mexicans feel about communicating with Mexican-Americans in the El Paso setting, and how they may react to the use of Spanish-English Code-switching. The items and the results are presented in Table 5.4. This table shows that slightly more than two thirds (69%) of the informants strongly agreed or somewhat agreed with Items 1 and 2. This majority of subjects reported that Mexican-Americans can actually speak Spanish, but that they refuse to use it or pretend to ignore it. On the other hand, only one out of five subjects indicated that Mexicans residing in El Paso do not have any knowledge of Spanish. Items 3 and 4 show that about one half of all the informants claimed not to understand Mexican-Americans when they switch continuously. Presented in an impersonal phrasing, these two items served to draw out a number of unsolicited comments regarding communication difficulties which were attributed to the "unexpected" change from one language to the other.

Several significant correlations with other variables help explain the reasons for some negative reactions toward the mixed language variety spoken in El Paso (see Table 5.5). Attitudes toward the Communicative Values of the Spanish spoken in El Paso is significantly correlated with English Use ($r = -.328$, $p < .01$). This negative correlation suggests that those with low scores in English Use tend to reject the Spanish spoken in El Paso because they do not understand Code-switching as well as those who have high scores. The Communicative Value of Spanglish is also correlated with Language Loyalty ($r = .400$, $p < .001$). This second correlation suggests that those who believe that the Spanish in Juárez has been maintained and should be maintained without the mixture of English also reject the variety of Spanish spoken in El Paso. A third correlation with the Inherent Values of Spanglish ($r = .386$, $p < .001$) hints that attitudes toward Code-switching are not only based on a limited knowledge of English and on Mexicans' attachment to their mother tongue, but also on considerations of a more subjective nature (see 5.1.4). The multiple regression analysis shows that English Use accounts for almost 11% of the total variance, Language Loyalty accounts for 13%, and the Inherent Values of Spanglish accounts for 6%. The three variables in combination make a multiple regression coefficient of almost 0.55. Table 5.5 presents the steps and the analysis.

Table 5.4 Response Percentages: The Communicative Values of Spanglish

Items	1	2	3	4	5
1. Those Mexicans who emigrate to El Paso never forget their language	40	29	9	14	7
2. Mexicans from Juárez do not really need to know English since they can communicate in Spanish with Mexicans from El Paso	61	8	9	14	7
3. It is impossible to understand what Mexicans from El Paso say when they mix the two languages	24	29	8	15	22
4. One can mix the two languages—English and Spanish—as the Mexicans of El Paso do, and still understand what people say	21	22	11	20	22
Scale: 1=Strongly disagree; 2=Rather disagree; 3=Uncertain; 4=Somewhat agree; 5=Strongly agree					

Table 5.5 Multiple Regression Analysis: The Communicative Values of Spanglish

Step	Variables entered in the equation	R	R^2	ΔR^2	r	F
1	Sex	0.328	0.107	-0.107	-0.328	10.33
2	Language Loyalty	0.488	0.239	0.131	0.400	4.97
3	Inherent Values of Spanglish	0.549	0.301	0.062	0.386	7.25

5.2.1. English as a barrier to communication

Actual problems of communication at the level of interpersonal relationships may arise in the El Paso area depending on the setting, the person spoken to and the code selected for communication. Most Mexicans from the Mexican side of the border would expect Mexicans from the American side to speak in Spanish, since they believe that Mexican-Americans have not lost the language of their ancestors. These expectations are sometimes contradicted by the facts, since many second and third-generation Mexican-Americans are not as fluent in Spanish as recent immigrants or Mexican nationals. Encounters of all types occur in this area between Mexican nationals, recent immigrants residing in El Paso, and Mexican-Americans. All these groups appear ethnically homogeneous, but they are in fact linguistically heterogeneous, varying along a continuum from predominantly monolingual in Spanish to predominantly monolingual in English. Interaction between these groups takes place in Spanish, in English, or in the mixture of both.

These linguistic differences, however, are not entirely acknowledged by many Mexican residents of Juárez, who tend to approach any "Mexican-looking" person in Spanish, expecting him/her to respond in Spanish also. Mexican-Americans, on the other hand, tend to make the same "mistake," that is, they also fail to notice that not all Mexicans in the El Paso area are fluently bilingual and competent code-switchers. Reactions and attitudes of all sorts may ensue if the language the individuals anticipate is not reciprocated in the encounter. When individuals know each other the process of communication is ameliorated, but when fortuitous, unexpected encounters occur, Mexicans and Mexican-Americans tend to dissociate from each other.

The "Theory of Speech Accommodation" proposed by Giles et al. (1977) may help explain the attitudes of Mexicans toward the mixture of Spanish and English. This theory proposes that

> the extent to which individuals shift their speech style toward, or away from the speech style of their interlocutors is a mechanism by which social approval or disapproval is communicated. A shift in speech style toward that of another is termed convergence, whereas a shift away from the other's styles represents divergence (p. 322).

Under this framework and taking into account the various degrees of bilingualism of the entire population of Mexican origin inhabiting the area, I will endeavor to describe the obstacles that Mexicans and Mexican-Americans encounter when they engage in verbal interplay. One of the most obvious impediments is the use of continuous Spanish-English Code-switching by groups of native code-switchers who tend to maintain their code assuming that everyone else code-switches. This speech style often irritates predominantly monolingual individuals who fail to understand the part of the messages transmitted in English. Furthermore, a good proportion of the Juárez residents claimed that Mexican-Americans do not make any distinctions between Mexicans who know English and Mexicans who ignore it. Failures in communication between groups are perceived as originating from Mexicans' limited abilities in English, or from Mexican-Americans' limited abilities in Spanish. The most common opinions were expressed in the following statements:

> *No todo se entiende. Muchas veces hay que adivinar lo que la gente quiere decir cuando mezcla los dos idiomas.*

> *A veces ellos no nos entienden a nosotros. Hay que decir las cosas de varias maneras, y cuando uno no sabe inglés hay que darle muchas vueltas en español.*

Other informants believe that Mexican-Americans do know Spanish but refuse to use it because they feel ashamed of it, as stated in the following comment:

> *A nadie se le olvida el idioma de sus padres. La gente no habla porque no quiere o porque le da vergüenza.*

The truth is that Mexican-Americans find themselves in a conflict when selecting their codes. Elias-Olivares1 (1976) informants expressed their concerns about the issue emphasizing that they speak English because they do not want to give the impression that they are ignorant of this language, and they also speak Spanish because they do not want to be identified as too Americanized (p. 21).

Mexicans react negatively toward Code-switching because they are predominantly monolingual, and as such, they are unable to code-switch. Even in a city like Juárez where English is available in many different ways, the opportunities to become fluently bilingual are limited, and the great majority of the residents of this border community are monolingual or possess limited registers of English. The population with an active/productive knowledge of English is a minority. Moreover, those who claim to be fluently bilingual find it hard, if not impossible, to switch to English and switch back to Spanish. Barriers to cross-cultural communication may reside in the discrepant processes of language acquisition since Mexicans learn English as a foreign language whereas Mexican-Americans learn both languages in a bilingual environment. Elias-Olivares (1976) also makes this distinction stressing the point that bilingual Mexicans lack the sociolinguistic competence in Code-switching. As a result, many of these individuals are unable to participate in conversations where Spanish-English Code-switching is utilized (p. 21).

Those individuals from Juárez who claimed to be highly bilingual—the Good or Excellent type described in Chapter 3—reported that they switch codes in a distinct way. The opinion of one informant with secondary education entirely in English and formal knowledge of several other languages describes very accurately the difference between the Mexican and the Mexican-American types of switching:

> *En El Paso la gente cambia del español al inglés y del inglés al español en la misma oración. En Juárez cambiamos cuando terminamos la oración en uno de los dos idiomas.*

The same insightful subject also pointed out the differences of social functions of Code-switching:

> *En El Paso los mexicanos hablan los dos idiomas entre ellos mismos. Nosotros hablamos español con los mexicanos e inglés con los americanos.*

This natural linguist also added that bilingual Mexicans learn English through constant translation from the mother tongue, whereas Mexican-Americans learn it through both formal and informal exposure in the environment where the language is spoken by native speakers. The differences in bilingualism between the two groups are manifold: Mexicans make intersentential switches whereas Mexican-Americans make intrasentential switches. Mexicans use English with native speakers of this language whereas Mexican-Americans use it for intragroup communication. Mexicans typically learn English at school whereas Mexican-Americans may be native speakers of English. These and other differences are in operation when Mexicans and Mexican-Americans communicate with each other, and under certain circumstances, bilingual Mexicans find themselves speaking only Spanish to competent code-switchers. Inasmuch as they understand the messages uttered in English, they report minor difficulties of communication with Mexican-Americans. Bilingual individuals also report, however, that they can switch continuously when they feel the pressures of their interlocutors. Under these conditions many bilinguals would unwillingly and grudgingly make intersentential switches. It thus seems that in addition to a lack of competence in Code-switching, most bilinguals from the Mexican side of the border do not switch because they do not want to switch. Most of the highly bilingual subjects—the Good or Excellent type—claim to prefer the use of Spanish with Mexican-Americans, even if Mexican-Americans respond in English or in Code-switching. The five students from The University of Texas at El Paso report that their communication around this campus takes place in Spanish, in English, or in the mixture of both, being themselves the speakers who maintain only-Spanish speech style, whereas their Mexican-American peers address them in English or in Code-switching.

The reports provided by the bilingual informants lead me to assume that those Mexicans who are proficient in English adopt one of the two following verbal strategies: (1) They switch their only-Spanish style to Spanish-English intersentential code-switching, showing an attitude of convergence. This form of behavior was reported as a rare instance of interpersonal pressure. (2) They maintain their only-Spanish speech style and respond to messages in English or in Code-switching in their own style. This form of behavior was the most commonly reported by bilinguals. This would be a typical example of no accommodation.

Monolingual individuals from Juárez claimed, on the other hand, to feel annoyed and sometimes abused by the use of continuous Spanish-English Code-switching. Inasmuch as they realize that part of the messages are in Spanish words, and inasmuch as they are unable to understand entirely the messages transmitted in English, they feel that Mexican-Americans do know Spanish but fail to use only-Spanish speech style for diverse attitudinal reasons (e.g., because they do not like people from Mexico, or because they want to boast that they speak English, etc.). Monolingual individuals are therefore more likely to feel disoriented and dissociated from speakers of Code-switching in the context of El Paso. They report major difficulties of communication which could be categorized as cases of divergence.

5.2.2 Language loyalty: a predictor of communicative values of Spanglish

Not only English Use but also Language Loyalty intervenes in the prediction of the Communicative Values of Spanglish (see Table 5.5). The relationship between the latter two variables can be explained in terms of ethnic identity. When Mexican-Americans code-switch continuously, Mexicans tend to remain aloof. If, on the other hand, Mexican-Americans show that they can maintain the only-Spanish style to which the Mexicans claim to feel strongly adhered, the latter may readily identify with the former. There is, in fact, evidence from various sources that language is one of the fundamental components of identity, and that individuals tend to identify with those who speak the same language rather than with those who share the same cultural background. This is the case of French-Canadian subjects who perceive French-Canadians speaking English as highly dissimilar (Taylor, Bassili and Aboud 1973:191) and that of monolingual English Welshmen who feel closer to English-only speakers of Welsh origin but psychologically removed from those who speak only Welsh (Giles, Taylor and Bourhis 1974). These examples add support to my own assumption that Mexicans do not identify with Mexican-Americans because of their common cultural heritage but because they may share a common language.

Other studies have been carried on in the same cultural settings mentioned above in order to investigate listener's reactions to different types of shifts in speech style (Bourhis, Giles and Lambert 1975). The first of the two experiments conducted by Bourhis and associates was so designed that French-Canadian subjects would hear a speaker of formal Canadian French style accommodating to a speaker of European French by either switching from his formal Canadian French to European French (upward convergence), by switching from his formal Canadian French to popular French (downward divergence), or by showing no accommodation. The purpose of the second study was to investigate the listener's evaluative reactions to similar types of accent change in the context of Britain. The South Welsh accent was the regional variety of English chosen for empirical investigation since a broadening of Welsh accent in English can be taken as a reflection of an individual's desire to emphasize his national identity. In the second study South Welsh listeners heard a mild Welsh accented speaker accommodating to a speaker of standard accent or Received Pronunciation by switching to this prestigious variety (upward convergence), by switching to a broader Welsh accent (downward divergence), or by showing no accommodation (i.e., making no change from a mild Welsh accent).

It was found in both Canada and Britain that upward convergence was associated with an increase in perceived intelligence by listeners. Although cross-national consistency is apparent in that upward convergence is associated with increased intelligence in both cultures, in Britain a speaker adopting a standard speech style will, in addition, be perceived as less trustworthy and kind than someone who maintains his own speech style. If a speaker in the Britain setting emphasizes his identity with a member of the out-group (by means of downward divergence), he will be perceived as more trustworthy and kinder than had he just maintained his identity through speech (i.e., used his mild Welsh accent). Apparently in Wales, a broad accent may be perfectly acceptable as a medium for expressing one's national identity. This is not the case, however, among people in Quebec.

These two studies looked into the social consequences that follow when a speaker accommodates or fails to accommodate his speech style with reference to his interlocutor. In applying these propositions to the El Paso-Juárez setting I assume that Mexicans fail to switch from Spanish to English and vice versa (even when they are in fact bilingual), because Code-switching is not the speech style which reflects social status, or intelligence, or any other positive moral trait. On the contrary, they consider that adopting such speech style when involved in verbal interplay with Mexican-Americans downgrades their own language. At the same time, Mexicans perceive that Mexican-Americans do not accommodate to only-Spanish speech style because they do not do not identify with it. In sum, there seems to be more of a dissociative motivation and behavior between Mexicans and Mexican-Americans. According to Bourhis, Giles and Lambert (1974), speech divergence is adopted when the speaker wishes to emphasize his group identity or when he disapproves of his listener for attitudinal-personality reasons (p. 57). The assumption that Mexicans and Mexican-Americans tend to dissociate from each other finds corroboration in the fact that Spanish-English Code-switching is not simply another code among the many that Mexican-Americans have available in their repertoire, but the code through which they manifest their in-group membership (Gumperz and Hernández-Chávez 1975; Elias-Olivares 1976; Huerta 1978). Thus, language divergence between both groups may well be related to a desire of expressing their own authenticities and loyalties. Furthermore, ethnic affiliation may be important for both groups, as they constantly interact with each other and may consider the "other" group a relevant out-group from which they both want to distinguish themselves. Under these circumstances, it has been argued, members of contrasting ethnic groups may accentuate the values of ethnic distinctiveness and use them in an attempt to maximize their differences (Giles 1979).

The literature on Code-switching reports, nevertheless, that native code-switchers select one code influenced by the particular proficiency of their interlocutors (Valdés-Fallis 1976; Poplack 1981), and that they are in fact, capable of sustaining long and rather elaborate conversations without switching to English. The case studies reported by Valdés-Fallis and Poplack are based, however, on one highly proficient bilingual individual. The question that sociolinguists have not answered is: Are all Spanish-English bilinguals capable of sustaining long and complex conversations in only one language?

From the point of view of the layman, this form of verbal behavior—sustaining long conversations in one language—is rather difficult, if not impossible, in a community like El Paso where the essence of bilingualism is precisely manifested through continuous Code-switching (Huerta-Macías 1981). Thus, whereas Mexican-Americans attempt to maintain the ancestral tongue by utilizing Code-switching as *one* single language, Mexicans perceive it as alternating performances in *two* languages. Mexicans seem to react negatively towards Mexican-Americans' code because they do not clearly understand why and how Code-switching takes place.

In the previous sections it has been pointed out that attitudes toward Spanish-English Code-switching are based on both subjective biased judgements of a rather complex nature and objective obstacles such as the limitations of Mexicans in their bilingual competence. Paradoxically, the overall evaluation of Mexican-Americans did not turn out to be related, in this study, to the evaluation of Spanish-English Code-switching. This does not mean, however, that such relationship does not exist. On the contrary, Mexican judgements regarding Code-switching and the assumptions drawn from diverse studies dealing with the evaluation of nonstandard language varieties provide the data to assert that the association between a group of people and the language they speak is apparent.

5.3. Beliefs about Mexican-Americans

Four questionnaire items focus on the process of de-ethnification which supposedly affects Mexican-Americans when they cross the border and become immersed in the American way-of-life. The items and the results are presented in Table 5.6. Table 5.6 shows that nearly two thirds (63%) of the eighty-five informants strongly agree that Mexican children brought up in the United States run the risk of forgetting their ancestry. With respect to Item 2, the opinions are equally divided between agreement (44%) and disagreement (46%). Similarly, almost half of the sample (49%) disagree that Mexican-American children feel proud of being Mexicans, and another third (32%) was uncertain about this issue; only one out of five persons felt that Mexican-American children are proud of their Mexican heritage. Somewhat less harsh opinions were expressed on Item 4 which explores Mexican-Americans' utilitarianism. Though more than half of the subjects (56%) disagree with the statement proposing that Mexicans residing in the United States only think of money while forgetting other values, fully a third of the respondents were willing to express agreement with this statement.

Table 5.6 Response Percentages: Beliefs about Mexican-Americans

Items	1	2	3	4	5
1. If Mexican-American children learn English in early childhood, they run the risk of forgetting they are Mexicans	43	20	12	11	14
2. When Mexicans emigrate to the United States, they lose Mexican customs and values	19	25	11	15	31
3. The children of Mexican parents who emigrated to the United States feel proud of being Mexicans	12	9	32	28	21
4. When Mexicans emigrate to the United States they forget Mexico and only think of money	13	21	11	25	31
Scale: 1=Strongly agree; 2=Somewhat agree; 3=Uncertain; 4=Rather disagree; 5=Strongly disagree					

The subjects who evaluated Mexican-Americans more positively are those who belong to the upper and middle social strata and those who have more years of formal education. The stereotypes of Mexican-Americans are positively correlated with SES ($r = .381$, $p < .001$), Formal Exposure to English ($r = .279$, $p < .025$) and Education ($r = .184$, $p < .05$). In general, these subjects analyzed the statements, and concluded that Mexican culture has not disappeared in the United States thanks to those Mexican-Americans who constantly travel between the two countries. Educated Mexicans were able to observe that Mexican-Americans have maintained, to a certain extent, some moral and cultural traits characteristic of their own culture: food, music, family structure, religious and national festivities were frequently pointed out.

Educated middle-class informants do not consider utilitarianism a negative moral trait but justify their countrymen in the United States for pursuing material success and upward mobility in American society. Dramatically contrasting are the opinions of a handful of outspoken lower-working class informants who were able to externalize a variety of conflicts between themselves and Mexican-Americans. Item 4 in Table 5.6 worked as an effective elicitor of one common stereotype among factory workers. This segment of the population openly verbalized their resentment against relatively successful Mexican-Americans, who, according to them, feel superior to poor Mexicans coming from Mexico. These informants had had contact with Mexicans residing in the United States while working in this country legally or illegally.

Similar evaluations have been detected among 360 assembly plant workers interviewed by Castellanos (1981). This researcher explores more deeply the conflicting relations of legal and illegal temporary Mexican workers in the United States and well-established Mexican-Americans. Mexican workers seem to perceive Mexican-Americans as highly ethnocentric, arrogant and conceited (Castellanos 1981:210-12). Though in a lesser degree, feelings of solidarity and comradeship are also displayed toward Mexican-American workers (Castellanos 1981:212).

On the whole, when judging outsiders, be it Americans or Mexican-Americans, Juárez residents are divided into two major groups: upper and middle class versus lower-working and lower-class individuals. The latter group seems to have more reasons to convey resentment, anger or dissatisfaction against outsiders, since they have been systematically exposed to economic exploitation in both Mexico and the United States. The judgements about Mexican-Americans are insignificantly correlated with the Inherent Values of Spanglish ($r = .004$) and with the Communicative Values of Spanglish ($r = .032$). These results do not necessarily indicate that the values of Spanglish are disconnected from the group of people who speak it. Spanglish has not acquired the same neutral status as English; on the contrary, it has gained a negative reputation due to the multiplicity of adverse connotations associated with this variety. The absence of a relationship between the Values of Spanglish and Beliefs about Mexican-Americans is, however, consistent with the finding of Section 3.8 focusing on the connection between Attitudes toward English and Beliefs about Americans.

This writer must also report that whereas a good number of the subjects were able and willing to externalize their fixed opinions about the variety of Spanish spoken in El Paso, they were at the same time reluctant to comment negatively about the speakers of the language. These inhibitions might have to do with the fact that a significant proportion of the Juárez residents have close relatives in El Paso (e.g., parents, children, brothers, sisters), and may therefore feel inadequate making judgements about Mexican-Americans.

5.4. Conclusions

The main purpose of this chapter was to show that the variety of Spanish spoken in El Paso is perceived by Mexicans from the Mexican side of the border as a code which does not carry the values of status and solidarity discussed at the onset of this dissertation. The values of the Spanish spoken north of the border were explored bi-dimensionally: (1) through direct questionnaire items focusing on inherent attributes assigned to languages and language varieties, and through questions addressing its communicative values in the El Paso-Juárez area. In this chapter I have dwelt on the attitudinal rejection of Spanglish, alluded to general beliefs on inherent values of languages, and, as a case in point, singled out the demographic and linguistic dimensions that impinge on such rejection.

(a) One demographic and one attitudinal dimension turned out to be the best predictors of attitudes toward the inherent attributes of Spanglish: Sex and Language Loyalty. In the first sections of this chapter it has been highlighted (1) that language loyalty is a deeply ingrained sentiment which impedes individuals from appreciating other linguistic codes; (2) that the social norms and cultural pressures governing general attitudes toward languages in both the United States and Mexico may explain the disparagement of Spanglish on the Mexican side of the border; and (3) that the negative attitudes of Mexican women towards the variety of Spanish spoken in El Paso seem to conform to the conventional linguistic behavior of females reported in diverse universal settings.

(b) Language Loyalty, together with the Use of English and the Inherent Values of Spanglish, turned out to be the best predictors of attitudes toward the Communicative Values of this mixed language variety. It has been illustrated that in the El Paso context Mexicans find linguistic and attitudinal conflicts which hamper verbal communication at the level of interpersonal relationships. Differences in bilingualism and in bilingual competence have been accentuated in order to exemplify the dynamics of intergroup and interethnic relations in the El Paso setting. The use of English has been considered as one of the most significant contributors to the reported difficulties of communication between Mexicans and Mexican-Americans. Language loyalty on the part of both groups has been equated to ethnocentric attitudes. Ethnocentric attitudes are in turn considered partially responsible for failures in convergence between ethnic groups. Following the "Theory of Speech Accommodation," several hypotheses have been proposed; (1) Bilingual Mexicans may adopt a series of speech strategies when involved in verbal interplay with Mexican-Americans: (a) divergence, (b) convergence, and (c) no accommodation. (2) Predominantly monolingual subjects and subjects who report high attitudinal language loyalty tend to adopt a strategy of divergence, emphasizing with this attitude their desires to distinguish themselves from the out-group, Mexican-Americans.

(c) In the Juárez setting, beliefs about outsiders seem to be determined by demographic factors rather than by attitudes toward the language spoken by other groups. The results of section 5.3 in conjunction with the results of Chapter 3 (section 3.8) suggest that two major social groups emerge in the evaluation of Mexican-Americans (and Anglo-Americans): upper-and middle-class individuals and lower-working and lower-lower class subjects. The reactions of the latter group reflect economic as well as ethnic conflicts of a very complex nature.

Chapter 6

Conclusions

In studying the sociolinguistic setting of the Mexican border, the crucial task of this investigator was to determine which sociodemographic factors would account for the use of language and for attitudes toward the three codes spoken in the Juárez-El Paso metropolitan complex, and which interrelationships between those factors and language use and language attitudes would be relevant for the population under study. In order to investigate these two issues, this writer posited a number of assumptions based on sociolinguistic and language attitude theory. The research embodied in the present study leads to the conclusion that the city of Juárez proved to be a highly appropriate location for testing the majority of my initial assumptions.

6.1. Assumptions about language

(a) The original proposition of section 1.6 about the functions of English in Juárez was demonstrated in this study. The data reveal that Juárez residents tend to use this other language of wider communication in certain domains associated with the Anglo-American culture. Furthermore, specific areas within the city have been signaled as representative of diglossic phenomena, making it possible to argue that there exist in fact different functions of the foreign language, English, as opposed to the native language, Spanish. Similarly, border residents tend to regularly use the spoken and written media originating in the United States; this usage pattern seems to be conditioned by the environment rather than by the preferential selection of the American means of communication. This study demonstrates that the vast majority of the population of Juárez have access to at least one form of informal contact with the English language (e.g., radio). In addition, this study shows that the use of English on the Mexican side of the border is predicted by the socioeconomic and socioeducational background of the individuals. The distinction between Informal Language Experience and Formal Language Training turns out to be relevant for Juárez residents since both types of exposure have direct effects on language attitudes, as suggested by Gardner's model discussed in section 1.1.2. Formal Instruction in English predicts the use of that language as seen in the solid lines joining variables A and B and E in Figure 1. Thus, those individuals who use English more systematically tend to be the ones who are able to learn it in formal contexts in either Mexico or the United States.

The assumption, originally proposed in section 1.1.2, that the use of English on the Mexican side of the border would be an effective moderator of attitudes toward the three codes spoken in the area was demonstrated by the fact that English Use is one of the best predictors of Attitudes toward English, one of the best single predictors of attitudes toward the Communicative Values of Spanglish, and one factor that is significantly correlated with attitudes toward the correctness of Local versus National Spanish. (See Figure 1, the relationships of Variable E with Variables H, J and I.). In the milieu of Juárez, English is thus the most powerful sociolinguistic dimension impinging upon the language preferences of the border residents.

(b) Although this study was not intended to profoundly examine the use of Spanish by Juárez residents, in the course of the interviews, certain usage patterns became apparent.

For example, the quantitative data about English Use, especially those reported by individuals who *never* or only *sporadically* use English, provide indirect evidence of the pervasiveness of Spanish. In addition, the reports of the subjects interviewed in Juárez reveal that the proximity and vitality of both English and Spanglish have had an immeasurable repercussion on the use of Spanish. This language contact situation has affected the use of the mother tongue in such a way that native speakers of Spanish abstain from conspicuous switches to the outsiders' code, English, especially in interaction with members of the in-group. The language reports of the subjects also show that whereas in the city of Juárez, the majority of the people tend to display a relatively strong behavioral commitment to the national language, Spanish, in the context of El Paso, they claim to engage themselves in different styles of communication. When interacting with Mexican-Americans, Mexicans report: (1) switching intersententially between Spanish and English; (2) responding to messages in English or in Code-switching in their only-Spanish style; (3) withdrawing from verbal interplay when they do not understand English or Code-switching.

6.2. Assumptions about the relationship between attitudes and behavior

The findings on the relationship between language attitudes and behavior toward language question the proposition of section 1.5 that the two dimensions are imperfectly related to each other. This dissertation has in fact demonstrated that the Use of English in the milieu of the Mexican border is one of the best single predictors of Attitudes toward English, as shown in Figure 1 in the solid lines joining Variables E and H. It is thus proposed that there might be only one possible causal relationship between attitudes and use. Those who have learned English are capable of using it; those who use English regularly display stronger instrumental and integrative attitudes toward this language of wider communication. Again, it seems that the local environment fosters an active use of the English language. Liking the language is therefore the result of this active/productive use; using the language is the result of having learned it. Speculatively speaking, the process may also be reversed to hypothesize that a failure in learning English might well impede the active use of this language, and this limitation might engender negative attitudes toward the language.

6.3. Assumptions about language attitudes

(a) The close relationship between Attitudes toward English and self-reported use of the language is supported by another attitudinal dimension: Local Identity. In this study, Local Identity turns out as strong as English Use in the prediction of Attitudes toward English, as seen in Figure 1, Variables E, G and H. Positive judgements about the language spoken in the United States—be it instrumental or integrative—seem to be founded not only on frequency of usage, but also on diverse sociopsychological factors such as the adjustment to the local lifestyle, acceptance of the proximity of the United States, appreciation of the city for its mixed culture, and a positive identity as a border inhabitant. It thus seems that the local milieu furnishes the cultural beliefs which affect language attitudes, as proposed by Gardner's model in section 1.1.2. When migrants from Mexico's interior or native border residents perceive the border as an advantageous place to reside—economically or otherwise, they develop, as a result, good attitudes towards the foreign language with which the community is in close contact. The opposite may also be inferred: if migrants or native border residents happen to feel aversion to the border and its concomitants, they are more likely to reject the English language.

An additional assumption about Attitudes toward English, posited in section 1.1.2, is that Mexican residents of Juárez would claim to learn English due mainly to the unquestionable values of this language in the job market. Such an instrumental motivation was not validated in this study. Similarly, the methodology employed in this investigation failed to draw out strong integrative attitudes toward English. Finally, the appreciation for representative members of the only-English speaking community turns out to be irrelevant to attitudes toward English. All in all, the members of the community interviewed by this researcher did not display unfavorable sentiments towards the foreign language spoken in the immediate vicinity.

The positive evaluation of English emanates from its own role *vis-à-vis* Spanish. English remains a foreign, additional language which is not by any means imposed on the collectivity or on the individuals. The mandatory courses of English as a Foreign Language offered in Mexican schools are merely one of the many subjects required by the curriculum, and it is very unlikely that border residents would perceive them as a cultural imposition. In the Juárez setting, English stands close enough to be learned or acquired but distant enough to be liked or enjoyed by most border residents.

(b) The assumption of section 1.2 that prestigious, superimposed language varieties tend to be perceived as possessing superior qualities when compared to language varieties which did not evolve in centers of political and economic power was verified in this dissertation. Socioeconomic Status and Education turned out to be the best predictors of attitudes toward the local variety of Spanish versus the "official" variety, as seen in Figure 1, Variables B, C and I. In the present study, I have primarily documented the perceptions of educated middle class informants: about three fourths of them tend to believe that their own colloquial variety lacks the inherent values of correctness by virtue of the fact that it does not conform to the rules of the literary version of Spanish, to the rules of the version of Spanish spoken in the capital of Mexico, or to the rules of the most formal version of Spanish utilized in Juárez (e.g., the Spanish of the school or the Spanish of the government, but not the Spanish of the media).

(c) The values of status and solidarity discussed in section 1.2.1 were in fact assigned to Spanish, the national language of Mexico and the mother tongue of all the informants. The value of status is verified when language loyalty turns out twice to be the predictor of negative attitudes towards Spanglish, as presented in Figure 1, Variables F and J and K. Claiming loyalty to Spanish seems to be one of the means utilized by Mexicans to assert their ethnic identity. Disloyal behavior and/or attitudes toward Spanish are associated with other socioethnic labels, such as Chicano, Mexican-American or Pocho; these labels allude to a negative minority status with which very few individuals would eagerly identify themselves.

Based on the information obtained from the subject sample, I have interpreted attitudinal language loyalty to Mexican Spanish as a marker of in-group solidarity with the Mexican sociocultural system. The study suggests that feelings of solidarity derive from a subjective need of identification with Mexico. The assumption, proposed in section 1.3, that attitudinal language loyalty to Mexican Spanish would be positively correlated with an evaluation of Mexico as independent, stable and authentic was very weakly supported by the data. The present study only hints that the local milieu lends itself to the study of the connection between language loyalty and national ethnocentrism.

(d) The assumption of section 1.2.1 that Mexican residents of Juárez would downgrade Spanglish was validated by means of two dimensions: (1) through the denial of inherent values of pleasantness, beauty, ethnicity and correctness, and (2) through reported difficulties of communication with native Spanish-English code-switchers. (See Figure 1, Variables D and K; F and J and K; and E and J). At the onset of this research, it was not assumed that most women would cast off Spanglish as substandard nor was it assumed that predominantly monolingual individuals in conjunction with those who report the highest scores in attitudinal language loyalty would reject the Spanish spoken in El Paso. However, this survey reveals that a considerable proportion of Juárez residents dislike the mixed variety of Spanish spoken in El Paso. This majority rejection has to do with (1) the upbringing of an individual as either male or female; (2) a biased perception of inherent values of language and language varieties; (3) limited bilingual competence; (4) ethnocentric tendencies. It seems that almost all the residents of Juárez have at least one reason to evaluate Spanglish unfavorably. It also seems that, while English is perceived as a benefit, Spanglish is perceived as an imminent danger. Using and liking Spanglish represents a form of suspicious behavior because this code is associated with the ominous presence of a group of people who were originally Mexican, but who have evolved into another group with dissimilar and menacing linguistic characteristics. Border residents are aware that the use of "pure" English does not alter their ethnicity, but they feel that the mixture of the two languages may well infringe upon their identity.

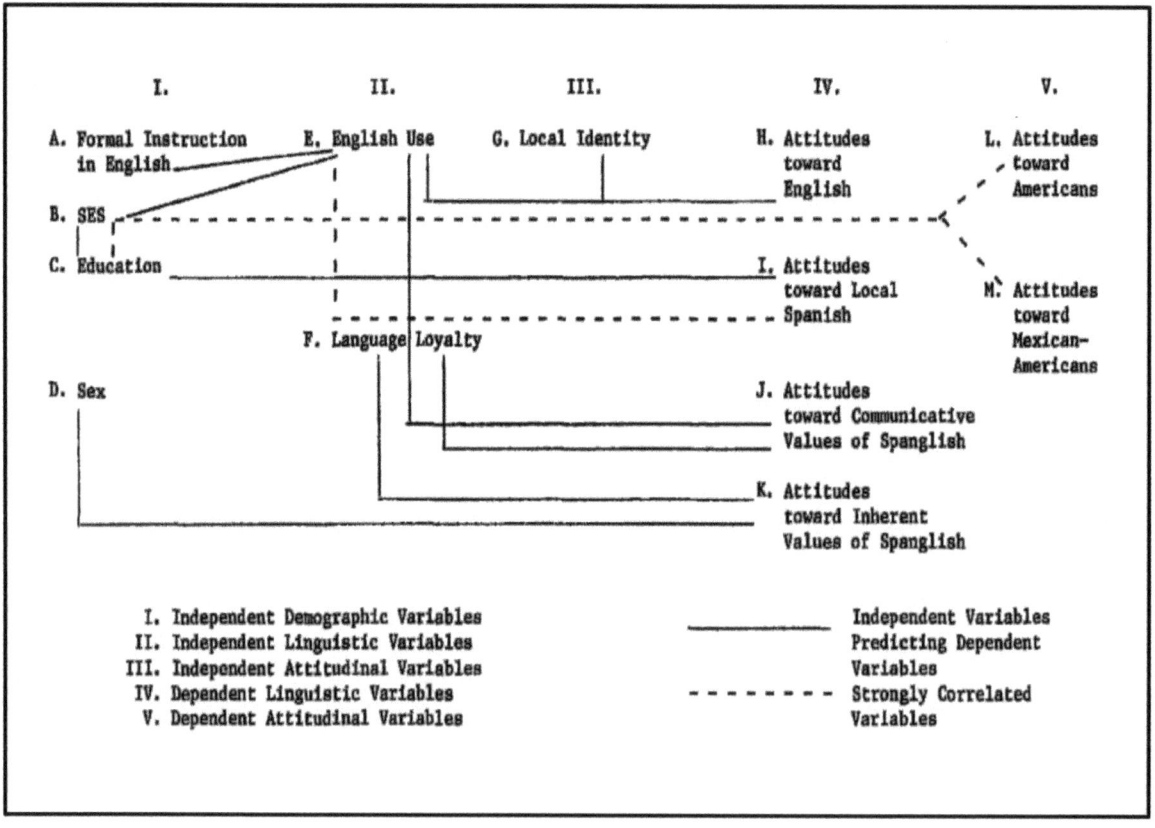

Figure 1 Graphic Summary of Findings: Language Use and Language Attitudes in Juárez

6.4 Implications

The conclusions of this investigation grew out of the methodology employed when designing the study, of the analyses and interpretations founded on language attitude and sociolinguistic theory, and of the opinions of the subject sample. The findings of this study imply that there does exist a causal link between sociodemographic factors and language attitudes and language use. In this case, socioeconomic background and formal exposure to the English language appear as directly affecting the use of English. In like manner, socioeconomic background and education predict attitudes toward local Spanish. Sex, on the other hand, seems to determine attitudes toward the inherent values of Spanglish. (See Figure 1, Independent Demographic Variables.) This unidirectional relationship (sociodemographic factors determining linguistic behavior) is not by any means the only approach to the findings of this study. It is my intention to emphasize the dynamic role of language as an independent determiner of attitudes and as a socioethnic identifier. This proposition is evidenced by the fact that the use of English in Juárez exercises a significant effect on attitudes toward the three codes utilized in the area, i.e., English, Spanish and Spanglish. This study also suggests that language loyalty must be considered an independent variable from sociodemographic factors. This proposition is supported by the fact that language loyalty, the most easily observable attitude in the milieu of Juárez, turns out twice to be an independent predictor of attitudes toward Spanglish. (See Figure 1, Independent Linguistic Variables).

Thus, if English Use and Language Loyalty are independent predictors of language attitudes, it is possible to propose a major theoretical implication: language *per se* plays an active, creative role in the formation of attitudes and in the definition of socioethnic categories. This is so in the milieu of the Mexican border due to the presence and vitality of the English language, which distinguishes, in sociolinguistic terms, the city of Juárez from other urban communities in Mexico's interior. As meaningful as the use of English is the affective loyalty to Spanish, the national language of Mexico. Language loyalty, a deeply rooted mental barrier in most border residents, may well be considered responsible for deterring a conspicuous and pronounced drift towards Anglicization. Both English Use and Language Loyalty are distinctive sociolinguistic dimensions of the city, which are derived by (1) contact with and dependence on the United States and by (2) the evolution of a group of speakers of Spanglish.

This study, therefore, contributes to sociolinguistic inquiry by highlighting the mutual interdependence of language and society and by drawing attention to the dynamic, independent functions of language in those milieus in which two or more clearly differentiated languages or language varieties come into close contact. The field of sociolinguistics needs a general theoretical framework reckoning the universality of sociolinguistic phenomena and principles. Smith, Giles and Hewston (1980) identify the problem:

> What we lack, and seek to locate, is a set of criteria for deciding which assumptions are warranted in trying to account for any particular piece of linguistic (or nonlinguistic) behavior. The cornerstone of our perspective is that language behavior is part of social situations, alternative (independent) or peripheral (dependent) in ways and under conditions that social psychological theory and methods can help make more specific (p. 286).

6.5 Suggestions for further research

This dissertation pinpoints sociolinguistic occurrences in an environment characterized by linguistic and cultural diversity. This diversity makes the Mexican border unique since it is not only a political boundary dividing the First World from the Third World, but also an area where economic dependency, and political and socioethnic conflicts and contrasts may be observed and examined. Furthermore, the area lends itself to the study of many facets of relationships between groups of people who happen to be speakers of two of the most prestigious languages spoken on a worldwide basis. The diversity and complexity of the Mexican border thus may provide the necessary data to investigate the universals of sociolinguistic phenomena and the numerous assumptions posited in the field of language attitudes.

Although I have dealt only with a small segment of the population of the city of Juárez, I have been able to detect more of its sociolinguistic and attitudinal aspects than I have been able to report. The city of Juárez may be very useful for the investigation of the following concepts:

(1) *The multidimensionality of language attitudes.*
Attitudes toward English, for example, can be assessed not only through the now classical instrumental versus integrative approach, but also through personal, affective and communicative dimensions. I base this proposition on the opinions of uninhibited informants who were able to elaborate their feelings when questioned on the values of English. Remarks such as "I would be a different person if I did not speak English" or "I would be missing something important if I did not know the language" reflect a more intimate, emotional type of orientation towards English. Statements such as "If I knew English better, I would not have any problems with the American clientele", reveal, on the other hand, the communicative values of this language of wider communication. Cooper and Fishman (1974) and Ryan (1979) have indicated the need for a multidimensional exploration of language attitudes.

(2) *The impact of local identity on linguistic behavior.*
Local identity has been reported to be a relevant dimension associated with unifying speech patterns. Labov (1972:1-42) makes a strong point about the social meaning of centralized diphthongs among those native Vineyarders who feel strongly attached to their island. In the case of Juárez, I have pointed out that local identity plays an important role in the formation of attitudes towards the foreign language, English, but this importance cannot be overemphasized. Local identity can indeed be utilized in the investigation of other language values, such as those assigned to the Northern variety of Mexican Spanish. Those values (discussed in the introductory section of Chapter 4) were externalized only by a handful of insightful, sophisticated and intellectually-oriented native border residents.

(3) *Covert prestige.*
This concept refers to hidden positive values of a nonstandard variety. The values exist but they are neither perceived nor overtly expressed by the speakers. Trudgill (1972) analyzes objective data which actually demonstrates that male lower-working class speakers of Urban British English use nonstandard speech which is covertly prestigious because of its "masculinity." In my own study I have discussed the fact that educated border residents

report using "incorrect" local speech forms which do not carry overt prestige. However, this local speech, also used by the spoken media, is the model for speakers of Mexican descent inhabiting El Paso, for uneducated migrants residing in Juárez and for speakers of rural and semi-rural communities with which Juárez is in close contact. Juárez is in fact the center from which numerous mass media productions irradiate. These productions not only reach remote towns throughout the states of Chihuahua, Durango and Sonora, but also the rural communities of West Texas and Southern New Mexico in which the population is predominantly Spanish-speaking. Thus, though educated border residents may consider their own language "incorrect," it serves as a prestige model for marginal speech communities.

(4) *Language attitudes and language use.*
This study has demonstrated that attitudes toward English can be predicted by English use. Further research in Juárez might well show that attitudinal language loyalty and behavioral language loyalty to Mexican Spanish are not imperfectly related to each other insofar as border residents language attitudes appear to be relatively consistent with their use of language. Inasmuch as the use of English and the use of Spanish are clearly differentiated at the level of interpersonal interaction, border residents are capable of reporting approximately how much English as opposed to how much Spanish they use on a daily basis. Subjects working in tourism or in the American assembly plants indicated to this writer the number of hours they would spend in a day using English in their places of employment. It would be of great significance to the field of sociolinguistics to investigate if a reported use of Spanish correlates with a reported affect towards the mother tongue.

(5) *Sociolinguistic variation.*
Inasmuch as the population of Juárez is comprised by both recent migrants from diverse regions of Mexico and lifelong urban dwellers, the city may serve to study the interplay, the dynamics and the societal values of regional and social dialects. To make this operative, the nonstandard features identified by the writer in Chapter 4 can be isolated and transformed into linguistic variables. Likewise, the language sensitivity existing in this community can serve to probe more deeply Mexicans' consciousness of varieties of Spanish and their beliefs in a "typically" Mexican style of language. Finally, the city of Juárez is ideal for investigating, through indirect instruments, a number of issues concerning the prestige of the "official" norm of Mexican Spanish. For instance, is Mexico City Spanish equivalent to the national standard, similar to Network English in the United States, or Received Pronunciation English in Great Britain? Is there, on the other hand, a national standard emanating from urban, formal, "provincial" domains indistinguishable from Mexico City formal Spanish?

References

Aboud, F. and R. D. Meade (1974) *Cultural Factors in Learning.* Bellingham, Washington: Western Washington State College.

Alarcón, A. (1978) *El habla popular de los jóvenes en la ciudad de México.* Tercera edición. México: C. B. Costa Amic.

Anderson, R. (1981) *New Dimensions in Second Language Acquisition Research.* Rowley, Mass.: Newbury House.

Barkin, F.; E. Brandt and J. Ornstein-Galicia (1981) *Bilingualism and Language Contact: Spanish, English and Native American Languages.* New York: Teachers College Press.

Blansitt, E. L. Jr. and R. V. Teschner (1980) *A Festschrift for Jacob Ornstein: Studies in General Linguistics and Sociolinguistics.* Rowley, Mass.: Newbury House.

Bourhis, R. Y. and H. Giles (1977) "The Language of Intergroup Distinctiveness," in H. Giles (ed), pp. 185-211.

Bourhis, R. Y.; H. Giles and H. Tajfel (1973) "Language as a Determinant of Welsh Identity," *European Journal of Social Psychology*, 3, 447-60.

Bourhis, R. Y.; H. Giles and W. Lambert (1975) "Social Consequences of Accommodating One's Style of Speech: A Crossnational Investigation," *International Journal of the Sociology of Language*, 6, 55-72.

Bowen, J. D. (1975) "Adaptation of English Borrowing," in Hernández-Chávez et al. (eds), pp. 115-121.

Boyd-Bowman, P. (1960) *El habla de Guanajuato.* Mexico: Imprenta Universitaria.

Brudner, L. A. and D. R. White (1979) "Language Attitudes: Behavior and Intervening Variables," in W. F. Mackey and J. Ornstein (eds), pp. 51-68.

Carranza, M. A. and E. B. Ryan (1975) "Evaluative Reactions of Bilingual Anglo and Mexican-American Adolescents toward Speakers of English and Spanish," *International Journal of the Sociology of Language*, 6, 83-104.

Casillas-Scott, C. (1969) *Spanish Language Maintenance and Loyalty in El Paso-Juárez: A Sociolinguistic Study of the Contact Situation in a Highly Bilingual Area,* Master's Thesis, The University of Texas at El Paso.

Castellanos, A. G. (1981) Ciudad Juárez: *La vida fronteriza.* México: Nuestro Tiempo.

Castellanos, A. G. and G. López y Rivas (1981) "La influencia norteamericana en la cultura de la frontera norte de México," en R. González Salazar (ed), pp. 68-84.

Censo para 1980. Dirección de Desarrollo Socioeconómico. Municipio de Ciudad Juárez. Ciudad Juárez, Chihuahua. Unpublished Manuscript.

Cohen, A. D. (1974) "Mexican-American Evaluational Judgements about Language Varieties," *International Journal of the Sociology of Language*, 3, 33-51.

Comisión para la Defensa del Idioma Español (1982) *La política lingüistica de México.* Primera parte, Tomo 8, Secretaría de Educación Pública: Mexico City.

Comisión para la Defensa del Idioma Español (1982) *La política lingüistica de México.* Segunda parte, Tomo 9, Secretaría de Educaci6n Pública: Mexico City.

Comisión para la Defensa del Idioma Español (1982) *La política lingüistica de México*: Tercera parte, Tomo 10, Secretaría de Educación Pública: Mexico City.

Conrad, A. W. and J. A. Fishman (1977) "English as a World Language: The Evidence," in J. A. Fishman et al. (eds), pp. 3-76.

Cooper, R. L. and J. A. Fishman (1974) "The Study of Language Attitudes," *International Journal of the Sociology of Language*, 3, 5-19.

Cooper, R. L. and J. A. Fishman (1977) "A Study of Language Attitudes," in J. A. Fishman et al. (eds), pp. 239-276.

Coppieters, F. and D. L. Goyvaerts (1978) *Functional Studies in Language and Literature*. Ghent: E. Story Scientia.

D'Antonio, W. V. and W. H. Form (1965) *Influentials in Two Border Cities: A Study in Community Decision Making*. Milwaukee: University of Notre Dame Press.

Davies, J. E. (1971) "The Spanish of Mexico: An Annotated Bibliography for 1940-69." *Hispania*, 54, 625-54.

De la Zerda, F., N. and R. Hooper (1975) "Mexican-American's Evaluations of Spoken Spanish and English," *Speech Monographs*, 42, 91-98.

Durán, R. (1981) *Latino Language and Communicative Behavior*. Norwood, N. J.: ABLEX Publishing Co.

Elías-Olivares, L. (1976) *Ways of Speaking in a Chicano Speech Community*. Unpublished doctoral dissertation. The University of Texas, Austin.

El-Dash, L. and G. R. Tucker (1975) "Subjective Reactions to Various Speech Styles in Egypt," *International Journal of the Sociology of Language*, 6, 33-54.

El Simposio de Bloomington (1967) Bogotá: Instituto Caro y Cuervo.

Escobar, A. (1972) *El reto del multilingüismo en el Perú*. Lima: Instituto de Estudios Peruanos.

Escobar, A. (1976) *Lenguaje*. Lima: Instituto de Investigaciones.

Escobar, A. (1978) *Variaciones sociolingüísticas del castellano en el Perú*. Lima: Instituto de Estudios Peruanos.

Escobar, A.; J. Matos Mar and G. Alberti (1975) *Perú, ¿país bilingüe?* Lima: Instituto de Estudios Peruanos.

Espinosa, A. M. (1975) "Speech Mixture in New Mexico: The Influence of the English Language on New Mexican Spanish," in E. Hernández-Chávez et al. (eds), pp. 408-28.

Ferguson, C. A. (1959) "Diglossia," *Word*, 47-56.

Fischer, J. L. (1958) "Social Influences on the Choice of a Linguistic Variant," *Word*, 14, 47-56.

Fishman, J. A. (1965) "The Status and Prospects of Bilingualism in the United States," *Modern Language Journal*, 49, 227-37.

Fishman, J. A. (1966) *Language Loyalty in the United States*. The Hague: Mouton.

Fishman, J. A. (1967) "Bilingualism with and without Diglossia: Diglossia with and without Bilingualism." *Journal of Social Issues*, 23, 28-33.

Fishman, J. A. (1970a) *The Sociology of Language: An Interdisciplinary Approach to Language in Society*. Rowley, Mass.: Newbury House.

Fishman, J. A. (1970b) *Readings in the Sociology of Language*. Second edition. The Hague: Mouton.

Fishman, J. A. (1971a) "Bilingual Attitudes and Behaviors," in J. A. Fishman et al. (eds), pp, 105-16.

Fishman, J. A. (1971b) "Societal Bilingualism: Stable and Transitional," in J. A. Fishman et al. (eds), pp. 539-56.

Fishman, J. A. (1971c) "Sociolinguistic Perspective on the Study of Bilingualism," in J. A.

Fishman et al. (eds), pp. 557-82.

Fishman, J. A. (1972) *Advances in the Sociology of Language*, Vol. 2. The Hague: Mouton.

Fishman, J. A. (1973) *Language and Nationalism*. Rowley, Mass.: Newbury House.

Fishman, J. A. (1974) *Advances in Language Planning*. The Hague: Mouton.

Fishman, J. A. (1977a) "The Spread of English as a New Perspective for the Study of Language Maintenance and Language Shift," in J. A. Fishman et al. (eds), pp. 108-36.

Fishman, J. A. (1977b) "Knowing, Using and Liking English as an Additional Language," in J. A. Fishman et al. (eds), pp. 302-28.

Fishman, J. A. (1977c) "Language and Ethnicity," in H. Giles (ed), pp. 15-52.

Fishman, J. A.; R. L. Cooper and R. Ma (1971) *Bilingualism in the Barrio*. Language Science Monographs. Bloomington: Indiana University Publications.

Fishman, J. A.; R. L. Cooper and A. W. Conrad (1977) *The Spread of English*. Rowley, Mass.: Newbury House.

Fishman, J. A.; R. L. Cooper and Y. Rosenbaum (1977) "English Around the World," in J. A. Fishman et al. (eds), pp. 77-107.

Fontanella de Weinberg, M. B. (1973) "Comportamiento ante –s de hablantes femeninos y masculinos del español bonaerense," *Romance Philology*, 27, 51-8.

Gardner, R. C. (1979) "Social Psychological Aspects of Second language Acquisition," in H. Giles and R. N. St. Clair (eds), pp. 193-220.

Gardner, R. C. and W. E. Lambert (1972) *Attitudes and Motivation in Second Language Learning*. Rowley, Mass.: Newbury House.

Giles, H. (1973) "Accent Mobility: A Model and Some Data," *Anthropological Linguistics*, 15, 87-105.

Giles, H. (1977) "Social Psychology and Applied Linguistics: Towards an Integrative Approach," *ITL: Review of Applied Linguistics*, 35, 27-42.

Giles, H. (1977) *Language, Ethnicity and Intergroup Relations*. European Monographs in Social Psychology. London: Academic Press.

Giles, H. (1979) "Ethnicity Markers in Speech," in K. R. Scherer and H. Giles (eds), pp. 250-80.

Giles, H. and P. T. Powesland (1975) *Speech Style and Social Evaluation*. European Monographs in Social Psychology. London: Academic Press.

Giles, H. and B. Saint Jacques (1979) *Language and Ethnic Relations*. Oxford: Pergamon Press.

Giles, H. and R. N. St. Clair (1979) *Language and Social Psychology*. Oxford: Basil Blackwell.

Giles, H.; D. M. Taylor and R. Y. Bourhis (1973) "Towards a Theory of Interpersonal Accommodation through Speech: Some Canadian Data," *Language in Society*, 2, 177-92.

Giles, H.; R. Y. Bourhis and A. P. Davies (1974) "Prestige Speech Styles: The Imposed Norm and Inherent Value Hypotheses," in W. C. McCormack and S. Wurm (eds), pp. 15-42.

Giles, H.; R. Y. Bourhis and A. Lewis (1974) "The Imposed Norm Hypothesis: A Validation," *The Quarterly Journal of Speech*, 60, 405-410.

Giles, H.; D. M. Taylor and R. Y. Bourhis (1974) "Dimensions of Welsh Identity," *European Journal of Social Psychology*, 7, 165-74.

Giles, H.; R. Y. Bourhis and D. M. Taylor (1977) "Towards a Theory of Language in

Ethnic Group Relations," in H. Giles (ed), pp. 318-36.

González Salazar, R. (1981) *La frontera del norte; integración y desarrollo*. Mexico: El Colegio de México.

Greenfield, L. (1972) "Situational Measures of Normative Language Views in Relation to Person, Place and Topic among Puerto Rican Bilinguals," in J. A. Fishman (ed), pp. 17-35.

Guitarte, G. L. and R. Torres Quintero (1974) "Linguistic Correctness and the Role of the Academies in Latin America," in J. A. Fishman (ed), pp. 315-68.

Gumperz, J. J. and E. Hernández-Chávez (1975) "Cognitive Aspects of Bilingual Communication," in E. Hernández Chávez et al. (eds), pp. 154-63.

Hannum, T. (1978) "Attitudes of Bilingual Students toward Spanish," *Hispania*, 61, 90-4.

Heath, S. B. (1972) *Telling Tongues: Language Policy in Mexico*. New York: Teachers College Press.

Henríquez Ureña, P. (1938) *El español en México, los Estados Unidos y la América Central*. Buenos Aires: Biblioteca de Dialectología Hispánica, 4.

Henríquez Ureña, P. (1940) *El español en Santo Domingo*. Buenos Aires: Biblioteca de Dialectología Hispánica, 5.

Hernández-Chávez, E.; A. D. Cohen and A. F. Beltramo (1975) *El lenguaje de los Chicanos*. Arlington: Center for Applied Linguistics.

Hill, J. H. and K. C. Hill (1980) "Mixed Grammar, Purist Grammar, and Language Attitudes in Modern Nahuatl," *Language in Society*, 9, 321-348.

Hofman, J. E. (1977) "Language Attitudes in Rhodesia" in J. A. Fishman (ed), pp. 277-301.

Huerta, A. G. (1978) *Code-switching among Spanish-English Bilinguals*. Unpublished doctoral dissertation. The University of Texas, Austin.

Huerta-Macías, A. G. (1981) "Code-switching: All in the Family," in R. Durán (ed), pp. 153-68.

Jiménez Sabater, A. M. (1975) *Más datos sobre el español de la República Dominicana*. Santo Domingo: Ediciones Intec.

Keller, G. D.; R. V. Teschner and S. Viera (1976) *Bilingualism in the Bicentennial and Beyond*. New York: Bilingual Press.

Kelman, H. C. (1971) "Language as an Aid and as a Barrier to Involvement in the National System," in J. A. Fishman (ed), pp. 185-212.

Labov, W. (1966) *The Social Stratification of English in New York City*. Washington: Center for Applied Linguistics.

Labov, W. (1972) *Sociolinguistic Patterns*. Philadelphia: The University of Pennsylvania Press.

Labov, W. (1972a) "Negative Attraction and Negative Concord in English Grammar," *Language*, 48, 773-818.

Lambert, W. E. (1967) "The Social Psychology of Bilingualism," *Journal of Social Issues*, 23, 91-109.

Lambert, W. E. (1974) "Culture and Language as Factors in Learning and Education," in F. Aboud and R. M. Meade (eds), pp. 233-265.

Lambert, W. E. (1979) "Language as a Factor in Intergroup Relations," in H. Giles and R.N. St. Clair (eds), pp. 186-192.

Lambert, W. E.; R. C. Gardner and S. Fillenbaum (1960) "Evaluational Reactions to Spoken Language," *Journal of Abnormal and Social Psychology*, 60, 44-51.

Lapesa, R. (1959) *Historia de la lengua española*. Quinta edición. Madrid: Las Américas.
Leal, L. (1964). "Recuerdos de Ciudad Juárez en escritores de la Revolución." *Hispania*, 47 / 2, 231-241.
Lope Blanch, J. M. (1970) "Las zonas dialectales de México: Proyecto de delimitación," *Nueva Revista de Filología Hispánica*, 19, 1-11.
Lope Blanch, J. M. (1971) "El léxico de la zona maya en el marco de la dialectología mexicana," *Nueva Revista de Filología Hispánica*, 20, 1-63.
Lope Blanch, J. M. (1972) *Estudios sobre el español en México*. México: Universidad Nacional Autónoma de México.
Lope Blanch, J. M. (1977) *El español hablado en las principales ciudades de América*. México: Universidad Nacional Autónoma de México.
Lope Blanch, J. M. (1977) "Anglicismos en la norma lingüística culta de México," en J. M. Lope Blanch (ed), pp. 191-200.
Lukmani, Y. M. (1972) "Motivation to Learn and Language Proficiency," *Language Learning*, 22, 261-274.
Mackey, W. F. and J. Ornstein (1979) *Sociolinguistic Studies in Language Contact. Trends in Linguistic Studies and Monographs* 6. The Hague: Mouton.
Malmberg, B. (1966) *La América hispanohablante: unidad y diferenciación del castellano*. Madrid: Istmo.
Martínez, O. J. (1977) "Chicanos and the Border Cities: An Interpretative Essay," *Pacific Historical Review*, 46, 85-107.
Martínez, O. J. (1978) *Border Boom Town. Cd. Juárez since 1848*. Austin: The University of Texas Press.
Martínez, O. J. (1980a) "El Paso and Juárez." Unpublished summary based on Border Boom Town, 1978.
Martínez, O. J. (1980b) "The Chicanos of El Paso: An Assessment of Progress," *Southwestern Studies*, The University of Texas at El Paso.
Mazon, M. R. (1976) *Swallow IV*. San Diego: Institute for Cultural Pluralism, San Diego State University.
McCormack, W. C. and S. Wurrn (1974) *Language in Anthropology IV*: Language in Many Ways. The Hague: Mouton.
Nadel, E. and J. A. Fishman (1977) "English in Israel: A Sociolinguistic Study," in J. A. Fishman et al. (eds), pp. 137-67.
Nie, N. H. et al. (1975) *Statistical Package for the Social Sciences*. New York: McGraw-Hill.
Neustupnŷ, J. V. (1974) "Basic Types of Treatment of Language Problems," in J. A. Fishman (ed), pp. 37-48.
Oller, J. W., Jr. (1981) "Research on the Measurement of Affective Variables: Some Remaining Questions," in R. Anderson (ed), pp. 10-22.
Oller, J. W., Jr.; L. Baca and A. Vigil (1977) "Attitudes and Attained Proficiency in ESL: A Sociolinguistic Study of Mexican-Americans in the Southwest," *TESOL Quarterly*, 11, 173-183.
Oller, J. W., Jr.; A. J. Hudson and P. F. Liu (1977) "Attitudes and Attained Proficiency: A Sociolinguistic Study of Native Speakers of Chinese in the United States," *Language Learning*, 27, 1-27.
Ornstein-Galicia, J. (1981) "Varieties of Southwest Spanish: Some Neglected

Considerations," in R. Durán (ed), pp. 19-38.

Ornstein, J. and P. Goodman (1979) "Socio-educational Correlates of Mexican-American Bilingualism," in W. Mackey and J. Ornstein (eds), pp. 393-424.

Ornstein, J.; G. Valdés-Fallis and B. L. Dubois (1975) "Bilingual Child Language Acquisition Along the U.S.-Mexico Border: The El Paso-Ciudad Juárez-Las Cruces Triangle," *Word*, Special Issue, 385-404.

Pap, L. (1979) "Language Attitudes and Minority Status," in Mackey and Ornstein (eds), pp. 197-207.

Parasher, S. V. (1980) "Mother Tongue-English Diglossia: A Case Study of Educated Indian Bilinguals' Language Use," *Anthropological Linguistics*, 22, 151-62.

Peñalosa, F. (1980) Chicano Sociolinguistics: A Brief Introduction. Rowley, Mass.: Newbury House.

Polizzi Holland, J. (1977) *Language Attitudes in the El Paso, Texas Newspapers: 1974-76*. Master's Thesis. The University of Texas at El Paso.

Poplack, S. (1981) "Syntactic Structure and Social Function of Codeswitching," in R. Durán (ed), pp. 169-84.

Probst Muro, G. (1982) *Attitudes and Motivation in Second Language Teaching*. Master's Thesis. The University of Texas at El Paso.

Riley, G. A. (1975) "Language Loyalty and Ethnocentrism in the Guamanian Speech Community," *Anthropological Linguistics*, 17, 286-92.

Riley, G. A. (1980) "Language Loyalty and Ethnocentrism in the Guamanian Speech Community: Seven Years Later," *Anthropological Linguistics*, 22, 329-333.

Rosenblat, A. (1965) *El castellano de España y el castellano de América*. Caracas: Instituto de Filología "Andrés Bello."

Rosenblat, A. (1967) "El criterio de corrección lingüística. Unidad o pluralidad de normas en el español de España y América," in El Simposio de Bloomington, pp. 113-146.

Ryan, E. B. (1979) "Why do Low-Prestige Language Varieties Persist?," in H. Giles and R. N. St. Clair (eds), pp. 145-157.

Ryan, E. B. (1981) "Language Planning from an Attitudinal Perspective." Paper read at the Conference for Interdisciplinary Research III, Cancún, México, December 16-19.

Sanou de los Ríos, R. M. (1981) "Variantes de /r/ en San Juan." Paper read at the II Congreso Nacional de Lingüística, San Juan, Argentina, September 16-17.

Scherer, K. R. and H. Giles (1979) *Social Markers in Speech. Cambridge*: Cambridge University Press.

Seckbach, R. and R. L. Cooper (1977) "The Maintenance of English in Ramat Eshkol," in J. A. Fishman (ed), pp. 168-78.

Secretaría de Educación Pública (1982) ¿Qué es la Comisión para la Defensa del Idioma? Mexico City.

Smith, P. M.; H. Giles and M. Hewston (1980) "Sociolinguistics: A Social Psychological Perspective," in R. N. St. Clair and H. Giles (eds), pp. 283-94.

Solé, Y. (1976) "Language Attitudes towards Spanish among Mexican-American College Students," in M. R. Mazón (ed), pp. 327-48.

Solís Garza, H. (1971) *Los mexicanos del norte*. México: Nuestro Tiempo.

St. Clair, R. N. and H. Giles (1980) *The Social Psychological Contexts of Language*.

Hillsdale, N. J.: Lawrence Erlbaum.

Stewart, W. A. (1970) "A Sociolinguistic Typology for Describing National Multilingualism," in J. A. Fishman (ed), pp. 531-45.

Stoddard, E. (1969) "The United States-Mexican Border as a Research Laboratory," *Journal of Inter-American Studies*, 11, 477-88.

Stoddard, E. (1978) "Mexican-American Attitudes toward Mexican Migration along the United States-Mexico Border," Paper read at the Social Science Association, Denver, Colorado, April 27-29.

Taylor, D. M. and L. Simard (1975) "Social Interaction in a Bilingual Setting," *Canadian Psychological Review*, 16, 240-54.

Taylor, D. M.; J. Bassili and F. E. About (1973) "Dimensions of Ethnic Identity: An Example from Quebec," *Journal of Social Psychology*, 89, 185-92.

Thorne, B. and N. Henley (1975) Language and Sex: Difference and Dominance. Rowley, Mass.: Newbury House.

Thorne, B. and N. Henley (1975) "Difference and dominance: An Overview of Language, Gender and Society," in B. Thorne and N. Henley (eds), pp. 5-42.

Trudgill, P. (1972) "Sex, Covert Prestige and Linguistic Change in the Urban British English of Norwich," *Language in Society*, 1, 179-95.

Trudgill, P. and H. Giles (1978) "Sociolinguistics and Linguistic Value Judgements: Correctness, Adequacy and Aesthetics," in F. Coppieters and D. Goyvaerts (eds), pp. 167-90.

Tucker, G. R. and W. E. Lambert (1969) "White and Negro Listeners' Reactions to Various American English Dialects," *Social Forces*, 47, 463-68.

Ugalde, A., et al. (1974) *The Urbanization Process of a Poor Mexican Neighborhood*. Institute of Latin American Studies, Austin: The University of Texas Press.

Valdés-Fallis, G. (1976) "Social Interaction and Code-switching Patterns: A Case Study of Spanish / English Alternation," in G. D. Keller et al. (eds), pp. 52-65.

Valdés, G. (1982) "Bilingualism in a Mexican Border City: A Research Agenda," in F. Barkin et al. (eds), pp. 3-17.

Webb, J. T. (1980) "Pidgins (and Creoles?) on the United States-Mexican Border," in E. L. Blansitt and R. V. Teschner (eds), pp. 325-31.

Weinrich, U. (1968) *Languages in Contact: Findings and Problems*. The Hague: Mouton.

Williams, G. (1979) "Language Group Allegiance and Ethnic Interaction," in H, Giles and B. Saint-Jacques (eds), pp. 57-66.

Wölck, W. (1972) "Las lenguas mayores del Perú y sus hablantes," in A. Escobar (ed), pp. 189-216.

Wolfram, W, A. (1969) *A Sociolinguistic Description of Detroit Negro Speech*. Washington: Center for Applied Linguistics.

Appendix I

English Translation of Questionnaire

I. Demographic Information

1. Name (optional)
2. Sex   F   M
3. Age
4. Birthplace
5. Father's regional origin
6. Mother's regional origin
7. Father's occupation
8. Mother's occupation
9. Length of residence in Juárez
10. Other places of residence
11. Occupation in Juárez
12. Occupation in El Paso
13. Forma education in Mexico
14. Formal education in the United States
15. Monthly salary. If you do not work, what is the head of household salary?
16. Do you own a house?
17. In which neighborhood do you live?
18. Which of the following activities do you carry out in El Paso
    - **a.** Shopping   **b.** Entertainment   **c.** Work
    - **d.** Education   **e.** Business   **f.** Visits to family and / or friends
19. What is the frequency of your activities in El Paso?
    - **a.** Daily   **b.** 2 or 3 times per week   **c.** 2 or 3 times per month
    - **d.** Sporadically   **e.** Never

II. Information on the Formal Acquisition and the Informal Use of English

1. Have you ever studied English?   Yes   No
2. If your answer is negative, can you say why not?
3. Where have you studied English?
    - **a.** El Paso   **b.** Juárez   **c.** Other
4. What kind of courses have you studied?
    - **a.** Those offered in secondary and preparatory school in Mexico (time)
    - **b.** Those offered in academics in El Paso or Juárez (time)
    - **c.** Elementary school in El Paso (time)
    - **d.** High School in El Paso (time)
    - **e.** College in El Paso (time)
    - **f.** Other (specify)

5. How long have you studied English?
   - **a.** Daily
   - **b.** 2 or 3 times per week
   - **c.** 2 or 3 times per month
   - **d.** Sporadically
   - **e.** Never
6. How often do you speak to native speakers of English?
   - **a.** Daily
   - **b.** 2 or 3 times per week
   - **c.** 2 or 3 times per month
   - **d.** Sporadically
   - **e.** Never
7. How often do you speak English to native Spanish speakers?
   - **a.** Daily
   - **b.** 2 or 3 times per week
   - **c.** 2 or 3 times per month
   - **d.** Sporadically
   - **e.** Never
8. How often do you listen to the American radio?
   - **a.** Daily
   - **b.** 2 or 3 times per week
   - **c.** 2 or 3 times per month
   - **d.** Sporadically
   - **e.** Never
9. How frequently do you watch American television?
   - **a.** Daily
   - **b.** 2 or 3 times per week
   - **c.** 2 or 3 times per month
   - **d.** Sporadically
   - **e.** Never
10. How often do you go to see American movies?
    - **a.** Daily
    - **b.** 2 or 3 times per week
    - **c.** 2 or 3 times per month
    - **d.** Sporadically
    - **e.** Never
11. How often do you read books and magazines in English?
    - **a.** Daily
    - **b.** 2 or 3 times per week
    - **c.** 2 or 3 times per month
    - **d.** Sporadically
    - **e.** Never
12. How often do you write in English?
    - **a.** Daily
    - **b.** 2 or 3 times per week
    - **c.** 2 or 3 times per month
    - **d.** Sporadically
    - **e.** Never
13. In general, your knowledge of English
    - **a.** Excellent
    - **b.** Good
    - **c.** Adequate
    - **d.** Poor
    - **e.** Never

III. Attitudinal Variables

The following key was explained to the informants: **1** means that you strongly agree; **2** means that you somewhat agree: **3** means that you are uncertain; (except in Variable E, Local versus National Spanish, where it means that they are the same); **4** means that you are rather opposed; **5** means that you strongly disagree. The opposite key was also presented.

Attitudes toward English

A. Integrative Orientation (Scale: 1=Strongly disagree; 5=Strongly agree)
  1. I study/have studied English to better understand the American people and their way of life
  2. English will enable me to gain good friends among Americans
  3. Knowing English will enable me to think and behave as American people do
  4. English will allow me to meet and converse with interesting and different people

B. Instrumental Orientation (Scale: 1=Strongly disagree; 5=Strongly agree)
1. I need English in the El Paso-Juárez area to get a good job
2. I need English to keep the job I have
3. I need English for interrelationships with people in the El Paso-Juárez area
4. English will make me a better educated person

C. Evaluations of Americans (Scale: 1=Strongly agree; 5=Strongly disagree)
1. Americans are more sincere than Mexicans
2. Mexicans are more fun-loving and creative than Americans
3. Mexicans are more organized and efficient than Americans
4. American education is superior and more disciplined than Mexican education

D. Local Identity (Scale: 1=Strongly agree; 5=Strongly disagree)
1. I find it difficult to live in this area where two such different cultures exist
2. I am *juarense*, and I feel very proud of it
3. Despite the problems of delinquency and family disintegration the border is to me the best part of Mexico.
4. The border has the advantage that people are able to get acquainted with another culture

Attitudes toward Spanish

E. Local versus National Spanish (Scale: 0=Did not know; 1=Strongly disagree; 3=They are the same; 5=Strongly agree)
1. The Spanish spoken in Mexico City is more correct than that spoken in Juárez
2. The Spanish spoken in Juárez is more correct than that spoken in Chihuahua City
3. The Spanish spoken in other important cities in Mexico is more correct than the Spanish spoken in Juárez, e.g., Guadalajara
4. The Spanish spoken in Juárez is more correct than that spoken in Mexico City

F. Language Loyalty (Scale: 1=Strongly disagree; 5=Strongly agree)
1. It is very important that border Mexicans maintain the Spanish language just like other Mexicans
2. Border Mexicans are able to talk just like other Mexicans although sometimes they know English
3. In Juárez people speak half English and half Spanish
4. I sometimes talk half English and half Spanish

G. National Ethnocentrism (Scale: 1=Strongly disagree; 5=Strongly agree)
1. I think that the most important thing for Mexico is to be an independent country from any other
2. Mexico is not a perfect country, but it is the most stable in Latin America
3. The proximity of the United States has damaged Mexican culture
4. It is certain that Mexico is very far from Heaven and very close to the United States

Attitudes toward Spanglish

H. Inherent Values (Scale: 5=Strongly agree; 1=Strongly disagree)
1. The Spanish spoken in El Paso is more correct than the Spanish spoken in Juárez
2. It sounds pretty when people from El Paso talk half English and half Spanish
3. It bothers me that Mexicans from El Paso talk half Spanish and half English
4. The Mexicans from El Paso should imitate the Mexicans from Juárez when they speak Spanish

I. Communicative Values (Scale: 5=Strongly agree; 1=Strongly disagree)
1. Those Mexicans who emigrate to El Paso never forget their language
2. Mexicans from Juárez do not really need to know English since they can communicate in Spanish with Mexicans from El Paso
3. It is impossible to understand what Mexicans from El Paso say when they mix the two languages
4. One can mix the two languages—English and Spanish—as the Mexicans from El Paso do, and still understand what people say.

J. Evaluations of Mexican-Americans (Scale: 5=Strongly agree; 1=Strongly Disagree)
1. If Mexican-American children learn English in early childhood, they run the risk of forgetting they are Mexicans
2. Those Mexicans who emigrate to the United States never forget their language
3. The children of Mexican parents who emigrated feel proud of being Mexicans
4. When Mexicans emigrate to the United States, they forget Mexico and only think of money

Attitudes toward Education in English

Discuss:
    Why do you prefer Mexican education over American education?
    Why do you prefer American education over Mexican education?

Appendix II
Correlation Matrix: Demographic and Linguistic Variables

	1	2	3	4	5	6	7	8	9	10	11	12	13	14
1. Sex	—	.125	-.001	.065	.083	.183	-.138	.027	-.198	-.069	-.129	.344**	.005	-.036
2. SES		—	.250	.622*	.543*	.175	-.217	.166	-.473*	-.028	.041	.165	-.084	-.381*
3. Education			—	.512*	.390*	.062	-.165	.047	-.463*	-.136	-.063	.053	-.040	.184
4. Formal Instruction in English				—	.621*	.231	-.086	.253	-.453*	.018	-.025	.048	-.155	.279
5. English Use					—	.410*	-.158	.116	-.380*	-.122	-.168	.007	-.328**	.148
6. Attitudes towards English						—	.063	.383*	-.213	.118	-.180	.181	.028	.105
7. Beliefs about Americans							—	.038	.199	-.007	.000	.034	.175	.023
8. Local Identity								—	-.200	.072	-.038	.048	-.022	.147
9. Local versus National Spanish									—	-.097	.028	-.187	.194	-.217
10. Language Loyalty										—	.175	.455*	.410*	-.012
11. National Ethnocentrism											—	.040	.120	.101
12. Inherent Values of Spanglish												—	.386*	.004
13. Communicativ lues of Spanglish													—	.032
14. Beliefs about Mexican-Americans														—

*Significance p < .001 **Significance p < .0

www.ingramcontent.com/pod-product-compliance
Lightning Source LLC
Chambersburg PA
CBHW041241240426
43668CB00025B/2459